THE IDEA THAT IS
AMERICA

THE IDEA THAT IS
AMERICA

Keeping Faith
with Our Values in
a Dangerous World

ANNE-MARIE SLAUGHTER

BASIC
BOOKS

A Member of the Perseus Books Group
New York

Books published by Basic Books are available at special discounts for bulk purchases in the United States by corporations, institutions, and other organizations. For more information, please contact the Special Markets Department at the Perseus Books Group, 11 Cambridge Center, Cambridge, MA 02142, or call (617) 252-5298 or (800) 255-1514, or e-mail special.markets@perseusbooks.com.

Design by Jane Raese
Text set in 12-point Garamond 3

Cataloging-in-Publication Data is available from the Library of Congress.
ISBN-13: 978-0-465-07808-0
ISBN-10: 0-465-07808-7

10 9 8 7 6 5 4 3 2 1

For my family,
far and near,
old and young,
past and present,
beloved all.

Contents

Preface

BROWSING IN A USED BOOK STORE in Los Angeles, I came across a dusty black book called *The March of Freedom: A Layman's History of the American People*. I opened it and read the story of "one man's hunt for what he felt he needed most to bring home to himself."[1] That man was William Harlan Hale—a journalist, classicist, broadcaster of the Voice of America, and, as I later found out, trusted adviser to President Harry Truman. But his credentials interested me far less than his prose. Writing in 1947, when America had emerged as the most powerful victor of World War II, he seemed to feel exactly as I do today, that the America he loved was turning into a country he no longer recognized.

Hale saw the looming forces of "greed, bigotry, and inertia." He saw a country with an atomic bomb capable of destroying anything on earth. He saw a country "accused of being overbearing and imperialistic," a country "so crisscrossed by our own divisions" that we were stuck fast, incapable of living up to our own ideal. Hale was not despondent, however, but determined. He turned to our past to find the energy and principles to spur renewed action. Across the decades, his account of those principles continues to inspire.

Today, America has emerged as the undisputed victor of the Cold War, and U.S. power and wealth are unparalleled. But when I read the papers in the morning, I often feel that I am in the midst of a bad dream. American soldiers and Iraqi civilians are dying daily in Iraq, in a war we rushed into under false pretenses and now can't get out of. We are so hated in many parts of the world that any policy initiative with our name on it is dead on arrival. Even the citizens of our fellow democracies see us as morally bankrupt, and not without reason.

Our Congress would allow the president to imprison any "enemy combatant" for life with no possibility of challenging his detention in court. We have denounced many of the international institutions that we worked so hard to build after 1945. We stand isolated in the world community, voting with countries like Libya, Yemen, and North Korea against all other NATO members and virtually all our other allies on issues like the establishment of a U.N. Human Rights Council. We have lost the diplomatic clout even to persuade a majority of Latin American countries to support our candidate for president of the Organization of American States. Worst of all, in large parts of the world, the image of America is not the Statue of Liberty, but rather the image of a hooded figure standing on a box with an electric cord trailing from under his gown. Yet rather than support efforts by leaders in Congress to reject and erase this image, our own vice president has insisted that our Central Intelligence Agency officers must be allowed to torture their captives.

I too have turned back to our past to help find the way forward. We can recover. We can regain our identity, our values, and our pride. Thirty years ago, millions of people around the world equated the United States with the picture of the naked little girl running down the road in Vietnam, fleeing a napalm attack. But this image then gave way to other images in the nation's and the world's consciousness: Ronald Reagan standing in Berlin and asking Mr. Gorbachev to "tear down this wall," and later joyous and unbelieving East Germans dancing on top of that same wall in 1989; the United States at the head of a global coalition under a U.N. flag driving Iraq back out of Kuwait; U.S. Ambassador Richard Holbrooke insisting at the United Nations that AIDS in Africa be treated as a global security issue; the Dayton Peace Agreement ending the war in Bosnia and later the NATO intervention in Kosovo to stop Slobodan Milosevic from one more horrific and bloody round of ethnic cleansing; and the unforgettable image of the Twin Towers burning on September 11, with all the world standing with us in shock and grief. More than five years after 9/11, we remember the horror of that indelible day. But in the intervening years of war and conflict, of unilateralism at home and anti-Americanism abroad, we have largely forgotten that all-too-brief moment of global solidarity, the opportunity to unite almost all nations in a fight against terrorism and its deeper causes. President Bush told our friends and our sympathizers and even the would-be neutrals that they had to be either with us or against us. Today, regardless of what their governments say, the people of almost every nation are against us.

We have lost our way in the world. To find it again, we must ask ourselves, and openly debate, a key question: *What role should America play in the world?*

For me, that question has a ready, though incomplete, answer. We should stand for our values, the values that this country was created to achieve and that define us as a nation. Standing for those values is both an end and a means. It reflects who we are as a people; it also serves our long-term national interests.

That answer may seem obvious, but many in my profession—scholars and practitioners of foreign policy—would argue instead that American political and economic interests often conflict with our values, and when they do, we should go with our interests. We cannot afford to be naïve or idealistic, they would say; we must recognize instead that the currency of international politics is power. The road to peace and prosperity requires amassing and holding on to more power than any other nation, regardless whether the means we use contradict our stated values. Hypocrisy, in this view, is the price of security.

Without question, America must have enough power to defend its territory and secure the lives and welfare of its people. This is the minimum responsibility of any American president. We must also have enough power to pursue our larger purposes at home and abroad. But those purposes go far beyond the self-interested accumulation of power. America has never fully accepted the traditional game of the international system. From George Washington to Woodrow Wilson to Ronald Reagan, we have claimed to stand apart from old-world power politics and stand for our values instead. Seeking power as an end in itself—even to balance the power of other states—seems, well, un-American.

So, for me, the question of what role America should play in the world becomes a more specific question: *How do we stand for our values in the world?*

Since 9/11, we have tried to stand for our values through a strategy of *regime change,* a fancy term for overthrowing governments we dislike and replacing them with governments that like us. Overthrowing the Taliban was a necessary response to the September 11 attacks; this group was harboring and actively assisting the attackers. By contrast, overthrowing Saddam Hussein as the first step toward building a democracy in Iraq was neither necessary for our security nor the only way to promote liberty and democracy in the Middle East. We have unwittingly, although not unforeseeably, plunged a country into steadily increasing violence and chaos, which has resulted in the deaths of thousands of American soldiers as well as many times more Iraqi civilians and the curtailment of liberty in day-to-day life for millions more.

The vast majority of our soldiers have done the best they could. These men and women have helped to rebuild the country's infrastructure, organized local governments and councils, and tried to safeguard Iraqi citizens from their fellow citizens. But by and large, they are viewed not as liberators but as invaders and occupiers. And most have been given missions they have not been trained for—nation building—and often do not have the proper guidance and supervision to carry out. I have taught some of these soldiers on their return from Iraq, as masters and Ph.D. students at the Woodrow Wilson School. They are extraordinary people, measured by both their talent and their dedication to duty. They deserve civilian leadership worthy of their sacrifice.

It is all the more unforgivable, then, that the actions of some of our soldiers have gravely—perhaps irretrievably—undermined our words and deeds in Iraq and everywhere else we fight. The pictures of torture and sexual and physical abuse from Abu Ghraib and Bagram air base in Afghanistan project around the globe images of the United States that could not be further from our values. These images dominated our headlines and television screens only briefly. But they remain vivid on the Internet and in the minds of millions around the world. They sully all of us, none more than the brave men and women who have put their lives on the line precisely to uphold and advance their vision of what America stands for. Instead of trying only a few actual perpetrators, conducting a token round of investigations, and calling the case closed, it is our responsibility as a nation to figure out how things could have gone so badly wrong—and to make them right again.

The question then becomes even more pointed: *How do we stand for our values in the world in a way that is consistent with our values?*

I wrote this book to answer that question—for myself and, I hope, for others. For me, it is a deeply personal as well as intellectual question. As an American, I have always been proud of being half-European; my mother left Brussels as a beautiful twenty-three-year-old ingenue to make her life in Charlottesville, Virginia, with my father. But in my many trips back and forth across the Atlantic to spend summers with my Belgian family, it was always clear to me that I was deeply and fundamentally American.

At lunch, which in Belgium was really dinner—the table set with white linen, china, silver, and glorious food and wine that were a far cry from the peanut butter and jelly I knew in Charlottesville—my family members had vehement debates in French over whether the Marshall Plan had really been altruistic or simply a vehicle for American economic interests. They argued over racism, the Vietnam War, fast food, rock music, and American tourists who descended by the busload on European monuments and seemed to assume that all the world spoke English.

My mother had all the zeal of the newly naturalized, and would speak of the warmhearted, generous, idealistic people she had found in her new life. My grandfather would pound his fist on the table and my uncle would expostulate about American cultural and political imperialism. In the end, though, these were family fights—within our own family and the larger transatlantic family. After all, my Belgian grandfather had been at Dunkirk, scrambling to get across the English Channel as the Germans advanced. He had fought with the British in the dark days before the Americans entered the war. My father, in turn, had served in the U.S. Navy after the Korean War and as a member of the Naval Reserve for decades afterwards.

Everyone around that table also knew that without the willingness of American soldiers and taxpayers to sacrifice their lives and dollars, Belgium would have become a German protectorate. America might not always live up to its own ideals, but overall, American power had made the world a better place.

Thirty years later, at the end of the 1990s, I found myself teaching American law to 150 foreign students every year at Harvard Law School. Almost half of them were young Europeans, often deeply conflicted. They had chosen to study at Harvard because they knew that it offered a better legal education than they could generally get at home; the prestige of an American degree was also undeniable. They would profit from their stay in America, intellectually and materially, and they saw much that they would later seek to emulate back home.

Yet they railed against what they saw as American hypocrisy. When I spoke of the rule of law and human rights, they would ask why the United States would not join the International Criminal Court or the Land Mines Treaty, why U.S. leaders sought always to make rules that would apply to everyone except Americans.

When I spoke of democracy and equal opportunity, the students wondered out loud about the huge disproportion of black Americans on death row, the appalling conditions in American prisons, and the refusal of American taxpayers to pay for decent schools or health care for vast numbers of American citizens.

When I spoke of generosity, they questioned why Americans have one of the lowest levels of foreign aid, as a percentage of gross domestic product, in the developed world. They admired

American ideals but insisted on measuring us by our perform-
ance; they increasingly saw us as an arrogant, hypocritical hy-
perpower.

I agreed with much of their criticism. Still, I could point to
much good that the United States was doing in the world—taking the lead on Somalia, Haiti, Bosnia, and Kosovo. Europe had
talked a good game on the Balkans, but had done very little actually to stop Milosevic. Rwanda was the mutual shame of Europe and the United States, but we had drawn a much more
activist lesson. When Secretary of State Madeleine Albright said
that America was the "indispensable power," she meant not that
we should go it alone, but that without us, nothing got done.

But those students were early indicators of a major decline in
America's international reputation. Millions—indeed billions—
of people around the world see us not as the indispensable power
but as the imperialist power, the arrogant power—the ignorant,
the immoral, and even the incompetent power. Too many Americans dismiss the antipathy against us as mere prejudice, ingrat-
itude, or even "hatred of freedom." In certain quarters, no
doubt, anti-Americanism is as necessary and fashionable as
dressing in black. But that kind of anti-Americanism is only a
fraction of the anger and disappointment welling up from every
corner of the world. Patriotic Americans need to understand
these critiques and take them to heart if we want our country to
remain true to its mission.

I want to be able to hold my head high again, not from pride
in American exceptionalism, but from common moral and political purpose with the vast majority of humankind. I want to
live in an America that inspires hope, not loathing or fear. I
want America to earn the faith it inspired in my mother. I want
my children to grow up happy to be Americans, not because it
makes them any better than anyone else, but because they can

say that their nation is true to its principles. That is why I am writing this book.

As I have turned the pages of our own history, I found myself taking comfort in the stories of the great men and women of our past, in the countless voices that have spoken so powerfully and movingly of our common human quest. I look to the many patriots who have criticized as well as championed, questioned their own certainties, acknowledged error, and sought truth. These are the voices of poets, politicians, song writers, storytellers, soldiers, social workers, judges, ministers, and memorial carvers. Their stories do not present America in its moments of victory, but in its times of struggle—not in its perfection, but in all the contending passions of its people. It is a better place to be from than the airbrushed videos of our lives and people that we send around the world today.

William Harlan Hale had his own vision of the role America should play in the world—an answer born directly of his experience in World War II. In his book, he tells of entering the German concentration camp at Dachau in 1945, on the heels of a battalion of American liberators. He describes the wraithlike prisoners scouring the camp grounds for rags and bits of colored cloth to make crude national flags—even before they searched for food. The prisoners then stood, in their thousands, in the Alpine rain, listening to speeches from different national leaders in a ceremony of liberation.

And then came the Americans.

An alley was made for the American commanding officer—a tall, gray-haired colonel who now climbed the platform, helmet in hand, and spoke a few words of greeting and fraternity. When he had finished, the great iron gate which the Nazis had built was swung open and three American soldiers marched in—a guard bearing the United States colors. They advanced toward the platform, and I thought they would climb up and mount our colors on it, impressively high. But at the last moment, upon the colonel's signal, they wheeled toward the assembled thousands, carried our flag into their midst, and placed it there with the banners borne by men in convict stripes from a dozen victim peoples. And at this there arose a shout—a general shout of brotherhood and joy that echoed around the sodden walls.

For Hale, that moment captured the very soul of America:

I thought as I came away: This is what we mean, this is what we are. Should we seem to be less than this—should we stand apart from the lowly, from the people oppressed for faith, from those who will not be bound—then, in spite of all our riches and our power, we are not what we set out to be. We were these people; we have led, and we can again lead, their common aspirations. If we forget this, we forget ourselves.

The country that I know and love is a country that flies its flag alongside other nations, not above them. It is a country that does not need to declare over and over again that it is the greatest power the world has ever seen. It is a country that accepts constraints in order to be able to constrain others, as the essence of the rule of law. My country is the country that young American men and women think they are fighting for around the world. It is the country that we can and will again be.

Introduction

Do we sacrifice our ideals in order to preserve security? Terrorism inspires fear and suppresses ideals like freedom and individual rights. Overcoming the fear posed by terrorist threats is a tremendous test of our courage. Will we confront danger and adversity in order to preserve our ideals, or will our courage and commitment to individual rights wither at the prospect of sacrifice? My response is simple. If we abandon our ideals in the face of adversity and aggression, then those ideals were never really in our possession. I would rather die fighting than give up even the smallest part of the idea that is "America."

> —*Captain Ian Fishback, 1st Battalion,*
> *504th Parachute Infantry Regiment, 82nd Airborne Division,*
> *writing to Senator John McCain, September 16, 2005*

AMERICA IS A PLACE, a country, a people, but also an idea. It is the idea of a nation founded on a set of universal values— self-evident truths—that come not from blood, or soil, or skin color, or wealth—but from the fact of our common humanity. It is the idea of a nation bound together not by territory or religion or ethnicity but by a self-conscious commitment to shared values, for ourselves and for all peoples.

But what are these values underpinning the idea that is America? If asked this question, virtually all Americans would talk about the American belief in liberty and democracy. Most would talk about equality; many would add justice. After all, the Pledge of Allegiance commits us to "liberty and justice for all," and the Declaration of Independence declares that "all men are created equal." We believe that we stand and fight for democracy around the world. These core values have been enshrined in two centuries of civics classes, Fourth of July speeches, inaugural addresses, poems, anthems, pledges, and creeds. They live in the memorial inscriptions carved into the granite and marble bases of statues in countless town squares.

Liberty, democracy, equality, and justice—certainly. But to this list I would add three more values that are essential to the idea that is America: tolerance, humility, and faith. Tolerance, because liberty and democracy are impossible without it. Humility, because, as an unrivaled superpower, we all too often forget the humility of our Founders and because humility is the flip side of our belief in progress. And faith, because faith in our ideals and in the very idea of progress is at the core of what many other peoples see as a distinctively American optimism. Faith conquers fear, fear that weakens our commitment to the American idea itself.

These values are not abstract concepts. They have taken on specific meanings through the stories that make up our American history, stories of struggle and persistence against all odds. Stories of Puritans, Quakers, Catholics, Presbyterians, Mennonites, Moravians, Lutherans, Amish, as well as Jews, Muslims, and countless other sects seeking liberty—the freedom to worship the god of their choice in the way they choose. Stories of relatively few propertied white men seeking to govern themselves in America's early days, and of white men of lesser means, black men, and women of all races and means determined to secure the right to vote in the decades and centuries that followed. Stories of slavery and war and segregation and protests and sit-ins and boycotts and the awakening of an entire nation to secure the promise of equality. Stories of lynching and internment, but also of prosecutions and subpoenas to secure justice and of a government of laws, not of men. Stories of tolerance not as a luxury, but as a necessary tool to weld a great multicultural nation together. Stories of humility, like the first governor of Massachusetts Bay Colony offering his shining vision of a city on a hill but telling its occupants to "walk humbly with their god." And stories of constant faith, faith in our values, faith in our own can-do spirit, faith that we shall overcome, faith in the idea of America.

These tales are plots and subplots in a larger story that continues. Revisiting and retelling them offers a moral, political, and practical compass to point the way to where we need to go today. We turn back to the past not to glory in it, but rather to remind ourselves and the world at large of our imperfections, our mistakes, and our struggles to live up to our own standards. Remembering and acknowledging those parts of our past will temper our view of ourselves and of other nations. But at the same time, summoning the stories of our past can help us recharge our dreams.

The American idea took shape at our nation's founding as a vision and a promise. The Founders foresaw a nation that could be different from any other. They wrote this vision into the Declaration of Independence, the Constitution, and the Bill of Rights. But in themselves, of course, these documents are only words on paper, however venerable the parchment and flourishing the signatures. The idea that is America may be written in words, but it is realized in our deeds.

AMERICA WAS FOUNDED ON A PROMISE, a promise to the American people and to the world. Our Founders promised deliberately and self-consciously that a government of the people—a republic—could succeed. They promised liberty, equality, and justice to all citizens of that republic. And they promised to demonstrate that such a government was the birthright of all human beings.

But these promises were not kept right away. It fell to Abraham Lincoln to reconcile, through the blood and fire of the Civil War, the contradiction between Jefferson's grand proclamation of human equality and the ugly, brutal reality of human slavery. In 1857, Lincoln acknowledged the gap between the lofty principles of the Declaration of Independence and the slave-holding practices of many of the Founders. In grappling with this issue, he expressed something essential about America:

> [The Founders] meant to set up a standard maxim for free society which should be familiar to all: constantly looked to, constantly labored for, and even though never perfectly attained, constantly approximated and thereby constantly spreading and deepening its influence and augmenting the happiness and value of life to all people, of all colors, everywhere.[1]

In other words, our history is a process of trying to live up to our ideals, falling short, succeeding in some places, and trying again in others. And our greatest patriots have often been those men and women—dark-skinned and pale-skinned and any color in between, immigrant and native-born, rich and poor, rural and urban, straight and gay, reformer and conservative, laborer and captain of industry—who have pointed out our shortfalls and insisted on holding our government and our people to their word.

———————

KEEPING THE PROMISE of our founding—the promise of America—means keeping faith with our values. But keeping faith, while often enormously difficult, is not a burden. It is our greatest source of strength. It is what knits us together, what motivates us and moves us forward, and what connects us to other nations.

Our values keep America strong by binding us together. By committing and recommitting ourselves to our ideals, we have forged a common American identity. It is what makes *e pluribus unum*—"out of many, one"—possible. That is precisely the message that Woodrow Wilson sought to communicate in May 1915, as he spoke to a group of newly naturalized Americans just after they took their oath:

> You have just taken an oath of allegiance to the United States. Of allegiance to whom? Of allegiance to no one, unless it be God. Certainly not of allegiance to those who temporarily represent this great government. You have taken an oath of allegiance to a great ideal, to a great body of principles, to a great hope of the human race.[2]

An ideal, a body of principles, a great hope: For Wilson, America represented a vision of the future and the hope that this vision could be achieved. He knew that America often stumbled in practice, but that the promise of our founding endured.

Our shared values also strengthen America by giving us something to hope and work for. Americans share an extraordinary faith in progress—to an extent perhaps unique among nations. This faith has its origin in the missionary zeal of our founding. "From its beginnings," wrote William Harlan Hale, "Americanism has been a denial that things could possibly stand still. We have a purpose here; we are going places. We are going to advance ourselves; we are thereby going to advance the country we live in; and by advancing this country, we shall eventually advance the world."[3]

Many observers—our own cultural critics and thoughtful commentators from other nations—are bemused, if not incredulous, at our insistence on seeing history as the march of progress, however unsteady, uneven, or halting. They point out, not unfairly, that it often leads us into trouble and makes us all too ready to oversimplify complex problems. On a deeper level, Americans sometimes seem simply unable to appreciate the magnitude of tragedy, evil, and injustice in the world. We want our stories to have happy endings.

Consider, for instance, the difference between the British Harry Potter novels and the American Star Wars films. Both are classic epics of good versus evil and are loved by children and adults alike. But in Harry Potter, death stalks Harry throughout the books. One after another, his protectors die, until, as he finally comes to understand in the sixth book, "he must abandon forever the illusion he ought to have lost at the age of one, that the shelter of a parent's arms meant that nothing could hurt him." He recalls Dumbledore's telling him that it is important "to fight, and fight again, and keep fighting, for only then could evil be kept at bay, though never quite eradicated."[4]

For Star Wars director George Lucas, on the other hand, evil can be vanquished once and for all. Luke Skywalker conquers the Sith, with the help of his father, Darth Vader, who has been to the Dark Side but is redeemed in his final act. Things may look bleak for the good guys at the end of one movie in the series to ensure that audiences come back for the sequel, but once the Jedi knights return, their ultimate and definitive triumph is never in doubt.

Harry Potter emerges from a nation that has known the Blitz, lost an empire, and ceded its position as the strongest power in the world to the United States. The British believe in the vital necessity of an enduring struggle against evil, but they are less automatically certain of the outcome. Hence, they pride themselves on their fortitude in the face of danger—the legendary stiff upper lip. Americans, by contrast, grew up on a vast, fertile continent of seemingly boundless opportunities. Though our nation made great sacrifices to defeat fascism and communism, we emerged virtually unscathed from the great conflicts of recent memory. We are motivated by our belief in the inevitability of victory—by blind faith in success, regardless of the odds.

People around the world are inspired by the extraordinary optimism of Americans—even though they may also mock it. Every year, tens of thousands of people around the world seek the opportunity to make a better life for themselves on American soil. Untold others fight valiantly in their own countries for the same freedoms and opportunities America affords. For all of these people, our great American epic—the story of our founding values and the progress that generations of Americans have made toward achieving them—is deeply compelling. It inspires them, on leaky boats or in dark jail cells, to believe that they can make their own lives better, either by emigration or revolution.

Finally, our shared values are essential because they link America to the world. The belief that American values are *universal* values—that *all* men and women are created equal, that

all are entitled to life, liberty, and the pursuit of happiness, regardless of race, creed, or nationality—connects us to other nations. From the early days of the nation, Americans understood
that the eyes of the world were watching our experiment—in
the hope that what worked for us could work for them as well.

On June 17, 1825, the fiftieth anniversary of the Battle of
Bunker Hill, the great American orator Daniel Webster laid the
cornerstone of the Bunker Hill Monument. His speech was intended to echo through the ages, as it has. Webster exulted "in
the conviction of the benefit which the example of our country
has produced, and is likely to produce, on human freedom and
human happiness." His emphasis on the American *example* to
the rest of the world is striking. For Webster, the survival and
success of the new nation had demonstrated to all people that
"representative and popular governments . . . are compatible,
not only with respectability and power, but with repose, with
peace, with security of personal rights, with good laws, and a
just administration." Webster understood that other countries
might prefer other systems of government. But the American
example demonstrated the validity of an idea that had been,
only five decades earlier, quite literally revolutionary: "that with
wisdom and knowledge men may govern themselves." It was
now the duty of all Americans to ensure the survival of this
shining example, and to "take care that nothing may weaken its
authority with the world."[5]

The deep connection between America and other nations is
too often overshadowed by what is sometimes referred to as our
"splendid isolation." An isolationalist strand does weave its way
through our history. Most famously, in his farewell address to our
young nation, George Washington counseled us to avoid entan-
gling alliances and to make a clean break between the old world
and the new.[6] But cosmopolitanism is the far stronger thread in

our national fabric. Thomas Jefferson, for instance, welcomed the revolutions in France and Holland that followed shortly after the success of the American colonists in overthrowing British rule. He proudly predicted that "this ball of liberty . . . is now so well in motion that it will roll round the globe, at least the enlightened part of it, for light and liberty go together. It is our glory that we first put it into motion."[7] We were not rejecting Europe, but rather the old monarchical politics of Europe. By the same token, we saw ourselves as immediately and automatically connected to our fellow democracies around the world.

Two centuries later, President Jimmy Carter also understood America's responsibility to the wider world in similar terms. He insisted on building advocacy of global human rights into American foreign policy in the face of detractors who scoffed at his "namby-pamby" liberalism. Carter recognized that supporting human rights globally was in the finest tradition of American history. He also knew that it would enhance our strength and bolster our credibility abroad. "To be true to ourselves, we must be true to others," he pronounced in his inaugural address. "We will not behave in foreign places so as to violate our rules and standards here at home, for we know that the trust which our Nation earns is essential to our strength."[8] Human rights, he later explained, are at the very root of what it means to be American: "America did not invent human rights. In a very real sense . . . [h]uman rights invented America."[9]

Remember the Declaration of Independence: *All* men (and women) are created equal. Believing in America means believing in values that apply to all people everywhere. Patriotism is love of one's own country, but American patriotism, because of what it stands for, is at its best a cosmopolitan patriotism.

Our pride in our values is a source of tremendous strength, but we often seem to talk as if we were the only nation in the world, or at least certainly the best. Perhaps not surprisingly, the end of the Cold War went to our heads. Instead of understanding these values as part of a process, we too often seemed to believe that we actually embodied them in perfected form. Instead of inviting others to strive with us in attaining our highest ideals, we came to believe that we had finished the job ourselves and demanded that others simply imitate us. Our confidence all too frequently came off as arrogance, damaging America's image abroad—at times with dire consequences. To cite an extreme example, Osama Bin Laden described his view of our nation's arrogance: "The collapse of the Soviet Union made the U.S. more haughty, and it has started to look at itself as a master of this world and established what it calls the New World Order."[10]

Let us make no mistake: America is still a work in progress. And unless we openly acknowledge our failings—failings such as our low voter turn-out, our political culture of special interests, the massive holes and inequalities in our health care and education systems, the state of our prisons—other nations will denounce us for our hypocrisy. Abraham Lincoln knew this problem all too well. In his famous 1854 debates with Stephen A. Douglas, he denounced the Missouri Compromise, which accepted slavery in the Southern states. He hated it not only "because of the monstrous injustice of slavery itself," he said, "but because it deprives our republican example of its just influence in the world—enables the enemies of free institutions, with plausibility, to taunt us as hypocrites—causes the real friends of freedom to doubt our sincerity."[11]

How those words resonate today. Guantánamo, Abu Ghraib, secret prisons, extraordinary renditions, detention without trial and possibly without end, tolerance of torture by others and even ourselves—all enable our enemies to taunt us as hypocrites and our friends to doubt our sincerity. Our power today is far greater and the world is far more complex than in Lincoln's time. And we act across a far broader range of issues. But the essential problem is the same. We must return to a foreign policy far more attentive to practicing what we preach.

If, in the international sphere, our nation succeeds in keeping faith with our values as we do at home—never perfectly, but consistently—it will be our greatest strength. If we do not, we will lose our way in the world, and our isolation may itself prove our undoing. We have already glimpsed the frightening possibility that in a world ever more hostile to America and thus ever more threatening, we will be ever more tempted to stray from the Constitution itself, to sacrifice liberty for security, democracy for efficiency, and justice for power. We may be tempted, in other words, to give up on the idea that is America.

TODAY IT IS MORE IMPORTANT than ever to regain our strength through a foreign policy based on our values. Measured by economic statistics and military might, our power is greater than ever. But measured by the commonsense measure of whether we can get others to do what we want them to do, we have clearly lost ground since the Cold War. If we are serious that our greatest strength is not our army, our land, or our wealth, but is instead our values, then we must rethink a whole set of current strategies and practices to reflect and promote those values.

To find the way forward, we need to look back and assess our own history honestly. We need to acknowledge just how long it has taken and how hard it has been to close the gap between our rhetoric and our lived reality in America, and how much work remains to be done. Admitting our own imperfections will not tarnish our ideals or ourselves in the eyes of the world. On the contrary, the world will find inspiration in the example of countless courageous Americans who, over the course of U.S. history, have forced the government and their fellow citizens to live up to proclaimed American ideals. Instead of hiding those struggles, many of which continue today, we should embrace and publicize them.

We also need to look back to understand exactly how we have defined and fought for our most cherished values over the course of our history. This understanding, in turn, will point the way to how we must now stand for those same values in the larger world. We must show one face—the same face—at home and abroad. And it must be an authentically American face, neither pious nor ashamed, that reflects who we are and have been as a people with both justifiable pride and much-needed humility.

But we must look forward, as well, and recommit ourselves to achieving our ideals at home. The most convincing argument for our way of life will lie in our ability to make it possible for more and more people to realize their American dreams. Our hold on people's hearts and minds around the world has always been rooted in the stories of their relatives and friends who made it to America and made a fortune, earned a degree, or simply gained the right to live free. Ensuring that this dream remains accessible today for both native-born Americans and immigrants may be the single best thing that we can do for ourselves in the world.

———

AMERICA NEEDS MORE PATRIOTS who understand the real meaning of American patriotism. In his famous poem "The Charge of the Light Brigade," Alfred Lord Tennyson describes the ultimate military loyalty: "Their's not to reason why, their's but to do and die." That kind of patriotism is not what America needs right now. If Ian Fishback, whose words inspired the title of this book, had followed that maxim, he would never have written his letter to John McCain urging a full investigation of the abuses at Abu Ghraib and explaining that his efforts to push an investigation within the army had fallen on deaf ears. He was protesting and exposing our flaws in time of war, pointing to behavior that deeply contravened American values. His was a deeply patriotic act, one that ultimately galvanized the Senate to take a stand against torture.

Our current government, however, does not always recognize the patriotism of such acts. The administration has denounced as disloyal and unpatriotic the politicians, reporters, and ordinary citizens who demand accountability for the disastrous prosecution of the war in Iraq and who challenge the constitutionality of aspects of the war on terror. But Americans who never question their government, regardless of the party or person in power, are avoiding their civic duty as Americans. In an unusually serious vein, our great folk hero Mark Twain put it this way. "Each must for himself alone decide what is right and what is wrong, and which course is patriotic and which isn't. You cannot shirk this and be a man. To decide it against your convictions is to be an unqualified and inexcusable traitor, both to yourself and to your country, let men label you as they may."[12]

In our history, the greatest patriots have been those leaders and ordinary citizens who have dared to hold America to our own highest standards—even at the cost of ostracism, punishment, imprisonment and, at times, even death. That, in the end, is what differentiates patriotism from nationalism. It is *not* "my country, right or wrong." It is, in the words of the great German American Civil War general, Republican senator, secretary of the interior, journalist, editor, and author Carl Schurz: "[Our] country, right or wrong; if right, to be kept right; and if wrong to be set right."[13]

This is a more humble and attractive patriotism, one that is particularly vital at a time of external threat, when criticism of any sort is generally silenced. Standing up for our country's ideals in the face of danger takes particular courage, the courage that Justice Louis Brandeis described as "the secret of liberty."[14] The stories on the following pages are accounts of great courage by great Americans, who criticized, agitated, marched, and fought for their cause. They were patriots in the spirit of James Baldwin, who proclaimed: "I love America more than any other country in this world; and, exactly for this reason, I insist on the right to criticize her perpetually."[15] That spirit itself is a vital part of the idea that is America.

"THE IDEA THAT IS AMERICA" can never be one idea. Our people, our landscapes, our families and cultures and experiences are far too diverse. Instead, many voices have sounded these ideas through our history, coming together over the centuries in a great chorus. As we listen to the speeches, the anthems, the sermons, the poems, the pledges, the ballads and the rallying cries across the land, we, like Walt Whitman in his famous poem *Leaves of Grass,* can hear America singing.

Yet this book is about far more than words, spoken or sung. Empty words yield hollow promises, breeding deep cynicism at home and abroad. We must translate our ideals into concrete plans and policies. And we must hurry, because the world is watching and the stakes could not be higher.

At the best moments in American history, we have, in Ralph Waldo Emerson's words, put our creed into our deed.[16] The manifest inconsistency between word and deed in the face of glaring injustice has produced a dynamic of protest and, ultimately, positive change. This change results not from our perfection or superiority as a people, but from the design of our political institutions, our collective shame when we fall short, and our collective conviction that, ultimately, we must be who we say we are.

A German friend of mine says that "beneath every hater of America is a disappointed lover of America." He is a German of the post–World War II generation, a man deeply devoted to American ideals and grateful for the role America has played in the German and European past. His sentiment captures how the members of his generation *want* us to live up to our ideals, to set an example and inspire others.

Young Germans today have a radically different view of America. They see us, quite simply, as having lost the moral high ground and, with it, any legitimacy to lead. During the Cold War, young Germans and young Europeans often marched in the streets to protest specific American policies that they disliked, but against the backdrop of an America standing for liberty and democracy against the Soviet Union. For the generations rising today in Europe, Africa, Asia, and Latin America, by contrast, the America they see arrogantly bestriding the world and using its military power without constraint is the only America they know.

Theirs are the minds we have to change. But to change the views of others, we must be able to look at ourselves with fresh eyes. To truly love our country, we must be willing to criticize, challenge, protest, and make democracy work—even in wartime. Finally, to regain our moral balance, we will need to learn as much as we teach, sometimes to play a supporting rather than a starring role, and even to set an example not through action but through self-restraint.

These are habits that often come hard to us. They are dusty from disuse. But to play the part we want to play in the world, they too must become part of the idea that is America.

Chapter 1

Liberty

My country, 'tis of thee,
Sweet land of liberty,
Of thee I sing;
Land where my fathers died,
Land of the pilgrims' pride,
From every mountainside,
Let freedom ring!

> —*Samuel Francis Smith,*
> *"America (My Country, 'Tis of Thee)," 1832*

Liberty is the universal longing of every soul.

> —*Secretary of State Condoleezza Rice,*
> *remarks at the American University in Cairo, June 20, 2005*

LIBERTY AND ITS NEAR SYNONYM, freedom, reside at the very heart of American identity. Our Constitution aims to "secure the Blessings of Liberty to ourselves and our Posterity." Our folk songs sing of the "sweet land of liberty" and the "land of the free." We have giant statues, cracked bells, airports, and even a professional basketball team named for liberty. A "freedom tower" will rise in the void left by the destruction of the World Trade Center.

Indeed, for many Americans, liberty and freedom are almost synonymous with America itself. When American relations with France soured in the lead-up to the 2003 Iraq war, jingoistic Americans did not speak of "American fries" or "American toast," but "freedom fries" and "freedom toast."

We come by this obsession honestly. The first Europeans came here seeking to worship as they pleased. Our founding revolution was a struggle for self-determination. Our Civil War was aimed—at least in part—at extending freedom to a wider swath of the population. The twentieth century's struggles against fascism and communism confirmed our self-image as defenders of the "free world," a duty we continue to believe in today.

Even more fundamentally, a commitment to liberty is woven into virtually every story we tell ourselves about who we are: every public oath, every popular account of American history, every inscription on our public monuments. American schoolchildren pledge allegiance to a nation "with liberty and justice for all."

That promise of freedom was written into our founding documents. The Declaration of Independence famously begins:

> We hold these truths to be self-evident, that all men are created equal, that they are endowed by their Creator with certain unalienable Rights, that among these are Life, Liberty and the pursuit of Happiness.

Liberty is also the founding commitment of the Constitution, which institutionalized the ideals proclaimed during the Revolution:

We the People of the United States, in Order to form a more perfect Union, establish Justice, insure domestic Tranquility, provide for the common defence, promote the general Welfare, and secure the Blessings of Liberty to ourselves and our Posterity, do ordain and establish this Constitution for the United States of America.

When it tolled after the first reading of the Declaration of Independence, the Liberty Bell rang with the message inscribed upon it: "Proclaim Liberty throughout All the land unto All the Inhabitants Thereof."[1] And over the course of more than two centuries, America has reiterated its commitment to liberty countless times. "Give me your tired, your poor, your huddled masses yearning to breathe free"—the famous lines by Emma Lazarus are inscribed on our Statue of Liberty, beckoning immigrants from across the oceans. More recently, President George W. Bush reaffirmed and broadened America's promise of liberty for the twenty-first century in his second inaugural address: "America, in this young century, proclaims liberty throughout all the world, and to all the inhabitants thereof."

And yet throughout American history, we have been far better at proclaiming our devotion to liberty than examining precisely what we mean by it. That's partly because once we try to translate our rhetoric into reality, liberty is not so easy to define. Absolute liberty for all citizens, for instance, will quickly degenerate into chaos. Alternatively, liberty for some can soon mean oppression for others. To achieve anything resembling liberty for all, individual liberty must be traded off against other values such as security, equality, justice, and tolerance.

Our Founders understood the need for these trade-offs and wrestled with them. Most fundamentally, they recognized the vital importance of *ordered liberty,* or liberty under law. As Thomas Jefferson wrote to a Greek patriot about the Greek revolt against Ottoman rule in 1823, America possessed the *"combined* blessings of liberty and order."[2] Jefferson and his fellow revolutionaries rejected order without liberty; that was the tyranny they had revolted against. But they understood equally that liberty without order would allow people's worst instincts to run unchecked. In George Washington's first inaugural address—the first presidential address by our first president—he counseled our young nation to attend to the supporting values that make liberty possible, among them "the eternal rules of order and right."[3]

Those grand-sounding "eternal rules" are far more likely in practice to be regulations as simple as traffic lights and as complex and technical as tax codes. What Washington had in mind was more likely the legal translations of the moral injunctions found in all great religions—thou shalt not kill or steal. But the order necessary for liberty to flourish includes the entire spectrum of the rule of law.

Liberty is a far more romantic and compelling battle cry than order, of course. Patrick Henry's words would not have resonated through the ages if he'd said: "Give me ordered liberty or give me death!" Yet ordered liberty is what liberty must mean in practice, for Americans and for all people. Equally important, ordered liberty can never be static. An established order enshrines a particular definition of liberty at a particular time in a society's history—just as our Constitution constituted liberty only for white men. But liberty itself is an ideal; its practical contours are continually defined and redefined.

Take, for instance, Franklin Delano Roosevelt's famous enunciation of "the four freedoms" in 1941: freedom of speech, freedom of religion, freedom from want, and freedom from fear. Freedom of speech and freedom of religion are largely uncontroversial among Americans as essential components of liberty, although the boundaries of these liberties are continually contested in the courts and Congress. Freedom from want, however, resonated throughout the country in the wake of the Great Depression, but today would be seen by many Americans as an economic right rather than a civil and political right guaranteed by the Constitution. And freedom from fear had a very different meaning in 1941 than what the Bush administration means today. Then, in the midst of a war against Nazism, it meant a stout defense of our way of life against militant fascism. Today, in the wake of 9/11, it means reducing the fear of a terrorist attack, in part by restricting the liberties that underpin our way of life.

Debating the practical meaning of liberty as it is defined and implemented in our Constitution and laws has profoundly catalyzed social and political change. Just as the Founders' urge for freedom proved stronger than the limits imposed on it, succeeding generations of Americans have used the promise of liberty to fight for their own freedom, from religious minorities to slaves to women and to various groups today seeking the liberty they believe is their due under the Constitution. This process has driven American history, but has hardly been a smooth or steady progression. We have made great strides in some places and backslid in others: freeing the slaves and promising them equal rights but then denying their descendants the right to vote or to get an education or a job; guaranteeing freedom of speech but then blacklisting or even imprisoning groups of Americans who say unpopular things; promising all citizens the liberty to marry and raise a family but then denying this liberty to those who seek committed and loving relationships with members of their own sex.

The stories of some of our greatest struggles to define and implement liberty are instructive. We have always defined liberty to mean freedom of mind and body for individual citizens, and freedom of our country from any foreign rule. But freedom of mind had to be fought for against a theocracy, freedom of body had to be secured through the bloodiest war our nation has ever known, and freedom for our country coexisted with our rule over other countries. These are stories we need to remember when we try to advance liberty in the larger world.

———————

THE AMERICAN CONCEPT of liberty is founded on freedom of expression—the freedom to think and to say what you think. It is no accident that the first right in the Bill of Rights, the first amendment to the Constitution, guarantees freedom of speech and religion. Freedom of religion, properly understood, is really freedom of conscience: the freedom to believe—or not to believe—in God, in a particular government or political order, in a set of principles or ethical beliefs for governing ourselves. It means the right of every man and woman to commune with his or her own soul, to decide on his or her deepest beliefs, to reason through or intuit a set of practices that govern relations with nature, with other beings, and, for many, with a higher being.

Freedom of conscience is, first of all, the freedom to decide what you believe, but it is equally important to be able to express your beliefs—through worship, writing, or public proclamation. In this sense, freedom of expression plays a dual role. It is a necessity for individual self-definition and flourishing; it is also, as we shall see later, an essential instrument for establishing and maintaining a democracy. But none of these aspects of perhaps our most fundamental liberty were obvious or uncontested.

The founders of the Massachusetts Bay Colony, pursuing a "purer" alternative to the Church of England, came to this continent seeking freedom to worship as they pleased. They were not, however, planning to extend this liberty to other sects, at least not at first. On the contrary, they created a strict theocracy.

Anne Hutchinson learned of Puritan intolerance firsthand. A devout woman, Hutchinson left her life in England to join the religious experiment taking place in North America. Her beliefs, however, differed slightly from the Puritan establishment. Whereas mainstream Puritans taught a "covenant of works"—that salvation came to those whose actions furthered God's will—Hutchinson believed that salvation could only come from a "covenant of grace," a profound, personal spiritual connection to God. More damningly, at least in the eyes of the Puritan elders, she, a mere woman, held theological discussion meetings in her house.

In November 1637—only eight years after the establishment of the Massachusetts Bay Colony—Governor John Winthrop called Hutchinson to trial. He accused her of troubling the peace of the commonwealth and saying things "prejudicial to the honour of the churches and ministers." Worse, Hutchinson held religious discussions in her house that were not "comely in the sight of God" and perhaps, above all, not fitting for her gender.[4]

In a remarkable show of lawyerly instinct, Hutchinson refuted Winthrop's charges, exasperating her prosecutors for two days with her sharp wit and knowledge of Scripture. In the end it did not much matter, for the court had reached its conclusion before the trial began. Hutchinson, who came to America seeking freedom, found herself banished from the Massachusetts Bay Colony.

Cast into the wilderness, she made her way south to a small settlement founded by another refugee from Massachusetts, the

Reverend Roger Williams. Williams had fled the Bay Colony a few years earlier, on the verge of being deported back to England for his strong belief in religious freedom and the separation of church and state. He saw his new settlement as a refuge from Puritan prosecution. Named Providence, the town was envisioned as a democratic community in which the state had authority only over public matters. The signers to the original charter pledged to submit themselves to the decisions of the majority of heads of families, but "only in civil things."[5]

The last phrase is key. By only submitting to the common will in "civil things," the inhabitants of Providence became the first Americans to separate church from state, conscience from political authority. They were the first to understand that freedom of worship had to mean not just that one group of people were free to worship their god, but that all groups of people had to be free to decide whether to worship any god.

Williams's views on religious freedom were profoundly controversial in his day. Quakers, Catholics, Jews, Lutherans, Methodists, and many other denominations jostled for space in different colonies. But by the time America grew into a country, the framers of the Bill of Rights had written religious rights into the Constitution: "Congress shall make no law respecting an establishment of religion, or prohibiting the free exercise thereof." The words were there; religious groups and secular authorities have been arguing over their meaning ever since.

Today we struggle over the meaning of the phrase "under God" in the Pledge of Allegiance and the posting of religious symbols in public buildings. And even with religious tolerance commanded by law, in our social and even political relations we are often highly suspicious of religious minorities, be they Catholics, Jews, Muslims, atheists, or Evangelicals.

Beyond religion, we insist on speaking our minds. But freedom of speech is hardly absolute either. Libel, slander, incitements to violence, even false advertising—all are regulated types of speech. Hate speech, on the other hand—speech that causes pain and injury to different groups in our society—is permitted far more in the United States than in most other democracies. These issues, as we will see, are fundamental to both our liberty and our democracy.

Freedom of mind is the ultimate liberty. Even a prisoner can still think and believe. But freedom of body is hardly negligible. Physical freedom is an essential component of liberty, but one that was denied to a significant proportion of Americans for almost a century after the nation's founding. This story is worth remembering as we ponder the meaning of liberty.

A FREE CONSCIENCE in a captive body is not liberty. A free body means freedom of choice, to choose where we live, what we do, how we pursue happiness. Freedom of choice allows us to define who we are, to live with purpose and meaning.

Such liberty is not license, however. Again, true liberty is ordered liberty. Free choice must mean responsible choice. And responsible choice does not infringe on the equal rights of fellow citizens. Thinking of America's endowment of natural resources, Thomas Jefferson asked, "What more is necessary to make us a happy and a prosperous people?" His answer: "a wise and frugal Government, which shall restrain men from injuring one another, shall leave them otherwise free to regulate their own pursuits of industry and improvement."[6]

According to the Declaration of Independence, this wise and ordered liberty is the birthright of all Americans. Here again, however, America's history belies its rhetoric. Those grand phrases coexisted with men and women in chains, sold like animals on the auction block, forced to work in the fields and the houses of their masters, with no liberty even to raise their own children. Slavery was our national shame for almost a century after our founding; the battles to overcome the legacy of slavery reignited a century after the Civil War and continue today.

A scant eleven years after the Declaration of Independence pronounced it a "self-evident" truth that "all men are created equal," the framers of the Constitution apportioned both representatives and taxes based on the number of "free Persons" of a particular district and "*three fifths* of all other Persons."[7] Those "other" persons were slaves, human beings with no liberty at all.

This clause was the subject of the most heated debates at the Constitutional Convention. While many in non-slave-holding states were more concerned with preserving their legislative strength against the South—where institutional slavery swelled the population—than defending the rights of blacks, the discrepancy between the lofty principles enshrined in the Constitution and the limited scope of those same principles was not lost on the Founders.

Jefferson perfectly embodied this paradox. How could he, a slaveholder, have written "that all men are created equal, that they are endowed by their Creator with certain unalienable rights"? Only with a troubled heart. As a Southerner, he saw no social or political alternative to slavery. But as a philosopher, a moralist, and a human being, he understood that his young nation was courting disaster. Writing about slaves and slavery in his 1781 *Notes on Virginia,* he worried that slavery degraded master and slave alike: "permitting one half of the citizens . . . to trample on the rights of the other, transforms those into despots, and these into enemies."

Jefferson believed that America itself would one day face divine justice. "Can the liberties of a nation be thought secure," he asked, "when we have removed their only firm basis, a conviction in the minds of the people that these liberties are the gift of God?" Such a conviction, he knew, meant that depriving some human beings of their liberty could only result in divine wrath: "Indeed I tremble for my country when I reflect that God is just: that his justice cannot sleep forever: that considering numbers, nature and natural means only, a revolution of the wheel of fortune, an exchange of situation, is among possible events."[8]

Eighty years later, Jefferson's foreboding would prove well placed. It took four years of war and the blood of nearly 700,000 Americans—almost one for each slave brought to North America—to wash the stain of slavery from the Constitution. America paid an awful price for what has been described as our country's "original sin."[9]

While it ultimately took the Civil War to end American slavery, abolitionists fought human bondage for decades before the opening salvos at Fort Sumter. Freedom-loving Americans invoked the nation's founding principles to challenge the evil institution they saw as an insult to the Constitution and to morality. Slaveholders responded in kind, defending slavery as a fundamental part of the American way of life. This debate pitted American values against American traditions, with both sides claiming the mantle of patriotism.

No one made the case against slavery more powerfully than Frederick Douglass, a former slave whose rhetorical eloquence made him one of the most prominent abolitionists of the day. In his 1852 Fourth of July address to the Rochester Ladies' Anti-Slavery Society—actually delivered July 5—he sharply denounced an America whose "character and conduct never looked blacker." He asked the rather proper and well-intentioned ladies sitting before him why they had asked him to speak on this day. He pointed out that justice, liberty, prosperity—all the things that Americans celebrate on the Fourth of July—did not belong to his people. The Fourth of July itself "is *yours,* not *mine,"* Douglass told the audience. He condemned slavery in the name of liberty, humanity, the Constitution, and the Bible, calling the practice "the great sin and shame of America."[10]

Douglass's anger did not come from hatred of the land that had once held him in bondage, but rather a burning frustration that America had failed to live up to its defining principles. Most whites, even those opposed to slavery, saw the Fourth of July as a time to express their patriotism by celebrating their common heritage. Douglass's patriotism, deeply rooted in American values, instead compelled him to expose the hypocrisy of that heritage. "America is false to the past," he cried, "false to the present, and solemnly binds herself to be false in the future."

Loyalty to a shared history was a powerful theme that slavery's advocates invoked in its defense. Perhaps none did so more eloquently—a dubious honor—than Senator John C. Calhoun of South Carolina. His famous 1837 speech on the Senate floor argued for slavery on economic and legal grounds, but became most passionate when defending the Southern way of life, above all its "peculiar institution," from Northern hostility. The system of slavery, he insisted, "be it good or bad, . . . has grown up with our society and our institutions, and is so interwoven with them, that to destroy it would be to destroy us as a people."

Douglass's insistence on America's ideals and Calhoun's insistence on American tradition crystallized the nation's struggle to reconcile its commitment to liberty with the essential economic and social institution of the Southern states. Calhoun was right; slavery could not be abolished without drenching the country in blood. More Americans died in the Civil War than in all the other wars America has fought combined.

Halfway through the war, on September 22, 1862, President Abraham Lincoln issued the Emancipation Proclamation, declaring that on January 1 of the coming year, "all persons held as slaves . . . shall be then, thenceforward, and forever free." Later in 1863, four and a half months after the largest and bloodiest battle of the Civil War, Lincoln delivered the Gettysburg Address, calling on all Americans to dedicate themselves to the "unfinished work" that the men who fell at Gettysburg had died to advance. He asked his audience to resolve "that this nation, under God, shall have a new birth of freedom."

But Lincoln was assassinated, and the new birth of freedom was not so easy. How much did liberty really mean to a poor black sharecropper or to a black citizen who, first barred from voting because he was a slave, was now barred because he could not read? How much did it mean at the height of the Ku Klux Klan's reign of terror? True liberty for the former slaves was a long time coming, and equality, democracy, and justice were still a long way down the road.

What good does it do citizens to be free in mind and body if their entire country is enslaved? From the revolution forward, we have always understood liberty to include the freedom of an entire country to govern itself. The Declaration of Independence is a public justification of the decision to break free of English rule, written in terms that apply to all people:

> whenever any Form of Government becomes destructive of [the unalienable rights of life, liberty, and the pursuit of happiness], it is the Right of the People to alter or to abolish it, and to institute

new Government, laying its foundation on such principles and organizing its powers in such form, as to them shall seem most likely to effect their Safety and Happiness.

When those words were written in 1776, America was a weak nation with republican tendencies—a loose confederation, really—challenging mighty, monarchical England. Our moral commitment to self-determination was clear—and easy.

As it grew into a continental, then hemispheric, and then global power, however, America succumbed to the temptation to deny other nations the right we claimed at birth. The Founders would have regarded American imperialism as an oxymoron, and American leaders tried to paint our colonizing in other colors. The fierce debate over our role in the world in the late nineteenth and early twentieth centuries became yet another arena in which we wrestled with not only the meaning of liberty but also its scope.

In 1895, the people of Cuba revolted against their Spanish colonial masters, who brutally attempted to put down the rebellion. Since 1823, the United States had followed a policy—the Monroe Doctrine—of preventing European meddling in the Americas. Though Spanish rule of Cuba dated from before President James Monroe's manifesto, U.S. public opinion turned strongly against Spain.

American newspapers, especially the sensationalist "yellow press," stoked this sentiment by publishing exaggerated accounts of Spanish oppression in Cuba. One paper screamed, "The horrors of a barbarous struggle for the extermination of the native population are witnessed in all parts of the country. . . . Blood on the roadsides, blood in the field, blood on the doorsteps: blood, blood, blood!"[11] The mysterious explosion of the American battleship *Maine* in Havana's harbor was all that was needed to turn public anger against Spain into open hostility.

America quickly deprived Spain of its colonial possessions, taking Cuba and Puerto Rico in the Caribbean and Guam and the Philippines in the Pacific. Briefly, it seemed as if the United States was acting according to its belief in self-determination, liberating smaller nations from the yoke of colonialism.

But then the liberators stayed. Of the four "freed" colonies, only Cuba was given nominal independence, and even then the United States inserted a clause into the Cuban constitution allowing America to intervene whenever it deemed appropriate. The other three islands were made effective colonies of the United States—though never officially described as such—and served as important bases for the expansion of U.S. naval power, particularly in the Pacific. In the Philippines, we used force to maintain control over the island nation, our troops fighting the same patriotic Filipinos we had previously assisted in their struggle against the Spanish. As the American flag rose above foreign lands, the irony was palpable: A war justified in the name of liberty was revealed to be an imperialist bid for power.

Fortunately, some Americans recognized this contradiction. In 1898, the industrialist Andrew Carnegie offered to buy Filipino independence from the U.S. government for $20 million. Carnegie was also active in the American Anti-Imperialist League, an organization dedicated to resisting the annexation of the Philippines. This group began as a small gathering of intellectuals and businessmen in Boston and grew to a national membership of thirty thousand after the U.S. occupation of the Philippines. In addition to Carnegie, its members included such notables as Mark Twain, psychologist William James, America's "mother of social work" Jane Addams, lawyer Clarence S. Darrow, and labor leader Samuel Gompers. George S. Boutwell, former secretary of the treasury and congressman from Massachusetts, served as president.

The league insisted that a free people could not hold another nation in bondage without risking their own liberty. Indeed, three and a half decades after the Civil War, the words of Abraham Lincoln again sounded in defense of freedom. At the Chicago Liberty Meeting, held at the Chicago Central Music Hall in April 1899, the league members took as their creed two quotes from the sixteenth president: "No man is good enough to govern another man without that other's consent. When the white man governs himself, that is self-government, but when he governs himself and also governs another man, that is more than self-government—that is despotism." And, "Those who deny freedom to others deserve it not for themselves, and under a just God cannot long retain it."[12]

By marshalling Lincoln's arguments against slavery for their own cause of freedom, the league made an important connection between America's own struggle to ensure freedom for its citizens and the struggle of people around the world to achieve that same goal. They recognized, as Lincoln had before them, that the American government was sometimes inimical to both.

The final shout at the meeting was a fierce fighting slogan taken from Patrick Henry, who first uttered it in the Virginia House of Burgesses after being called a traitor for advocating American independence from Britain. Harking back to America's own struggle against a colonial power, the conventioneers shouted, "If this be treason, make the most of it."[13]

However ardent its rhetoric and committed its members, the Anti-Imperialist League failed to prevent America from joining the ranks of imperialist powers. The United States did not relinquish its hold on the Philippines until almost four decades later. Guam and Puerto Rico remain U.S. protectorates to this day.

As these territories were pondering and struggling against their status as American colonies, the world fought a "Great War" so that the world could be made "safe for democracy."[14] Woodrow Wilson's sweeping vision included self-determination for all European peoples ruled by a foreign power, including Romania, Serbia, Montenegro, and Poland. Wilson laid out this goal in his famous fourteen-point plan, which, he told Congress on January 8, 1918, rested on "the principle of justice to all peoples and nationalities, and their right to live on equal terms of liberty and safety with one another, whether they be strong or weak."[15]

Wilson's vision was bold, but bolder still was his estimate of the support for this principle in the world and in America itself. He was certain that Americans "could act upon no other principle." But he reckoned without his fellow victors, and ultimately without Congress itself. Britain, France, and other victors were more interested in strengthening their own colonial holdings around the world and taking their defeated enemies' possessions than in promoting self-determination. Moreover, the Congress to which Wilson had directed his lofty words balked at various parts of Wilson's plan, especially his efforts to create a collective security organization—the League of Nations—to protect weak states. Instead of proving willing to sacrifice everything for other nations' independence, the United States turned inward, embracing isolationism.

Not until after World War II could America more confidently and consistently champion decolonization, offering support to the scores of former European and Asian colonies fighting to be free. This time America did found and join a collective security organization, the United Nations, which was dedicated to the sovereign equality of all member states. The United Nations was also charged with a powerful mandate for decolonization through its Trusteeship Council, which, despite the complications of the Cold War, successfully helped scores of colonies become independent countries in the decades following the war. The U.S. track record certainly was not perfect, but in critical cases like the Suez Crisis of 1956, the United States stood against France and Britain—close allies but colonial powers—and sided instead with Egypt.

Unfortunately, just as we were forswearing formal imperialism, the struggle against the Soviet Union during the Cold War led us to support and even to install puppet governments in countries we deemed important to our security. The democratically elected government of Iran was an early casualty. In 1953, President Eisenhower agreed, at the request of the British government, to use the Central Intelligence Agency to topple the nationalist government of Prime Minister Mohammad Mossadegh, which had nationalized British oil companies working in Iran. Truman, Eisenhower's predecessor, had refused to take on this mission, but Iran's shared border with the Soviet Union and the socialist leanings of Iran's government led the new administration to agree. The coup went rather smoothly, restoring Mohammed Reza Pahlavi as shah and crushing Iran's democratic aspirations. Resentment against the shah and his Western backers festered over the following years before exploding in the Islamic Revolution of 1979. As Washington struggles over how to contain Tehran's nuclear aspirations today, I cannot help but wonder what might have happened had we remained true to our values in 1953.

As we looked around the world through Cold War lenses, we repeatedly chose authoritarianism over communism, preferring a friendly government over one that provided even the most basic liberties for its citizens. Franklin D. Roosevelt summed up this attitude well in his reported description of the Nicaraguan dictator Somoza: "He may be a son of a bitch, but he's our son of a bitch." Somoza had plenty of company. U.S. support helped create and maintain a crazy quilt of dictatorships across the globe. The list includes Chile, Argentina, Indonesia, Guatemala, Iran, Egypt, Nicaragua, Paraguay, Bolivia, Angola, Zaire, Saudi Arabia, Kuwait, Morocco, Tunisia, Algeria, Jordan, Panama, Haiti, the Dominican Republic, Honduras, El Salvador, Nepal, Brazil, Uzbekistan, South Africa, and Saddam Hussein's Iraq.

Many of these choices, made by both Democratic and Republican administrations, seem easy to second-guess now, but to the men and women who made them they seemed the lesser of two evils. The alternative, they thought, would have been the expansion of Soviet totalitarianism, another kind of oppression. Today, however, what is most important is to understand how U.S. support for these governments appeared to their citizens, all of whom were denied freedom of expression and many of whom suffered directly at the hands of secret police and death squads for daring to mount political opposition. These physical and mental scars make it hard for millions of people around the world to believe U.S. claims of support for liberty.

O BEAUTIFUL FOR SPACIOUS SKIES, for amber waves of grain." Most Americans know the first verse of "America the Beautiful." But the second verse is more relevant to the U.S. role in the world today.

> O beautiful for pilgrim feet, whose stern, impassioned stress
> A thoroughfare for freedom beat across the wilderness!
> America! America! God mend thine every flaw,
> Confirm thy soul in self-control, Thy liberty in law!

This verse captures the apparent paradox of ordered liberty. The first two lines describe America marching with the forces of history—a pilgrim's progress toward ever greater liberty. While the "thoroughfare for freedom" had many twists and turns, it was never blocked completely. The great struggles recounted here are all of a slow, difficult, periodically backsliding, but ultimately steady progression toward greater freedom of conscience, choice, and country—first within America and then beyond our borders.

In contrast, the second two lines of the verse speak to George Washington's "eternal rules of order and right." Liberty requires restraint: self-restraint first, and then the capacity to restrain those who cannot exercise self-restraint. The entire concept of the rule of law is a collective precommitment to obey the law and to accept that if we violate it, the law will be enforced against us. We enjoy liberty because we accept the necessity of ordered liberty.

Domestically, the order that is enshrined and enforced in our Constitution and laws safeguards our individual liberty. Internationally, however, we have found the formula of ordered liberty much more problematic. Within countries, as much as we may desire to help their citizens gain the liberty we enjoy, the calculations of power and stability among nations have often led us to turn a blind eye to stifled minds and shackled bodies and to ally with the governments we find rather than the governments we want. In relations between countries, we have often been tempted to ignore the international law that guarantees freedom of country for all nations.

We stand now at a time in our history when we must resist this temptation. Keeping faith with our values means seeking and securing a world of ordered liberty. Such a world would also serve our interests, both because people around the world would see us standing for our ideals rather than merely mouthing them and because power without law ultimately becomes tyranny or empire.

As a young—and weak—nation, the United States championed international law as armor against intervention by Britain, France, and Spain—first in North America and later, in the nineteenth century, in South America. As the United States became a major power itself, Americans became interveners and, as we have seen, even imperialists. Only after two world wars did Americans come to appreciate the virtues of international law and institutions even as a strong nation.

After World War II, the United States, though more powerful than any other nation, wisely realized that its power was greatest when integrated into a system of "order and right." We worked closely with other nations to create a host of multilateral institutions and programs, including the North Atlantic Treaty Organization (NATO), the World Bank, the International Monetary Fund, the General Agreement on Trade and Tariffs (the precursor to the World Trade Organization), the Marshall Plan, human rights conventions, and, most importantly, the United Nations.[16] These projects, which became the infrastructure of international order for over half a century, often checked and balanced America's scope of action abroad. We deliberately consulted and worked with allies to pursue common ends, and we promised to uphold common standards.

We chose this route because we knew that power alone was not enough to keep us safe. Indeed, we knew that too much power could be a problem. By engaging the other nations of the world as equal partners, we reassured them that the United States would not seek domination; we showed that American power was no threat to countries interested in working to promote peace and stability. By building constraints on our own power, we created at the international level a system of ordered liberty that advanced our own interests and those of our allies. For every increment of power we gave up, we gained an equally valuable—and indeed indispensable—increment of legitimacy.

"No matter how great our strength," said Harry Truman to the assembled delegates of the nascent United Nations in 1945, "we all have to recognize . . . that we must deny ourselves the license to do always as we please." He rejected the idea of special privileges for any one nation or regional group that would harm any other nation. His reasoning was not idealistic, but intensely practical: "If any nation would keep security for itself, it must be ready and willing to share security with all."[17]

After the Cold War, however, the United States again bestrode the world like a colossus, so much so that many Americans began to wonder if the United States could not establish and maintain international order all by itself. And after September 11, 2001, the majority of Americans considered any constraints on the government's freedom of action, even self-imposed restraints, as threats to U.S. security, not safeguards. Consequently, from 2002 to 2005, the Bush administration decided, in its view, to unshackle American power and to pursue our interests as we pleased, accompanied by whichever other nations decided to join us in various "coalitions of the willing." Indeed, some Americans went further and openly embraced the idea of an American empire, resurrecting—and for some reason interpreting literally—Jefferson's metaphorical description of America as an "empire of liberty."[18]

It is in this vein that far too many people around the world heard President Bush's second inaugural address, in January 2005, in which he dedicated America to a global struggle for liberty. Speaking explicitly to "the peoples of the world," he made a promise. "When you stand for your liberty," he proclaimed, "we will stand with you." It was a short speech, but he mentioned the words "liberty" fifteen times and "freedom" twenty-seven times.

Unfortunately, the principal result of the U.S. campaign for global liberty is a bloody, fractured, and increasingly dangerous Iraq. Without an appreciation of the need for ordered liberty in Iraq, the administration radically underestimated the need for troops. With similar disregard, Washington failed to produce a clear and effective postwar plan to prevent the destruction of the institutions that had established order under Saddam Hussein. In Afghanistan, too, the Taliban originally came to power through its ability to provide even minimum security for ordinary Afghans, a harsh and even brutal order that was nevertheless preferable to the anarchy of contending warlords. Today, the Taliban movement is resurgent, and the weak central government cannot maintain order or protect its supporters much beyond Kabul, the capital.

On top of these specific crises, we now face a whole host of threats, from terrorism to global pandemics to the proliferation of nuclear weapons, for which power alone is not enough. These issues, like the process of building order and securing liberty in countries ravaged by conflict, require long-term, institutionalized cooperation between as many nations as possible. Repairing and reforming the international rules and institutions that anchored international order during the Cold War would be a start. But those institutions were built for a very different configuration of power in the world than either the unipolar era currently coming to an end or the multipolar era rising with a united Europe across the Atlantic and China, India, and Japan across the Pacific.

America needs a new plan. It must be a collective plan, one that requires us to work closely with other nations. It must be a plan for ordered liberty *among* nations that will allow us to stand with as many other countries as possible to help create, protect, and sustain ordered liberty *within* nations.

To formulate and implement this plan, America must once again, as a nation, be willing to commit itself to a set of international rules concerning the use of force. We must be prepared to live by these rules if we can strike the right bargain with other nations. The best way to craft the elements of that bargain is to design a set of rules and institutions adapted to the needs and threats of the twenty-first rather than the twentieth century. Specifically, those rules must permit far more intervention into the domestic affairs of states that pose a major danger to other states. The rules must be applied and enforced by institutions capable of much faster, more flexible, and more effective action than current institutions.

Other nations are afraid of us. A 2003 survey of Europeans, conducted after the Iraq war, showed that America was considered as much a threat to world peace as North Korea and Iran, slightly ahead of countries like Iraq and Afghanistan, and a good 20 to 25 percent above China and Russia. Over half the respondents to a similar poll in Lebanon, Jordan, Kuwait, and Morocco were worried about U.S. military threats to their own countries.[19]

President Bush reacts to such polls with incredulity. Like most Americans, he cannot imagine how other nations could really think we would ever threaten others. But in the world of the twenty-first century, in which a growing majority of the global population does not even remember the Cold War, we *must* see ourselves as others see us. Their newspapers show many pictures we never see or we glimpse only briefly: photos of civilians killed or maimed by our bombs or by our allies' bombs; pictures of abused detainees at Abu Ghraib; or the rare but nevertheless real image of a girl raped and, along with the rest of her family, killed by U.S. Marines in Iraq. And when we then declare the right to wage preventive war, to invade and topple other governments before they actually attack or prepare to attack us, the world begins to see us as Goliath and to cheer for any nation or group that can take us down.

If liberty requires order, and order requires constraint, then we must begin by proposing and accepting constraints on our own right to use force in our international relations. When we signed the U.N. Charter in 1945, we agreed not to use force against the territorial integrity or political independence of any state except in self-defense or as authorized by the Security Council. The formula needs to be amended to permit the use of force to stop the perpetration of genocide or other crimes against humanity whenever the use of force is collectively authorized by a representative regional or global institution. If the Security Council is deadlocked, then a decision to act by NATO, an organization of twenty-six democracies that stretches from Ottawa to London to Ankara to Riga; the Organization of American States; or the African Union could substitute.

At the same time, the United States should sponsor and strongly support reform of the Security Council in ways that will make it both more representative and more effective. This is no easy task; it will require restricting the use of the veto and bringing additional important countries like Germany, Japan, Brazil, India, and South Africa into the council as at least the equivalent of permanent members. But if we cannot live by the current rules, the right response is not to reject them and thus any hope of an international order that works both for us and for other countries, but to amend the rules in ways that we are genuinely prepared to live by.

It's the hard stuff that matters most. The fundamental structure of international order is determined by the rules governing the use of force. Our current rules must be revised to allow the international community to take prompt and effective action against (1) a government that has failed in its most fundamental obligations to protect its people or (2) armed gangs who have effectively taken over a country. And the institutions to enforce these rules and to build the cooperation necessary to fight crime, disease, poverty, illiteracy, and environmental disasters must be decentralized, fast, and flexible.

Flexibility will be key, but cannot come at the expense of legitimacy or effectiveness. We once lived in a world where communication was provided by centralized hierarchical companies—Ma Bell in the United States and the PTT (Post, Telephone, Telegraph) in various European countries. We now live in the world of the Internet, which allows countless groups to come together in various ways and for various purposes in almost infinite combinations. Yet the Internet is structured by rules—basic technical rules, security rules, and values-based rules that govern behavior from pornography to basic civility on various Web sites. It is an order fixed enough to make things work, but flexible enough to accommodate the speed and scope of human ingenuity. It is ordered liberty for the twenty-first century.

The world needs an international order that is similarly adapted to the needs of the twenty-first century. The United States should lead the way and rally other nations to reform the current international order—which looks much more like the old world of centralized, monopolistic telecommunications—based on a clear set of goals and a clear alternative strategy. Much of the rest of the world suspects that we have been halfhearted about U.N. reform, because our preferred reform would be for the United Nations simply to disappear. This is a strategy not for a leader but for a spoiler.

If we are willing to adopt rules that bind ourselves as well as others, and to put in the work and the will to create an international order that will liberate nations and the people within them, then we can hold our heads high in the international community. And if we cannot convince 191 nations to adopt meaningful reforms, then we should negotiate new treaties and institutions with as large a group of like-minded nations as possible. We should begin with the 25 nations of the European Union and the 26 (significantly overlapping) nations of NATO, as well as nations such as Japan, Australia, India, South Africa, Brazil, and Mexico. It may be necessary to build ordered liberty at the international level by turning first to nations committed to ordered liberty domestically.

We should not expect to succeed overnight. Nor should we expect anything like perfect success. We continue to conduct our own "experiment in ordered liberty" domestically and to try to live up to our founding commitments. But the world's first attempt at a genuine global institution that would create sufficient security for ordered liberty internationally—the League of Nations—was made not even a century ago. The attempt failed; its successor, the United Nations, has done better but has far to go. Success may take generations or even centuries. But as a nation "brought forth in liberty" and committed to building the conditions at home and abroad in which it will flower, America has to try.

———————

We AMERICANS ARE OPTIMISTS. When they see the citizens of other nations fighting for their freedom, American presidents, both Republican and Democratic, have an unfortunate tendency to think of liberty as simply spreading through the world like ripples emanating from a pebble in a pool. Recall

Jefferson's metaphor of a "ball of liberty" that will simply "roll round the globe" once it has been put in motion. But as we have seen, Jefferson well understood the critical importance of ordered liberty. And as is so violently and painfully obvious in Iraq and Afghanistan, order is the hard part.

No surprise there—it was similarly far easier for our Founders to wave the banner of liberty than to construct the rules and institutions that have, over two centuries, allowed freedom to flourish for more and more Americans. But without order, and the basic security that order provides, liberty is all too often just an empty phrase. And if, in practice, liberty for all means chaos and anarchy for all, then most people will trade some degree of liberty for stability and order, even if they can see that they are sliding down the slippery slope to oppression.

For Americans, the lesson might seem to be that spreading liberty around the world will take a bigger army than we thought— one big enough to create and enforce the order necessary for ordered liberty. But that's not enough. Ordered liberty within countries will also require a measure of ordered liberty *between* countries.

Ordered liberty between countries, in turn, requires America to accept constraints on its behavior in the same way that individual Americans must accept the rule of law at home as both the price and the prerequisite of their liberty. To the citizens of the most powerful nation in the world, this necessity is likely to seem paradoxical. But we will not be the most powerful nation in the world—measured by guns and dollars and people— forever. On the contrary, our best hope flows from strengthening and husbanding the power and authority that flows from our values. To build and keep that power, we must confirm our soul in self-control, and our liberty in law.

Chapter 2

Democracy

We are a Republican Government. Real liberty is never found in despotism or in the extremes of Democracy.

> —*Alexander Hamilton,*
> *speaking at the Constitutional Convention, 1787*

Democracy is on the march.

> —*George W. Bush,*
> *speech at Moosic, Pennsylvania, September 3, 2004*

HAVING DECLARED INDEPENDENCE and won the revolution in the name of liberty, the Founders were faced with the task of organizing thirteen former colonies and their principles into a workable nation. Freedom had been dearly won from the British, but now arose the even more difficult task of institutionalizing it. How to create a government that would, in the words of the preamble to the Constitution of 1789, "secure the blessings of liberty to ourselves and our posterity?" What would liberty under law actually look like?

The answer, of course, was what followed the preamble, the revolutionary plan for popular government that has guided the nation ever since. Largely the work of James Madison, the Constitution stands as the foundation of what has come to be known as American democracy.

This legacy might have shocked its writers. For its first century, America did *not* promise democracy to its people. Search in vain for a reference to democracy in any of our founding documents, anthems, or patriotic verse. Nary a mention in the Declaration of Independence, which simply speaks of governments deriving "their just powers from the consent of the governed." Nor in the Constitution, which promises a republican form of government designed to secure the blessings of liberty. We sing of the "sweet land of liberty," but not of democracy; the Star-Spangled Banner waves over the "land of the free and the home of the brave" but not the government of the people.

This was not an accident. George Washington, James Madison, and Alexander Hamilton all saw big and important differences between a republic and a democracy. The revolutionary principle that they had fought for was *self*-government: government by the consent of the governed. Republican government and democratic government were both forms of self-government. A republic was a government in which voters must elect people to represent them. Democracy, on the other hand, meant pure majority rule—direct rule by the people themselves. The Founders firmly wanted a republic, in which elected representatives could deliberate over what was best for the country rather than responding automatically to the will of their constituents.

Yet today, America stands proudly for democracy throughout the world; President Bush typically uses "liberty" and "democracy" as synonyms, but, like most Americans, is less fond of "republic." He is not alone—indeed, this tendency harks back to

Woodrow Wilson, Franklin Roosevelt, John F. Kennedy, and Ronald Reagan, all of whom identified America as a champion of "democracy" around the world. So what exactly do we mean, as a nation, when we talk about democracy?

Democracy today means self-government by *all* citizens, which means, above all, granting all citizens the right to vote. This right has been fought for and won by successive groups of disenfranchised Americans—white men who were laborers rather than landowners, black men, and then women of all races. Today, when people say they stand for democracy in the world, they usually mean that they stand for universal suffrage.

The quality and stability of our own democracy, however, depends on much more than free and fair elections. Democracy in this country also means divided government. America emerged out of a revolution against the absolutist rule of King George III, who ultimately held all the power of state in his unelected hands. In creating the new country, the Founders strove to ensure that no one person—or group of people—would ever be able to amass so much power. Their great innovation was checks and balances, a system of both shared and divided powers among the three branches of government. We Americans take this arrangement for granted as part of the backbone of our democracy, but many other democratic countries do things differently, concentrating governing power in a single parliament.

American democracy also rests on a foundation of guaranteed rights, ensuring that minorities and other individuals are safe from the tyranny of the majority. The first amendment to the Bill of Rights (the first ten amendments to the Constitution) proclaims the right to dissent, the right of all citizens to speak against the government when they disagree with what it is saying or doing. This right is another crucial check on government power: the right to sound the alarm at the first sign that government is overstepping its Constitutional bounds and the right to let all government officials know that the public is watching.

Together these aspects comprise what political scientists call liberal democracy. Before promising to stand for democracy throughout the world, we Americans need to reflect on our own form of democracy to understand just what we are, or should be, promising. We must remember all the different pieces of our democratic experiment and the decades and even centuries that the struggle has taken. And while Americans often use "democracy" and "freedom" in the same breath, we must remember that one is actually a means to achieve the other.

———

WHEN AMERICAN PATRIOTS dumped 342 chests of British tea into Boston Harbor in 1773, their battle cry was "No taxation without representation." Representation is the soul of republicanism; those who are to be subject to rules must have a say in making them through their elected representatives. For Madison, representation of the many by the few was one of the "two great points of difference between a democracy and a republic." The other was a republic's ability to extend over a greater number of citizens and territory than a democracy could, precisely because not all citizens had to speak directly for themselves.

Representative government was a lofty and genuinely revolutionary principle. For the Founders, white men with property could legitimately represent all citizens: husbands would represent their wives, and property holders would represent the best interests of society as a whole. In a bitter twist, even enslaved black men helped determine how much representation their states received in the federal government—they were counted as three-fifths of a man. But with all its inequities by modern standards, the system of government that the Founders created reflected the consent of at least *some* of the governed. The relevant standard of comparison is the standard eighteenth-century form of government: hereditary monarchy.

The concept of representative government immediately raises the question of who is entitled to be represented. Our founders unwittingly created a tide of change that roiled through the country over the next century and a half and still makes waves today. Unrepresented minorities demanded a voice to defend their rights and interests against the majority. And in one critical case, an entrenched, ruling minority denied rights to a group that actually comprises a slight majority of Americans—women. The story of women's suffrage reminds us of the long road we have traveled to what we mean by democracy today: representative institutions chosen by universal suffrage. And as we shall see, universal suffrage is itself only part of the story.

THE CONSTITUTION DOES NOT offer much guidance about who is allowed to vote, saying only that "Electors in each State shall have the Qualifications requisite for Electors of the most numerous Branch of the State Legislature." In 1789, these "qualifications" required that voters be white, male landowners. Nonpropertied white men were not allowed to vote in many states until the middle of the nineteenth century. Black men were not enfranchised until the Fourteenth Amendment was ratified in 1868, though many continued to be excluded from voting by insidious Jim Crow restrictions. And, it was not until 1920 that women—that is, the majority of Americans, since women make up slightly more than half the population—gained suffrage through the Nineteenth Amendment.

The seeds of women's suffrage, however, were planted far earlier and in fact had their origin in the struggle against slavery. In 1840, Lucretia Mott and Elizabeth Cady Stanton were among the American delegates to the World Anti-Slavery Convention in London. The convention organizers, dedicated to the brotherhood of man, refused to seat the women abolitionists, on account of their sex. The hypocrisy was not lost on Stanton and Mott, and the pair resolved to convene a meeting to call attention to the situation of women.

This they accomplished eight years later, drawing together a modest crowd of three hundred men and women in the farming town of Seneca Falls in upstate New York. Though this humble setting seemed an unlikely backdrop for the start of a national movement, the discussions at Seneca Falls proved earth-shattering. Taking the Declaration of Independence as her guide, Stanton drafted, and the convention approved, a "Declaration of Sentiments" that laid claim to America's promise of democracy in the name of womankind. She began with a simple edit to the Declaration of Independence: "We hold these truths to be self-evident: that all men *and women* are created equal; that they are endowed by their Creator with certain inalienable rights; that among these are life, liberty, and the pursuit of happiness."

The rest of the declaration reads very differently when women are included alongside men as bearers of rights. To begin with, women must count among those who have the right to revolt whenever a government fails to secure their inalienable rights. Indeed, Stanton continued, again repeating most of the words of the original Declaration, when women are oppressed and threatened with despotism, "it is their duty to throw off such government, and to provide new guards for their future security. Such has been the patient sufferance of the women under this government, and such is now the necessity which constrains them to demand the equal station to which they are entitled." Inspired by this call to a new American revolution, the delegates passed a series of resolutions calling for, among other rights, suffrage.

As news of the scandalously bold Seneca Falls Convention spread, eliciting mostly scorn and ridicule, it came to the admiring attention of one Susan B. Anthony. Impressed by the conventioneers' audacity, Anthony would later become one of the women's movement's greatest leaders and orators, founding the American Equal Rights Association with Stanton in 1868 and publishing the newspaper *The Revolution,* whose masthead read "Men, their rights, and nothing more; women, their rights, and nothing less."

In 1872, Anthony, much to the discomfort of local election officials in Rochester, New York, attempted to register herself and her two sisters to vote. When the startled officials refused, she read them the Fourteenth Amendment and warned them that she would sue if prevented from registering. Finding no explicit legal reason to deny her, the officials grudgingly registered Anthony and forty other women inspired by her example. On November 5, 1872, she had the satisfaction of seeing a woman's ballot—her own—slide into the collection box.

The uproar was immediate. Newspapers across the country called for Anthony to be arrested and punished. The *Rochester Union and Advertiser* condemned her "female lawlessness" and, the day after the election, editorialized sternly about what it thought should be done to female voters: "Citizenship no more carries the right to vote than it carries the power to fly to the moon. . . . If these women in the Eighth Ward offer to vote, they should be challenged, and if they take the oaths and the Inspectors receive and deposit their ballots, they should all be prosecuted to the full extent of the law."[1]

Two weeks later, Anthony was ordered to appear before the

district attorney, where she was arraigned for voting illegally. In the weeks before her trial, Anthony took to the road to press her case and her cause with a new speech, entitled "Is It a Crime for a Citizen of the United States to Vote?" Invoking the immortal words of the Founding, just as Stanton had at Seneca Falls, she reminded her audiences of the Preamble of the Constitution, with its ringing claim that "We, the people of the United States, in order to form a more perfect union . . . do ordain and establish this constitution for the United States of America. "It was *we, the people,*" she continued,

> not we, the white male citizens, nor yet we, the male citizens; but we, the whole people, who formed this Union. And we formed it, not to give the blessings of liberty, but to secure them; not to the half of ourselves and the half of our posterity, but to the whole people—women as well as men. And it is downright mockery to talk to women of their enjoyment of the blessings of liberty while they are denied the use of the only means of securing them provided by this democratic-republican government—the ballot.[2]

Anthony's trial had enormous implications. If acquitted, she would have opened the door to electoral representation for women everywhere. If found guilty, she could go to jail.

Unfortunately for American women, the trial was fixed from the start. Associate Justice Ward Hunt, who tried the case, was a determined antisuffragist. He refused to allow Anthony to testify, declaring her an incompetent witness. After hearing the defense, Judge Hunt read out an opinion—conveniently prepared before the trial had begun—arguing that though the Fourteenth Amendment guaranteed equal rights, the right to vote was not part of the Constitution and thus need not be applied equitably. To the shock of all assembled, he then ordered the (all male) jury to return a guilty verdict, despite some of the jurors' protests that they were entitled to return any kind of verdict they deemed just.

Before pronouncing the predetermined sentence, Judge Hunt made the mistake of asking Anthony, "Has the prisoner anything to say why sentence shall not be pronounced?"[3] Indeed she did. Recalling the trial of Anne Hutchinson more than two centuries earlier, Anthony refused to be silenced by Hunt's repeated orders, and in her clear and forceful orator's voice gave a lengthy enumeration of how the trial had violated her civil rights. Showing no remorse for voting, Anthony used her own trial to indict the unjust laws that had brought her to the court. She referred to the recently overturned law that punished those who aided slaves fleeing their masters:

> Every man or woman in whose veins coursed a drop of human sympathy violated that wicked law, reckless of the consequences, and was justified in so doing. And then the slaves who got their freedom had to take it over or under or through the unjust forms of law, precisely as now must women take it to get their right to a voice in this government; and I have taken mine, and mean to take it at every opportunity.[4]

In the end, Anthony won the day, but not until the passage of the Nineteenth Amendment in 1920.

Nor was universal suffrage truly won. African Americans and other people of color still faced enormous practical obstacles in exercising their right to vote, through such measures as poll taxes and grandfather clauses. These restrictions were challenged and eliminated with the voting rights acts of the civil rights movement, but new ones have emerged—often in the form of malfunctioning voting machines in inner cities or a paucity of machines so that predominantly African American or Hispanic voters face far longer lines and waiting periods than do most white voters.

Indeed, in a living, breathing democracy, the question of who is to be represented can never be static. During the Vietnam War, at a time when most states set the voting age at twenty-one, many soldiers were infuriated that eighteen was old enough to be drafted to die for one's country but not to vote for or against the government sending young men to war. The Twenty-sixth Amendment, allowing all citizens eighteen or older to vote, was added to the Constitution in 1971.

Accidents of birth are not the only factor that have denied citizens the right to vote. Today, forty-eight states restrict the voting rights of convicted felons, a system that prevented 5.4 million people from voting in 2004.[5] Yet if in fact we believe that a prison sentence or a fine repays a criminal's debt to society, and if we truly seek to rehabilitate those who have paid that debt, can they never participate in the political life of the nation again? Should those making our laws only be those who have never been on the wrong side of them? Are those worthy individuals truly representative of our entire society? I do not have firm views on these issues, but they certainly seem worthy of debate—debate once again about the full meaning of citizenship and representation in a democracy.

———

DEMOCRACY DOES NOT DEPEND on elections alone, much less on majority rule. On the contrary, our Founders were highly attentive to minority rights. Every high school history class reads Federalist No. 10, in which James Madison appeals to his fellow revolutionaries to support the Constitution. He deplores the inevitable existence of *faction*—what today we would call partisanship or special interests—and explains that when a faction is in the majority, the majority is likely to ride roughshod over the minority.

This fear of faction came from the Founders' doubts about human nature. They revered "the spirit of America," a spirit "which nourishes freedom, and in return is nourished by it."[6] But they put little faith in virtue alone, even American virtue, to make a government work. On the contrary, their vision of American democracy was founded on a commitment to good institutions, not good people.

This is the subject of the second Federalist paper that every high school student must read, Federalist No. 51. Again it is James Madison writing, this time expressing a view of human nature well honed by careful study of the rise and fall of ancient civilizations, as well as his astute observation of his contemporaries in Virginia and Philadelphia. "If men were angels," he noted, "no government would be necessary." On the other hand, "if angels were to govern men, neither external nor internal controls on government would be necessary." But since angels were notably lacking in the colonies, the task before Madison and his fellow Founders was to design a government that would control both the citizens—the governed—and itself. They were certainly aware of the value of elections as a set of external controls, but Madison also believed strongly in a vigorous internal system of checks and balances.[7]

The American commitment to democracy is thus a commitment to institutions rather than to human nature, be it the nature of Americans or any other people. But the only way to create such a system is to recognize that institutions themselves are only as incorruptible as the people who run them. So they must be set at odds with one another, to temper and block the usurpation of power. The result was the distinctively American device of checks and balances, designed to make our institutions work through a system of shared and separated powers. John Adams had described the separation of powers succinctly in Article 30 of the Massachusetts Constitution, a passage Madison cited approvingly in Federalist No. 47:

> The legislative department shall never exercise the executive and judicial powers, or either of them; the executive shall never exercise the legislative and judicial powers, or either of them; the judicial shall never exercise the legislative and executive powers, or either of them; to the end that it may be a government of laws, and not of men.

While Madison and the other framers designed our Constitution to distribute power carefully among the various branches, it was not clear exactly how the checks and balances they constructed would work out in practice. Democracy on such a scale had never been tried before.

For instance, though the Constitution clearly granted the Supreme Court the ability to review and, if necessary, invalidate state laws, different parties held different views about whether the Court held such power over Congress. The Federalist Party, eager for a stronger national government, believed the Supreme Court should exercise judicial review over federal laws, while the Jeffersonian or Republican Party feared that an overly strong judiciary would prove antidemocratic. This conflict came to a head in 1801 and led to the famous case of *Marbury v. Madison.* Although the dispute was between a justice of the peace and a secretary of state, it was really our system of checks and balances that was on trial.

The story is fairly straightforward. The Federalists had just lost an election to the Jeffersonians, but on their way out appointed a number of new federal judges, including one William Marbury. However, the Jeffersonians took office before the actual letters of appointment could be delivered. The new government, in which James Madison served as secretary of state, saw no need to strengthen its opponents' already dominant position in the federal judiciary and decided not to deliver the appointments. Marbury sued, requesting that the Court issue a special "writ," ordering Madison, whose office was responsible for the delivery of the appointments, to carry out the previous government's orders. Congress, seeking to check the executive, had specifically authorized the Court to issue such writs in the Judiciary Act of 1789.

The 1803 case of *Marbury v. Madison* presented a dilemma for the Supreme Court and its chief justice, the Federalist John Marshall. If the Court issued the writ, Madison might well simply refuse the order, weakening the Court's stature and undermining the rule of law generally. But if the Court did not issue the writ, it would be seen as fearful of the administration. Either way, the Court seemed to have little chance of serving as an effective check on the executive branch.

Marshall's solution was ingenious and has become the foundation of judicial review and the rule of law in America today. He refused to issue the writ, not because he sided with Madison on the merits of the case, but because the law allowing the Court to issue such writs had expanded judicial power by more than the Constitution allowed. As Marshall wrote in his opinion, "It is emphatically the province and duty of the judicial department to say what the law is. Those who apply the rule to particular cases, must of necessity expound and interpret that rule. If two laws conflict with each other, the courts must decide on the operation of each."

Similarly, if a rule stated in a particular law conflicted with a rule set forth in the Constitution, the courts would have to decide which rule should apply. And since the Constitution was by its terms the "supreme law of the land," then courts had to choose the rule of the Constitution over the rule in a statute and thereby invalidate the statute. Indeed, on this account, the Supreme Court had not only the power but the *duty* to invalidate federal laws that it deemed unconstitutional.

While the decision was technically a victory for the Jeffersonians—preventing Marbury's appointment and removing the Supreme Court's ability to issue writs of mandamus—it was a Pyrrhic one. By claiming the power to invalidate congressional laws, Marshall made his Supreme Court the ultimate arbiter of constitutionality and a strong check on both Congress and the executive branch.

While the Court did not exercise the power of judicial review again until 1857, it has since weighed in on legislation numerous times, often to protect minorities from the excesses of the majority, just as Madison envisioned. It is surely fitting that he gave his name to the precedent-setting case that serves as the base of judicial power, though perhaps a bit ironic that he appears as defendant. *Marbury v. Madison* reminds us that the beauty of Madison's design for the federal government is that *everyone* can be checked and balanced—even the man who came up with the idea in the first place!

CHECKS AND BALANCES are only part of the system the Founders designed to ensure the preservation of American democracy. They also wanted the entire government to be put under the direct surveillance of the people. Here is where freedom of expression comes in. Freedom of expression allows individuals to be exactly who they are by thinking what they want and saying, writing, painting, singing, dancing, rapping, or chanting what they think. But it also plays a genuinely indispensable role in a democracy by creating and protecting spaces for dissent. Because we are citizens of a democracy, dissent is not only our right but also our duty if our government does not represent us accurately or fairly. No matter how difficult or uncomfortable the job, true patriots should be prepared to challenge the status quo.

The Founders believed that dissent and debate are the keystones of American democracy, but not every American political leader has shared that view. Frank Hague was one of the party bosses who plagued local politics during the early twentieth century, running Jersey City like a feudal fiefdom. Infamous for his declaration "I am the law!" he also held a dim view of political dissent: "We hear about constitutional rights, free speech and the free press. Every time I hear those words I say to myself, 'That man is a Red, that man is a Communist.' You never heard a real American talk in that manner."[8]

This sentiment, that constitutional rights of freedom of expression are un-American when they are used to advocate certain views, has been, unfortunately, common in American political history, particularly in times of war. Perhaps the best-known example is Senator Joseph McCarthy, who at the outset of the Cold War carried out a terrifying witch hunt against suspected communists in Hollywood, in the intelligentsia, and in the government. Feeding off rising public fear of communism, McCarthy used scanty evidence and hearsay to destroy the reputations of countless individuals. For him, these investigations were "Americanism with its sleeves rolled."[9]

McCarthy's Senate colleague Margaret Chase Smith, the first woman to serve in both houses of Congress, disagreed, earning national fame with her "Declaration of Conscience Speech" of June 1, 1950:

> Those of us who shout the loudest about Americanism in making character assassinations are all too frequently those who, by our own words and acts, ignore some of the basic principles of Americanism:
>
> > The right to criticize;
> > The right to hold unpopular beliefs;
> > The right to protest;
> > The right of independent thought.
>
> The exercise of these rights should not cost one single American citizen his reputation or his right to a livelihood nor should he be in danger of losing his reputation or livelihood merely because he happens to know someone who holds unpopular beliefs. Who of us doesn't? Otherwise none of us could call our souls our own.[10]

Perhaps no issue highlights the interplay of patriotism and dissent as much as flag burning. Can desecrating the physical symbol of our nation represent a commitment to the values for which that symbol stands, or does it undermine those values?

During the 1984 Republican National Convention in Dallas, a group of about one hundred rowdy protesters marched to City Hall, where they formed a circle around an American flag they had torn down from a nearby bank building. Chanting "Red, white, blue, we spit on you. You stand for plunder, you will go under" (a direct if not particularly poetic slogan), the crowd watched a man named Gregory Lee Johnson set the flag alight.

After spitting on the charred bits of cloth, the crowd tried to cool down in a nearby fountain, where dozens of them, Johnson included, were arrested for disorderly conduct. A passing Korean War veteran, angered by what he had seen, took the flag's ashes home and respectfully buried them in his backyard.

Most of the charges of disorderly conduct related not to flag burning but to minor acts of vandalism that the protesters had inflicted on businesses along their marching route. These charges were soon dropped. Johnson, however, found himself saddled with a new charge, a Class A misdemeanor offense of "desecration of a venerated object." In 1989, his case came before the Supreme Court.

Justice Brennan wrote for the Court: "If there is a bedrock principle underlying the First Amendment, it is that the government may not prohibit the expression of an idea simply because society finds the idea itself offensive or disagreeable."[11]

Burning a flag, however "offensive or disagreeable," expressed an idea—a strong idea of opposition to the government. The right to burn the flag is part of "the constitutionally guaranteed 'freedom to be intellectually . . . diverse or even contrary.'" Even more fundamentally, it is part of "the 'right to differ as to things that touch the heart of the existing order.'" Here the twin roles of freedom of expression converge: the right to dissent also protects the right of individuals to define themselves squarely in opposition to their government or even their society as a whole.

The Court's decision provoked immediate outrage. The House of Representatives voted 411 to 5 to express "profound concern" with the court's ruling. President George H. W. Bush pronounced flag burning "dead wrong" and called for a constitutional amendment to overturn the decision, a move supported by 69 percent of the American people, according to a *Newsweek* poll.

Instead of beginning the lengthy process of amending the Constitution, Congress instead passed the Flag Protection Act in October 1989, which made mutilating or burning flags a federal crime punishable by fine or imprisonment. The law also provided for expedited judicial review, meaning that challenges would be put before the Court quickly.

Indeed, before the month was out, a bevy of flag-burning protests had taken place across the country, including one on the very steps of the Capitol Building, in which the "revolutionary artist" Shawn Eichman took part. The Supreme Court heard his case, *United States v. Eichman,* in May of the following year, but the justices' minds remained unchanged: "We are aware that desecration of the flag is deeply offensive to many. But the same might be said, for example, of virulent ethnic and religious epithets . . . vulgar repudiations of the draft . . . and scurrilous caricatures."[12]

The flag is the symbol of our Constitution itself, including the First Amendment. In consequence, the Court noted, "Punishing desecration of the flag dilutes the very freedom that makes the emblem so revered, and worth revering."

Our democracy has many moving parts. Elections—as our primary means of assuring popular representation—play a vital role. But those whom we elect are deliberately set against each other in various ways. Unlike in parliamentary systems, where the prime minister is the leader of the party that has a majority in the legislature or that has put together a governing coalition, we can, and often do, elect a Congress of one party and a president of the other. Our Constitution gives each branch separate but also overlapping powers, to allow them to check and balance one another. And then the courts, with judges appointed by the president and confirmed by the Senate, have the power to review and reject laws made by both those branches.

That's the basic machinery. In addition, as *Marbury v. Madison* shows, it works best when operated by smart and politically astute men and women who know when to compromise and when to lose a skirmish to win a longer-term victory. It also depends on the continual oversight of the people—all of us. We can vote, we can petition, we can sue, we can write and talk and protest and challenge. And even when some of us do that in ways that offend the rest of us, such as burning the flag, the judicial branch of government protects our freedom of expression against efforts by Congress or the president to curtail it.

Our democracy has always been and remains a work in progress. It is a dance between the government and the governed; it controls us and we control it, just as Madison intended. Who "we" are is continually contested and redefined as the meaning of universal suffrage changes. The balance of power between elected and appointed officials changes; election rules change both for members of Congress and for the president. Congress expands and limits the powers of the courts; the courts expand and limit the powers of the executive branch. When we seek to support democracy abroad, we must remember these moving parts, and remember that they are always in motion.

THE STORY OF DEMOCRACY in America underlines the difference between democracy and liberal democracy. The framers of our Constitution wanted a republican government that would represent the people, but represent them in a way that protected against mob rule and maximized opportunities for careful deliberation in the best interests of the country as a whole. They insisted on a pluralist party system, a Bill of Rights limiting the power of the government, guarantees for free speech and a free press, checks and balances to promote a government more transparent and more accountable, and a strong rule of law enforced by an independent judiciary. These rules and institutions are as essential to sustained rule by the people as elections are. They ensure that democracy remains an instrument to secure individual liberty rather than a recipe for tyranny of the majority or simply a stop on the road to renewed dictatorship.

The principal problem in championing democracy abroad is that it is often easier and faster to organize and hold elections than it is to build the necessary supporting institutions for stable liberal democracy. As moving as it was to watch Iraqis hold up their purple thumbs to mark their vote in a free and fair election, both they and we had inflated expectations, and perhaps even dangerous ones, about what the election could accomplish in a landscape so physically and politically stunted. In Afghanistan, too, elections have proven to be no match for determined warlords.

Democracy is *hard*. Even in Germany and Japan, the Bush administration's poster children for the potential of democratizing despotic regimes, the road to liberal democracy took military defeat, lengthy occupation, economic renewal, the scrutiny and support of institutions like the nascent European Union and NATO, and constitutional disarmament, not to mention a long history of developed state institutions. Proclaiming the blessings and bounty of democracy without tempering expectations about the time frame and work necessary to achieve it and providing the sustained economic, political, and even military support the task may require is at best irresponsible and at worst immoral.

Which is not to say that America should not stand for democracy in the world and support democratic people and institutions everywhere that we can. We should; we *must*. Democracy and liberty are deeply intertwined in our history and our national identity as Americans. Our Declaration of Independence declares that *all* have the right to reject governments that do not secure their rights and to replace those governments with ones based on the consent of the governed. Support for democracy in other countries means keeping faith with our heritage.

Supporting democracy effectively, however, also means being realistic. Democratization is an ongoing and often slow process, one that requires sufficient security to live by the force of law rather than of arms; tolerance for social, ethnic, and religious divisions; and a culture of accountability for the spending of public funds. States that hold elections without the supporting constitutional infrastructure and conditions are likely to be unstable and prone to belligerent nationalism. On the flip side, states with the best prospects for sustaining democracy have reasonably strong domestic groups prepared to embrace the limits on power entailed by liberal democracy rather than use democracy to gain and maintain power. Democracy must deliver tangible benefits for the population as a whole, beginning with security and extending to at least modest prosperity. And external support for democracy must be prepared to stay what is often a long and difficult course.

In short, we should not abandon support for democracy in the world, but we must rethink the *way* we provide that support and measure its results. Rereading our own history should make us much more attentive to the multiple dimensions of liberal democracy and the various metrics that track its progress. Three aspects need to be considered:

- *Popular government:* the extent to which a government actually represents its people through elected representatives,

advisory councils, and other decision-making bodies designed to give different segments of the population a
meaningful voice

- *Accountable government:* the extent to which citizens can
monitor the activities of their government (transparency,
absence of corruption) and hold it responsible, through
protests, elections, votes of no confidence, or the courts, for
failure to deliver on its promises or uphold the law

- *Rights-regarding government:* the extent to which a government upholds and protects the rights of all its citizens, as
guaranteed in a country's constitution, statutes, and
treaties to which it is a party

A government that is Popular, Accountable, and Rights-regarding is up to PAR as a liberal democracy. A government that
is below PAR might well have free and fair elections, but,
through corruption or deception, might not be accountable to
the people for its policies. Or it might consistently violate minority rights or the human rights of its citizens more generally.

Developing a PAR index—preferably with a group of other
liberal democracies—would be a new approach to promoting
democracy. It would allow advocates of democracy to gather and
distill all the knowledge that governments and nongovernmental organizations have developed about what has worked in the
many countries that have made successful transitions to democracy over the past three decades—as well as what has not worked.
It would allow us to evaluate governments on a range of dimensions, thereby avoiding the black-or-white label of whether a
country is a democracy or not. Such a cut-and-dry label is hard
to apply and understandably generates tremendous resentment
around the world from governments and citizens who find that
our own American democracy is less than perfect (consider the

Bush-Gore election and our system of campaign financing). Assessing whether a government is up to PAR would also break what often seems to the rest of the world like an obsession with elections, even when, as in Palestine, elections produce a Hamas government that openly supports terrorism.

Finally, a PAR index would acknowledge that successful liberal democracy comes in many forms. Some nations combine legislative and executive power in a single parliament led by a prime minister and cabinet. Democracies that have instead chosen to follow the U.S. model of a strong president separately elected from the legislature are often more vulnerable to coups. Some supreme courts exercise judicial review; others do not. Some countries have federalist systems with state or provincial subgovernments; others have centralized governments.

Liberal democracies also differ significantly in the precise range of rights they protect. Some, for instance, restrict hate speech much more than in the United States, but permit more of what the United States prohibits as pornography. European democracies typically restrict abortion more than most American states do, but do not have the death penalty. The South African constitution requires its supreme court at least to find out what foreign and international courts think on important constitutional questions before issuing an opinion under South African law, while some U.S. Supreme Court justices reject that practice. America is not the only or even the best model for new democracies.

This variety of forms and features of liberal democracy offers another reason that we should join with other countries in developing a PAR index. Much of the groundwork for developing such an index has already been laid; the nongovernmental organization Freedom House ranks all countries in the world according to whether they are free, partly free, or not free.[13] Transparency International, another civic organization based in Berlin, ranks countries on a corruption index that measures the prevalence of corruption, and public attitudes toward it. Moreover, many human rights groups evaluate countries on their specific human rights records. A group of liberal democratic governments working with these nongovernmental groups could formulate a PAR index that would have broad legitimacy and could be used by these governments and groups in deciding whether and how to support democracy in countries with different rankings.

Governments below PAR—and no government should get a perfect score—could make progress on finding ways to increase popular participation in government, accountability, or human rights and be recognized and credited for such progress. For example, the Chinese government worries about the implications of handing the vote to 1.3 billion people who have never governed themselves before. The Egyptian government worries about the electoral power of the radical Islamists. Both are worried even more about losing the privileges that political power has brought them. But both could nevertheless be encouraged or pushed to allow multiple parties in the elections that they do hold. Both could be brought to allow multiple currents of thought in their societies and politics. Both could develop mechanisms to combat corruption and improve transparency of government decisions, and to improve their human rights records—all as part of an evolution not only toward democracy but also toward liberal democracy.

The rankings would all be relative. The history of all liberal democracies, including our own, reveals the gap between the ideal of liberal democracy and the often checkered reality. Countries make progress, backslide, reform their systems, redefine their electorates, tie themselves to the mast of international human rights standards, and learn from other countries. Rather than championing democracy by preaching to the rest of the world, we should take the lead by being honest about the defects in our own practice.

IN JUNE 2005, Secretary of State Condoleezza Rice traveled to Cairo. She did not proclaim the virtues of American democracy and urge the Egyptians to follow suit. On the contrary, she admitted that for sixty years, the United States had "pursued stability at the expense of democracy" in the Middle East and "achieved neither." She strove to assure her audience that things would be different in the future. In doing so, she also spoke directly of America's promise to its own people, and of our ongoing struggle to uphold that promise.

> The moral worth of my ancestors, it was thought, should be valued by the demand of the market, not by the dignity of their souls. This practice was sustained through violence. But the crime of human slavery could not withstand the power of human liberty. What seemed impossible in one century became inevitable in the next.
>
> There was a time, even more recently, when liberty was threatened by colonialism. It was believed that certain peoples required foreign masters to rule their lands and run their lives. Like slavery, this ideology of injustice was enforced through oppression. . . .
>
> Today, liberty is threatened by undemocratic governments. Some believe this is a permanent fact of history. But there are others who know better. These impatient patriots can be found in Baghdad and Beirut, in Riyadh and in Ramallah, in Amman and in Tehran and right here in Cairo.[14]

These must have been welcome and surprising words for Secretary Rice's Egyptian audience. But the "impatient patriots" who Rice said could be found in cities across the Middle East have extra reason to be skeptical of U.S. motives these days. Large majorities in countries around the world scoff at the idea that the United States went to war in Iraq to promote democracy. Many Americans, however, continue to see the Iraq war as an act of benevolence, the world's mightiest nation freeing people halfway around the world from the yoke of a violent tyrant. The Pentagon's name for the war, Operation Iraqi Freedom, exemplifies that view. And our soldiers' commitment is sincere, even as they go to their deaths.

Yet polls show that majorities of Turks, Moroccans, Jordanians, and Pakistanis believe the entire war against terror—in which the Bush administration insists Iraq be included—is really aimed at securing oil, protecting Israel, or even "world domination." Further, majorities in all those countries, and in France, Germany, Russia, and even Britain, say that the Iraq war has made them *less* confident that the United States wants to promote liberty or democracy globally.[15]

This skepticism is largely fueled, as a Palestinian cabdriver in Copenhagen explained to me, by the way we chose to go to war. He was at pains to explain that he had no quarrel with the American people. But he asked how on earth America could say it was fighting for democracy in Iraq when it had completely ignored even the limited measure of global democracy established through the United Nations in choosing to go to war against the wishes of the Security Council. If the world didn't want war, he asked, including almost all of the closest U.S. allies, how could we go ahead? Surely, he thought, it was because we had other motives—oil, money, and power.

To combat this skepticism and, above all, to regain the global credibility required for any of our policies to be effective, we should start by accepting that honesty is the best policy. We should be very frank about our own failings—about our broken system of campaign finance, our gerrymandering, our vicious partisanship, our often politicized courts. We preach the virtues of an independent judiciary, but judges in forty-nine out of our fifty states are elected; many of them run for office on actual platforms outlining their political views—hardly a model of judicial neutrality!

Organizations like Freedom House can help. Though based in New York, it scrutinizes the United States just as it assesses other countries. Its 2005 report helpfully points out various U.S. failings, which range from the corruption scandal involving House majority leader Tom DeLay and lobbyist Jack Abramoff, the continuing controversies over the treatment of prisoners of the war on terror, the enormous influence of money in political campaigns, the gerrymandering of congressional districts, and the high prevalence of nonwhites on death row. The best thing we could do to give a PAR index global credibility and legitimacy would be to join organizations like Freedom House in documenting our own failures and then striving to change them. Only by accepting our own score and publicly committing to improve it through a series of specific actions can we make credible our rankings of others.

All the honesty in the world about our own failings, however, will not absolve us of the inevitable and necessary inconsistencies and even contradictions in our own policies. We must be honest with ourselves about our dealings with nondemocratic governments. Take Egypt, for instance. As much as Egyptian democratic activists listening to Secretary Rice may have wanted to take heart from her words, they must wrestle with the contradictions between our advocacy of freedom and the billions of dollars that successive U.S. administrations have sent the repressive Egyptian government for decades and that President Bush continues to send today. The United States has strong reasons to support the Egyptian regime; American support is the price Egypt demanded for its historic 1978 peace with Israel. Continued peace between the two countries is in the interests of the United States and the region, but comes at the high price of our supporting an unsavory regime. Being honest about our interests and intentions in Egypt is the least we owe to the impatient patriots Rice addressed.

We also have important and necessary reasons to deal with China (trade, East Asian stability, and China's status as an ancient civilization and a rising power), Saudi Arabia (oil), Pakistan (tracking down al-Qaeda), Sudan (valuable intelligence on global terrorist networks), and other nondemocracies. We often find it very awkward to combine the realpolitik language of interests with our preferred rhetoric of ideals, so we play down these strategic needs. But the result simply undermines our international credibility. Keeping our interests in the spotlight reminds the world we bear the regimes no special love and reminds ourselves that we need not do anything more than the minimum required to achieve those interests.

At the same time, we have a duty to talk to our nondemocratic partners about our dissatisfaction with their political systems. Diplomacy is not a binary choice. Governments have more options than just "deal with these countries, or not." Engaging in dialogue with nondemocratic nations does not mean that we embrace them without reserve. It is perfectly possible, even if uncomfortable, to engage with countries in some areas and address them frankly and even harshly in others. Autocratic regimes are understandably prickly about such criticism, but they must realize that such dialogue is a necessary element of working with the United States. And because they have at least as much interest in dealing with us as we do with them, they will have no choice but to listen. Ronald Reagan's approach to arms control was "Trust but Verify." Our approach to supporting democracy should be "Engage but Scrutinize."

We can also develop graduated tiers of engagement, so that our criticism points more constructively at what governments can do if they desire closer ties. With governments composed of competing moderate and hard-line groups, this approach can strengthen moderate voices. It is hardly foolproof, however, and some governments are unlikely to budge no matter what we say. In these cases, ostracism may be the only recourse, but, if so, it will be more effective if decided on and implemented collectively by regional or global organizations.

In talks with autocratic governments, it also behooves us to listen. Some of what we will hear we will reject, and rightly. Yet we may also hear and understand things that will help us help or push these countries to build the underpinnings of true liberal democracy. Understanding the origins of autocracy—to stifle ethnic or religious conflict, as with Tito in the former Yugoslavia; to feed one individual's megalomania, as with Hitler; or to satisfy one group's greed, as with many juntas—can help us and other liberal democracies to chart a better path from autocracy to democracy.

Even the most idealistic democrats acknowledge that America cannot wall itself off from nations whose domestic politics we dislike, especially when important interests are at stake. Pretending that is not so just exposes us as hypocrites. We must stand for democracy in the world by recognizing its complexity and its varied evolution and developing policy tools to support its different facets; by being honest and open about the imperfections of our own democracy and the length of our own journey; and by not pretending to perfect consistency in our dealings with other countries, but instead pushing the nondemocratic governments with which we engage to listen to dissenting individuals and groups within their own people who are pushing to bring their government up to PAR.

———————

WHAT A LONG, STRANGE TRIP IT'S BEEN. James Madison might well be appalled at many aspects of our government today, concluding that faction now runs rife and that we have sacrificed wise government for universal suffrage. Abraham Lincoln's government "of the people, by the people, and for the people" excluded the female half of the population. And the Reverend Martin Luther King, Jr., marched only decades ago for the real, as opposed to the paper, right of African Americans to vote.

Yet democracy is part of the American soul. Today, Americans believe that government by the people must mean government by *all* the people. We also believe that the right to self-government is universal, even if we have often been too hypocritical or preoccupied to act on our belief. Going forward, a U.S. foreign policy true to American values and our history as a nation must support popular, accountable, and rights-regarding government in countries around the world. That cannot mean democratization by force (a contradiction in terms) or by holding ourselves up as some kind of perfect model. Democracy for us has been the surest and best way of guaranteeing and preserving our liberty, but only when buttressed by a host of liberal habits and institutions that require constant maintenance. Democracy for others must similarly be an instrument to achieve liberty and justice for all.

Chapter 3

Equality

We hold these truths to be self-evident, that all men
are created equal.
>—*Thomas Jefferson, 1776*

I have a dream that one day this nation will rise up and live out
the true meaning of its creed: "We hold these truths to be self-
evident: that all men are created equal."
>—*Rev. Martin Luther King, Jr., 1963*

AMERICA BEGAN WITH A DREAM of equality, one that for
many Americans remains a dream. Perhaps no words resonate as
deeply in the American mind as Jefferson's ringing proclamation in the Declaration of Independence that all men are created
equal. The Founders embraced equality as a political principle,
the principle that no men were inherently ordained to rule over
other men. Governments could be established only by the consent of the governed.

Political equality begins with formal equality, equality in the
eyes of the law. In 1789, the first Congress wrote this promise

into the Bill of Rights, guaranteeing all Americans equal protection of the laws under the new federal government. In 1866, after the bloodiest war America has ever known was fought over the principle, Congress proposed the Fourteenth Amendment, which entered into force in 1868 after being ratified by two-thirds of the states. The amendment reiterated equal protection of federal law and, crucially, extended it to state governments. Henceforth, the Constitution required states from Alabama to Maine, South Carolina to Oregon, to treat all their citizens equally under the law.

In theory, and with independent, honest, and unbiased judges, equal protection of the laws means that all of our rights—the liberty to pursue happiness as we find it and to make our lives the best we can, the right to participate fully in determining our government, the right to fair trial if we are accused—extends equally to every citizen, regardless of color, creed, ethnicity, disability, and, as a majority of Americans believe, sexual orientation. No one can use the power and authority of the state to discriminate among groups or classes of citizens.

Equality under the law in this country is also bound up with equality in the eyes of our fellow citizens. The Founders intended to ignite a political revolution. What they did not foresee was that the forces they had set in motion would also launch a social revolution.[1] Americans of all social classes fought side by side during the American Revolution. Immigrants came from all over the world, lured by the promise that they could make better lives for themselves and their families. Masses of pioneers pushed westward, many remaking themselves and their fortunes. And even on the near frontier, day laborers could become homesteaders and in time prosperous farmers and property owners. Political equality meant equality in the eyes of the law;

social equality meant an equal opportunity to make good, regardless of birth or breeding.

In the century after the Revolution, landed gentry presidents—Washington, Jefferson, Madison, Monroe—were joined by log-cabin presidents, most famously Abraham Lincoln, but also Andrew Jackson. By 1900, when that most American of poets, Walt Whitman, wrote his most American of poems, "I Hear America Singing," he wrote of the common American worker:

> I hear America singing, the varied carols I hear;
> Those of mechanics—each one singing his, as it should be, blithe and strong;
> The carpenter singing his, as he measures his plank or beam,
> The mason singing his, as he makes ready for work, or leaves off work;
> The boatman singing what belongs to him in his boat—the deckhand singing on the steamboat deck;
> The shoemaker singing as he sits on his bench—the hatter singing as he stands;
> The wood-cutter's song—the ploughboy's, on his way in the morning, or at the noon intermission, or at sundown;
> The delicious singing of the mother—or of the young wife at work—or of the girl sewing or washing,
> Each singing what belongs to her, and to none else;
> The day what belongs to the day—At night, the party of young fellows, robust, friendly,
> Singing, with open mouths, their strong melodious songs.[2]

Whitman sang of a working-class America marked by exuberance, optimism, and plenty. The mechanic, the carpenter, the mason, the homemaker—all could make good and all could stand honorably beside the lawyer, the doctor, and the engineer.

Even today, unlike most nations whose leaders are perfectly happy to emphasize their elite education and background, our presidents portray themselves as men of the people. George W. Bush gained popularity by downplaying his patrician New England background and recasting himself as a Texas rancher. Bill Clinton's origins in a troubled, working-class home in Hope, Arkansas, earned him respect even from his political opponents. Our top public figures, business leaders, and celebrities have always taken pride in their humble beginnings, telling stories of how they started as the children of immigrants who arrived with little more than the clothes on their backs and yet worked their way to the top.

From nothing to something is what we mean by the American dream—from rags to riches, from a log cabin to the White House, from a Kansas farm to a Hollywood studio. It is a story of making and remaking ourselves as far as luck and hard work will carry us. This story is so deeply ingrained in our culture that we typically don't realize that it does not resonate everywhere, that the "self-made man," or woman, does not exert the same hold on European, Latin American, Asian, and African imaginations as it does on ours. But it is a story that deeply shapes our conception of what equality actually means.

The political and the social dimensions of the American idea of equality have a common core. With our declaration of political equality, we took charge of our destiny as a nation. With our concept of social equality, we sought to allow all citizens to take charge of their individual destinies. In both cases, we embraced an ideal of free will versus determinism, a vision of life-chances limited only by factors within an individual's control—hard work, thrift, self-discipline—and by factors outside any human's control: luck, weather, genes, and the forces of history. Europeans love to ask why it is that socialism, much less communism, never took root in the United States. The pages of many books and journals are filled with debates over this question, but surely part of the answer is Karl Marx versus Benjamin Franklin: the inevitable dialectic of class warfare versus "Early to bed and early to rise makes a man healthy, wealthy, and wise"!

Our stories, our proclamations, our laws, and our celebrities notwithstanding, the struggle for equality in America has been hard fought and slowly, incompletely won. Formal equality was written into the Constitution, yet it took another seventy-seven years and a horrific civil war before Americans achieved the same right of equal protection from state governments, many of which had permitted or encouraged slavery. Even then, in many states, equality remained a paper promise.

A century after the Civil War, in the 1960s, courts were still enforcing laws and contracts whose benefits explicitly applied only to white men or whose restrictions extended only to African Americans, Mexican Americans, Chinese Americans, or women. Further, as anyone who has ever been excluded from an "in" group knows, even after formal barriers are lifted, countless informal barriers can rise to take their place. From formal equality to real equality—in life chances, political power, economic opportunity—is a long road, one that still stretches before us.

On the social side, as we move into the twenty-first century, we are actually moving backward. We talk the talk of social equality, but the gap between the richest and poorest Americans grows ever wider. People may make it from rags to riches on reality TV, but fewer and fewer are managing in actual reality. And look at the face we are presenting to the world. The gap between what we pay workers and managers in our corporations is greater than in any other country. Do we really think it is OK for a CEO to be paid a thousand times more than a janitor as long as both people are on a first-name basis?

Today the country is richer than ever before, but somehow the American dream is slipping further from many Americans' grasp. Since the 1970s, the U.S. economy has grown steadily, but the gains have not been widespread. The bottom 20 percent of Americans saw their after-tax income rise by 9 percent between 1979 and 2000. Over the same period, the after-tax income of the top 1 percent grew 201 percent, or twenty times the increase of the poor.[3] We pride ourselves on social mobility, but the Organisation for Economic Co-operation and Development (OECD) has found that it is easier for families to climb out of poverty in countries like Denmark, the United Kingdom, the Netherlands, Ireland, Spain, Belgium, France, Germany, Italy, Canada, and Portugal than it is in the United States.[4] And yet Americans still cling to the dream: A 2005 *New York Times* survey found that 40 percent of Americans believed that the chance of moving up from one class to another had risen over the last thirty years, when in fact it did not increase at all.[5]

How can we explain these paradoxes? Part of the answer lies in Jefferson's phrasing. All men are *created* equal; they won't necessarily end up that way. Our concept of equality focuses more on starting points than endpoints. It is intertwined with our faith in opportunity and progress. For Americans, equality does not mean the eradication of differences in society—differences of wealth, class, education, and professional opportunities. But we believe that these differences are and must continue to be permeable and surmountable. Many Americans revere celebrities because they dream of becoming one. Some middle-class people and even some of the poor support tax cuts for the wealthy, because they hope to be counted among them one day.

Where we so often stumble is our refusal to see that equality of opportunity is not an automatic fact of American life. It is a promise made by the government to the American people, a promise the government has to work actively to fulfill. Over our history, settlers tilling the land have benefited from land grants. Manufacturers could count on investments in transportation infrastructure such as canals and railroads. Immigrants could send their children to free and good public schools and universities. Workers could be sure that if they were willing to work two and even three jobs, they could earn enough to give their children at least a chance.

It was never perfect. Virtually all Americans who have ever studied American literature will remember "I Hear America Singing." Few are likely to know of a very different side of Whitman revealed in his poem "I Sit and Look Out":

> I sit and look out upon all the sorrows of the
> world, and upon all
> oppression and shame;
> . . .
> I observe the slights and degradations cast by arrogant persons
> upon laborers, the poor, and upon negroes, and the like;
> All these—All the meanness and agony without end, I sitting,
>   look out upon,
> See, hear, and am silent.[6]

Those slights and degradations were also part of Whitman's America, and they remain part of ours. But at our best, when we have been willing to take a hard look not at the American dream, but at the reality of the many deep inequalities in American life, we have found the courage and the means to insist that our government and our society live up to their promises.

In the Whitman poem, the narrator remains silent. Many Americans, naively accepting the American dream as inevitable, have also kept silent in the face of our country's inequities. But across the span of two hundred years, many patriotic citizens have spoken out and fought to ensure that all Americans, men and women, of every color, creed, and national origin, enjoy equal rights and an equal opportunity to make a better life. To understand the idea and the ideal of equality in American life today, we must hear their stories.

———

As DESCRIBED IN the discussions of liberty and democracy, slavery—the most blatant denial of human equality imaginable—was embedded in the Constitution itself. As a result, the greatest struggle for equality in American history—one still ongoing—had to start with legal reform: the amendment of the Constitution itself. In addition to extending equal protection to the states, the Fourteenth Amendment of 1866 gave African American men the vote, a right and responsibility they used to send thirty black congressmen to Washington in the years following the Civil War. Additionally, many other black men during this period gained state and local seats.[7] It appeared that formal equality in the eyes of the law was indeed producing the political equality necessary for making future laws equitable.

Unfortunately, this triumph proved short-lived. In the late 1800s, white-dominated state governments across the South enacted insidious new restrictions on voting, schooling, interracial marriage, and other rights of citizenship. For example, in Mississippi, voters were required to "read and interpret" a passage from the state constitution before they could be registered. Besides the problem of black illiteracy—before the Civil War, it had been illegal to teach them to do so across much of the South—the interpretation requirement allowed state officials to fail whomever they pleased. While many educated blacks "failed" the test, most whites passed. In George County in the 1950s, one white applicant's interpretation of the section "There shall be no imprisonment for debt" was: "I thank that a Neorger should have 2 years in collage before voting because he don't under stand."[8] He passed.

In the decades after Reconstruction and the Union troops' withdrawal from the South, a new doctrine arose, disguised as the American promise of equality it quietly eviscerated. "Separate but equal" came from an 1896 Supreme Court case in which the nation's highest judicial body ruled that nothing in the Constitution prohibited states from forcing blacks and whites to ride in separate train cars. Separate lunch counters, drinking fountains, bathrooms, schools, and communities were already a fact of American life. The federal government had actively opposed state-sponsored discrimination in the years after the Civil War, but as the Civil War receded further into the past, the government increasingly turned a blind eye to so-called Jim Crow laws—named after a stereotypical black character made popular by white entertainers at the time.

The Jim Crow regime was enforced by the police and other official organs of the Southern states. But perhaps the most effective tool of repression was the campaign of terror that reactionary white paramilitary organizations like the Ku Klux Klan (KKK) carried out against blacks (and also some whites) who challenged the status quo. Literally thousands of black Americans were murdered by their white neighbors in the hundred years following the Civil War. Some were simply in the wrong place at the wrong time; others were singled out for standing up for their civil rights. Across the South, lynchings were as commonplace as they were terrifying. In 1940, the jazz singer Billie Holiday described the macabre landscape of the American South:

Southern trees bear strange fruit,
Blood on the leaves and blood at the root,
Black bodies swinging in the southern breeze,
Strange fruit hanging from the poplar trees.[9]

Like modern terrorist groups, the KKK and its sister organizations used fear as a weapon to try to force America to accept their backward vision of a "utopian" segregated society. And for the hundred years after the Civil War, they largely succeeded. But the story of formal equality, at least, was about to change. Many courageous Americans, black and white, fought in the Supreme Court, the voting booth, and the halls of Congress to make formal equality a legal reality, even if the lived reality for African Americans and many other Americans of color continued to fall short of the American dream.

IN 1951, a Santa Fe Railroad welder named Oliver Brown and twelve other residents of Topeka, Kansas, sued the local board of education for refusing to enroll their children in the school of their choice, which was reserved for whites. Brown's daughter Linda had to take a bus to get to the "colored" school, while the white school was only seven blocks from her house. The case was organized and led by the Topeka chapter of the National Association for the Advancement of Colored People (NAACP) and, under the organization's guidance, eventually arrived at the Supreme Court.

The Court issued its ruling in 1954—the first sign that important changes were in store for African Americans. Overturning its "separate but equal" doctrine, the Court ruled in *Brown v. Board of Education* that states could not prevent black children from attending the same schools that white children attended.

While the nine justices of the Court were ultimately responsible for the landmark decision, the opportunity to reach this decision resulted from the sophisticated legal efforts of the NAACP. Indeed, similar grassroots efforts were responsible for almost all the advances that would follow *Brown*. The American promise of equality was not granted from on high, but bitterly bought with the tears, sweat, and even blood of the most marginalized Americans.

The civil rights leaders of Montgomery, Alabama, hoped for a similar success in their fight against segregated public transportation. They needed a case that would spark the black community's anger and fuel a citywide bus boycott. In 1955, a year after *Brown v. Board of Education,* a Montgomery seamstress named Rosa Parks refused to give up her seat in the front of a city bus to a white passenger, despite a city ordinance reserving the front section for whites. She was arrested, and the fight was on.

With Parks's permission, black leaders encouraged Montgomery's entire African American community to avoid taking the bus until they could sit where they pleased. The minister of the local Dexter Avenue Baptist Church—one Rev. Martin Luther King, Jr.—emerged as one of the leaders of the movement.

The response from the black community was overwhelming. Seventeen thousand people stayed off the city buses at first, a number that would grow to forty-two thousand over the 381 days of the boycott. This swell of public protest astounded the Montgomery city leaders, who responded harshly by discontinuing bus service on predominantly black routes, harassing the informal carpool services that sprang up to replace the bus system, and even indicting eighty-nine of the boycott leaders on trumped-up charges (the leaders were subsequently released on bonds).

White paramilitary groups like the KKK took the law into their own hands and responded to the boycott with violence. In January, King's parsonage was bombed. The following night, another bomb exploded in the home of fellow boycott leader E. D. Nixon. In August, another minister's house was bombed twice, and in January 1957, after the boycott had ended, four black churches and two homes were bombed.

Despite the violence, despite having to walk long distances, and despite the city's efforts to disrupt the boycott, Montgomery's blacks stayed off city buses for over a year. Meanwhile, civil rights groups were challenging the segregation ordinance in federal courts. Relying on the *Brown v. Board of Education* decision, the NAACP argued that if schools must be integrated, then why not buses? In June 1956, the Montgomery district court ruled in favor of the boycotters, a decision quickly appealed by the segregationists. The boycott continued throughout the lengthy appeal process, which finally ended on November 13, 1956, when the Supreme Court ruled the segregation of public buses to be illegal. On December 21, Montgomery's black community again boarded the city's buses, sitting in the front, back, or anywhere in between.

The bus boycott inspired other Americans to chip away at the pillars of Jim Crow. Black students sat at whites-only lunch counters until they were served. Racially mixed groups of freedom riders tested the desegregation of interstate buses by attempting to ride with the blacks in front and the whites in back. Citizens groups attempted to register the enormous number of black voters who had never before exercised their constitutional rights.

These patriots often paid dearly for their courage. Snipers shot at integrated buses in several cities. In Rock Hill, South Carolina, an angry mob set fire to the bus carrying one group of freedom riders, while in Anniston, Arkansas, another mob savagely beat black and white passengers while police looked on. More civil rights leaders' houses and activist churches were bombed. Several whites and blacks working to register voters were murdered in cold blood.

Despite these assaults, the civil rights movement continued to flourish. By 1963, as the Kennedy administration was preparing a civil rights bill, it was ready to take the national stage. On August 28, 1963, a quarter million people marched on Washington to demand that America fulfill its promise of equality. At the event's closing, Martin Luther King, Jr., stood before the Lincoln Memorial and gave voice to the dream of every American and to the very promise of America itself:

> In spite of the difficulties and frustrations of the moment, I still have a dream. It is a dream deeply rooted in the American dream.
> . . .
> I have a dream that one day on the red hills of Georgia the sons of former slaves and the sons of former slave-owners will be able to sit down together at a table of brotherhood. . . .
> I have a dream that my four children will one day live in a nation where they will not be judged by the color of their skin but by the content of their character.
> I have a dream today.

King's message did not fall on deaf ears. In 1964, Congress passed a civil rights act that banned all discrimination in public places and in private hiring policies. That same year, the Twenty-fourth Amendment to the Constitution was ratified, eliminating the poll taxes that had been used to keep poor voters away from the polls. The following year, Congress approved the Voting Rights Act of 1965, which required the states to use standard voter registration tests and empowered the federal government to register voters whom the states failed to include on their rolls. In 1967, the Supreme Court ruled that states could not prohibit marriages between people of different races, and a year later, President Johnson signed a civil rights act that prohibited discrimination in the sale, rental, and financing of housing. By the end of the decade, the American dream of equality was looking much closer to American reality—at least on paper.

WHEN I WENT TO LAW SCHOOL in the 1980s, the stories of *Brown v. Board of Education* and the great line of civil rights decisions that followed it made us students feel great. We sat at the feet of professors who had participated in this struggle themselves or at least who had clerked for Justice Thurgood Marshall, the legal genius behind many of the NAACP victories. Their stories, and the ringing rhetoric of the decisions in our casebooks, told of the triumph of justice over racism and of words over swords. They convinced us that law was a mighty tool of social change and that lawyers could be white—and black—knights.

As comforting as these legends were, particularly to the legions of first-year law students wondering why on earth they had decided to come to law school, the tales capture at best a partial truth. Change in the law has to mean, ultimately, change on the streets, a much harder and slower struggle. When I became a law professor in my turn, I had my students study the great civil rights decisions. I exulted with my students in the extraordinary power of simply insisting, over decades and centuries, that words mean what they say. But I also assigned them the story of *Hansberry v. Lee.*

The story of Carl A. Hansberry, a prominent black real-estate developer, reminds us of the countless unsung struggles by individual African Americans and their allies across the country to claim what was theirs by right. It also points out the limits of fighting for formal equality through law alone.

In the 1930s, Hansberry wanted to move his family from one of Chicago's poor black neighborhoods to a nicer house in a community populated exclusively by whites. The white neighborhood's ethnic makeup was no accident; the homeowners had all signed an agreement pledging not to sell to black people, a common arrangement at the time.

The Hansberry family moved in anyway, and the neighbors sued to block them. The case went all the way to the Supreme Court, which in 1940 found in favor of Hansberry, but only on a technicality. The Court would not rule that so-called restrictive covenants were unconstitutional until 1948. Today, however, the decision in *Hansberry v. Lee* is assigned in property and constitutional law courses as a major milestone in the struggle for equal rights.

Carl Hansberry's daughter Lorraine, however, had a different view. Lorraine Hansberry became a celebrated playwright, fictionalizing her family's experience in one of the most important plays of the twentieth century. *A Raisin in the Sun* opened on Broadway in 1959. The play tells the story of a family, the Youngers, who are deciding what to do with an insurance check they have received from the death of their father. The son wants to use the money to start a business, the daughter wants it to fund her medical education, and the mother wants to move the family to a nicer house in a part of town reserved for whites. The family clashes over their differing dreams, but in the end decides to move into a nicer house, over the white community's objections. Though the Youngers' future remains uncertain, the play ends on a hopeful note: Even with the world against you, dreams should not be deferred.

Five years later, however, in a letter to the *New York Times,* Hansberry commented on the frustrations of pursuing equality through the system rather than against it: "My father was typical of a generation of Negroes who believed that the 'American way' could successfully be made to work to democratize the United States." He undertook a battle, she said, with NAACP lawyers to fight housing segregation in Chicago, a struggle that cost him

> a small personal fortune, his considerable talents, and many years of his life. . . . That fight also required that our family occupy the disputed property in a hellishly hostile "white neighborhood" in which, literally, howling mobs surrounded our house. . . . I also remember my desperate and courageous mother, patrolling our house all night with a loaded German luger, doggedly guarding her four children, while my father fought the respectable part of the battle in the Washington court.
>
> The fact that my father and the NAACP "won" a Supreme Court decision, in a now famous case which bears his name in the lawbooks, is—ironically—the sort of "progress" our satisfied friends allude to when they presume to deride the more radical means of struggle. The cost, in emotional turmoil, time and money, which led to my father's early death as a permanently embittered exile in a foreign country when he saw that after such sacrificial efforts the Negroes of Chicago were as ghetto-locked as ever, does not seem to figure in their calculations.
>
> That is the reality that I am faced with when I now read that some Negroes my own age and younger say that we must now lie down in the streets, tie up traffic, do whatever we can—take to the

hills with guns if necessary—and fight back. Fatuous people re-
mark these days on our "bitterness." Why, of course we are bitter.
The entire situation suggests that the nation be reminded of the
too little noted final lines of Langston Hughes' mighty poem:
What happens to a dream deferred? . . . . *does it explode?*[10]

The Hughes poem that Hansberry refers to gave her play its
title—*A Raisin in the Sun.* The title of that poem, however, is
"Harlem (2)." Its anger roils just beneath the surface.

What happens to a dream deferred?

Does it dry up
Like a raisin in the sun?

Or fester like a sore—
And then run?

Does it stink like rotten meat?
Or crust and sugar over—
like a syrupy sweet?

Maybe it just sags
like a heavy load.
Or does it explode?[11]

As Hughes reminds us, promises unfulfilled, or fulfilled only
on paper, can be worse than no promises at all.

TODAY, 230 years after Jefferson's declared equality, 150 years
after the Fourteenth Amendment officially granted it, 50 years
after Hughes worried that dreams deferred may fester, and 40
years after Hansberry warned that equality had been put off too

long, the American dream of equality remains out of reach for too many citizens. Black Americans are three times more likely to live in poverty than white Americans and twice as likely to be unemployed.[12] Black children are almost twice as likely to die before age four as white children.[13] Average mortality rates are higher for blacks than for whites and have actually *increased* since 1960; if this "mortality gap" were closed, we could save about ninety thousand lives per year.[14] Despite many gains, blacks continue to lag behind whites in nearly every measure of educational achievement.

Changing attitudes and affirmative action have changed the complexion of the graduating classes of our top universities, our news anchors, our advertisements, and our television shows. American attitudes toward race have shifted dramatically since the end of the civil rights movement, with effects that will probably take decades to become manifest. But somewhat ironically, the fall of official barriers has in some ways made it harder to promote equality today, because the causes of discrimination are more diffuse. They are now intertwined with patterns of residential housing, the plight of inner cities, the parts of the country least likely to get a measure of economic or legal protection against the impact of global outsourcing, and a host of other issues difficult to disentangle from the not-so-simple fact of race.

It took all the force of Hurricane Katrina in August 2005 to blow the dark underside of the American dream onto the national stage. Confronted with images of Americans fleeing their homes in tattered clothes, of Americans foraging for food and water in smashed storefronts, and of American bodies lying for days in the hot Delta sun, the country was forced to acknowledge that we had abandoned our poorest citizens, the great majority of them black, in their time of need.

We watched, day after day, with the eyes of the world on us, while the ugly truths hidden in sociological studies and economic statistics were laid bare. White, well-off citizens of New Orleans had gotten out. Poor black citizens had not, and our great army could not even get them water or helicopters *for four days*. Shame and grief and frustration lay over the country like a pall for months. But even then, these collective emotions failed to mobilize us to meaningful action. For all our claims of being the mightiest power on earth, the United States could not manage even to remove the rubble in New Orleans for over a year.

Far less have we probed the deeper causes of Katrina—the broken systems of government, the corruption, and the continuing racism that led to the poverty and aimlessness of life in much of the Lower Ninth Ward in the first place. Such a deep analysis would require more than just an honest national conversation; it would require a leader who could force us not only to face facts but to change them. We can do it. We've done it before, no matter how imperfectly. But we have to start by acknowledging that in America today, all people are *not* created equal.

RACIAL INEQUALITY AND class inequality have always correlated in our society; our poor have always been disproportionately Americans of color. Today, however, economic inequality extends well beyond race, in ways that are eating into the fabric of our society and undermining the foundations of our democracy. The Gilded Age of the late nineteenth century has come again, with a new class of not the rich but the superrich. Their mansions have given way to gated communities, and their Pullman cars to private jets, but as with their predecessors, they inhabit a world not only completely different from ordinary Americans, but even from well-to-do Americans.

President George H. W. Bush was ridiculed toward the end of his presidency when he visited a supermarket and did not know about bar codes, the package marking that allows cashiers simply to swipe the groceries rather than key in the amount. Bill Clinton used this incident against him in the 1992 presidential campaign, portraying Bush as living in a bubble far removed from ordinary Americans. Yet President Bush, surrounded by Secret Service agents and scheduled from dawn to dusk, had an excuse. Today, the top 1 percent of Americans who control 33 percent of America's wealth and wield tremendous political power have simply built a separate world with their money.[15]

To make matters worse, our government measures the state of the economy by macro measures—the overall levels of economic growth and unemployment. Those numbers hide the micro stories of millions of individual Americans. Overall, the economy has been quite good in recent years, growing steadily despite international turmoil, high oil prices, and other obstacles. But only about four in ten Americans think the economy is "good" or "excellent," compared with seven out of ten in 2001.[16] This change reflects the extent to which economic gains have gone increasingly to the very richest Americans. The levels of credit card debt and bankruptcy tell the other side of the story: how Americans simply trying to maintain their standards of living are gradually going under. Americans owed more than $800 billion on their credit cards in 2005, or more than $9,000 per family.[17] According to the Federal Reserve Bank of St. Louis, filings for personal bankruptcy increased 350 percent between 1980 and 2004.[18]

America is now the third-most unequal industrialized country in the world after Russia and Mexico. According to various analyses, on average our CEOs make 200 to 400 times more than the people who work for them. That is, the boss makes more in one day than the average worker makes all year. In 1965, it took the average CEO two weeks to make his workers' annual pay.[19] That's still the case in places like Europe and Japan, where CEOs typically make only 20 to 30 times as much as their workers.

But why should we care? The American vision of equality has never promised an equal standard of living for all. We are not, like Europe, the land of social solidarity, but of rugged individualism. As long as America is getting richer overall, what's the problem?

We should care because our society and our democracy depend on all citizens' having at least enough of a stake in the system to think collectively about our common interests, our national interests, our public interests. From the top down, if an entire class of citizens never actually *sees* the physical, educational, health, and recreational spaces that their fellow citizens see, then this top group will live in a different political sphere as well. If you never take the subway or the train or the bus, how can you know that the nation's infrastructure is crumbling? If you never darken the door of a public school, how can you understand the depths of our educational crisis? If you have the best private health care in the world, and it is paid for with private insurance, how can you even imagine the fear and despair of the uninsured when catastrophe strikes?

From the bottom up, if the workers at the bottom of the pay scale derive no benefits from the global economic forces that are building fortunes at the top, why shouldn't the workers fight these global forces? Endless lectures on the theory of comparative advantage cannot stop the tide of protectionism among voters who will never have the means to see India or China in person, but must see "made in China" stamped on virtually every good in Wal-Mart and hear Indian voices in call centers once located in Ohio or Texas. Similarly, while a corporate CEO might join with immigrants themselves to enumerate the ways in which immigration benefits this country, Americans who are financially struggling would disagree. This working class sees no benefit to admitting new citizens who will only undercut wages still further and crowd already underfunded schools and emergency rooms. Both free trade and immigration have been historically very good for America as a whole, but America as a whole must benefit from them. The case for globalization needs to be made in a way that takes all Americans into account.

Finally, inequality is feeding the seemingly unstoppable polarization of our politics, making it harder and harder to get anything done even when we can manage to agree on what should be done.[20] The growing segregation of our communities results in vastly different opportunities to get a good education, receive decent health care, and find jobs that produce not only income but meaningful and fulfilling work. Because our communities elect our politicians, fewer and fewer politicians see any reward in working to improve the lives of *all* Americans, as opposed to advancing the goals of a particular interest group or segment of society. The resulting stalemate in our political system makes us all worse off. As even the great individualist Theodore Roosevelt once said, "This country will not be a permanently good place for any of us to live in unless we make it a reasonably good place for all of us to live in."[21]

The traditional glue that has held our society together has been social mobility, the ability to climb the social and economic ladder by dint of a little luck and a lot of hard work. For two centuries, Americans pulled themselves up by working first the land that seemingly stretched out forever, and then the great manufacturing machines in countless factories across the country. Hard work still matters, but in the knowledge economy of the twenty-first century, an economy based on information and services, the most important determinant of future income is education. The more education a worker has, the higher the income he or she can expect.

In short, equal opportunity today means equal access to education. But although America has the best universities in the world and some of the best private secondary schools, tuition levels are steep even at public universities. Getting to university, of course, depends on a good secondary school education, which in turn depends on at least a decent elementary school education. And all of these steps, it has been shown, increasingly depend on children getting the right care in their earliest years. Here, sadly, our once great system of free public education is failing us miserably in many key cities and counties across the nation. An OECD study found that American fifteen-year-olds are among the worst prepared in the developed world. Out of 38 countries, they ranked 24th in mathematics, 19th in science, 12th in reading, and 26th in problem solving.[22] Civics is also suffering: A recent study of American college students found that many thought that Martin Luther King, Jr., was advocating an end to slavery in his "I Have a Dream" speech.[23]

Countless Americans today—individuals, foundations, corporations, nongovernmental organizations—are working to improve public education at the local, state, and national level. But the government must do far more. Guaranteed access to a good free education through university level is the twenty-first-century equivalent of land grants, the Homestead Act, or mining or meatpacking jobs. It is a gift and an incentive to those who will help themselves and help the nation.

Equal access to education is the civil rights challenge of the twenty-first century. In many school districts, the battle must start in court, with plaintiffs suing to equalize the distribution of funding across all school districts within a state. For example, a group called the Campaign for Fiscal Equity successfully sued the state of New York to provide more funding for schools in New York City, which, the group challenged, were not receiving the same resources as wealthier communities outside the city. In New Jersey, the case *Abbot v. Burke* led to a program through which state money is channeled to poor communities unable to fund decent schools on their own.

As in the civil rights movement, the formal equality that the courts can confer will not be enough. The quality—and the equality—of public education must change on the ground, classroom by classroom, student by student. But equal educational opportunity is the key to equal economic opportunity. Restoring equal economic opportunity is the only way to halt the spreading blight of social inequality, which undermines the promise of formal equality and erodes our liberty and our very national identity.

We can do it. We have done it before, with faith and a fierce commitment to make our values real. In 1938, when the country was still in the grips of the Great Depression, Langston Hughes penned a powerful appeal, "Let America Be America Again":

The free?

Who said the free? Not me?
Surely not me? The millions on relief today?
The millions shot down when we strike?
The millions who have nothing for our pay?
For all the dreams we've dreamed
And all the songs we've sung

And all the hopes we've held
And all the flags we've hung,
The millions who have nothing for our pay—
Except the dream that's almost dead today.

Today, in real terms, this nation has millions who are receiving less and less for their pay, and who, in countless ways, are less and less free. We must once again let America be America, this time by giving these struggling millions an education that can give them a realistic shot at the American dream.

AMERICA'S PROMISE OF EQUALITY is grandly broad. "All men are created equal" means that Americans are no better or worse, no more or less important, than Lithuanians, Chinese, Iranians, Uruguayans, or anyone else. Our Constitution, however, is not a global compact. "We the people" refers only to the American people. When our government must choose between a policy that favors Americans and one that would help people outside our borders but hurt Americans, it must choose to put Americans first.

How do we square this circle? How do we reconcile a belief in the equal rights of all human beings with a specific commitment to the human beings living within a defined territory? Why should the accident of birth—say, to be born in Haiti, one of the poorest countries in the world, versus the United States, one of the richest—entitle or condemn two human beings to such radically different life chances? Why should a U.S. citizen born in Maine owe so much more, in taxes, law, and loyalty, to a fellow citizen in faraway Arizona than to a fellow human being, of the same French Canadian ancestry and culture, a few miles across the border in Quebec?

One answer to this conundrum is a practical one. No one nation, no matter how rich or powerful, can possibly provide for the people of all nations. Even to try would simply dissipate that nation's resources in ways that would leave it unable even to take care of its own citizens and vindicate their rights. World government, on the other hand, is both unfeasible and undesirable. As the great philosopher Immanuel Kant pointed out over two centuries ago, such a global institution would be too big and too distant to be truly accountable to anyone and would quickly fall into tyranny.

A global governing body would also deny the "self" in self-government. Self-government means the ability to direct your own political fate, to participate with fellow citizens in managing the institutions that all of you have designed to take collective action and live as you want to live. Empires fall apart, in the end, because they are too large, too distant, and too centralized to withstand the universal desires of peoples to govern themselves.

But as another great political philosopher, John Stuart Mill, pointed out in the nineteenth century, the right of self-government cannot simply be given; it must also be taken and earned. A group of people must themselves decide that they want to govern themselves. And on their own, they must gain the experience and the wisdom that can only come with trying.

Come back now to the precise language of the Declaration of Independence, and recall the context in which Jefferson wrote it. We did not proclaim to the world that we believed "all men are created equal" simply as a moral principle, but as a political right. We said that all men are created equal, all have unalienable rights, *and that to secure these rights, governments are instituted with the consent of the governed.* Critically, we advanced this proposition to the world at large as the first step in our larger argument that when governments do not secure these rights, their citizens—that is, we, the oppressed subjects of the British king—are justified in revolting.

Our founding commitment to the equality of all human beings means that first and foremost, we must recognize the equal rights of all groups, nations, or peoples to take charge of their own governments, as long as they do so to secure the individual equal rights of their citizens. We must do everything we can to help other peoples secure their own equal rights, through whatever form of government the people themselves believe is best suited or most capable of undertaking that task. We must be certain, however, that it is actually the people themselves who are making the decisions through representative institutions, rather than one person or a small group claiming to speak on behalf of the people. We must help them to help themselves, when they seek our help.

In practice, as in our domestic politics, this understanding of global equality has both a procedural and a substantive component. On the procedural side, we may reject global government, but then we must ensure that national governments have a meaningful voice in global decision-making processes that directly affect their citizens. On the substantive side, it means doing everything that we can—as a nation and with other nations—to ensure that individuals all over the world have *an opportunity* to make a better life for themselves and their children. That means guaranteeing that the citizens of every country, including our own, have access to the necessities of life: food, shelter, basic health care, and the means to make a living.

IF YOU WERE BORN IN AMERICA, you were lucky enough to be born into a rich, powerful country. Even so, the massive migrations of money and people that have been a part of the most recent round of globalization since 1989 have caused many Americans to feel powerless and angry, at the mercy of forces beyond their or even their government's control. If you are not an American, you may recognize instantly what it feels like to be buffeted not only by all those forces, but also by American policy as well, by decisions taken in Washington, New York, Chicago, or Los Angeles. These are decisions in which you have no voice and over which you have no control.

To take just one example, if you are one of the 150 million Bangladeshis—half the population of the United States—substantial parts of your country could very well be submerged within the next fifty to one hundred years by rising seawater as a result of global warming. The United States is the largest single emitter of carbon in the world, and hence the largest single contributor to global warming. But you have absolutely no say in what the United States decides or does.

The Bangladeshis aren't the only ones at risk. Scientists predict that during our lifetime, parts of Florida, not to mention Manhattan, could well be underwater. Whether or not this happens is largely beyond our control. The Chinese are the second largest carbon emitters in the world and are likely to pass us in the near future, by 2015. The *New York Times* reports that over the next twenty-five years, the increase in global-warming gases just from China's use of coal is projected to exceed that of all industrialized nations combined and to surpass by fivefold all the reductions promised under the Kyoto Treaty.[24] We Americans have no control over what the Chinese do or decide. Next time you wonder why people around the world rail against America, imagine how you might feel about China in 2015 if your house is underwater.

I will talk about specific solutions to climate change later, but the point here is the importance of having a voice in decisions that directly affect you—the twenty-first-century equivalent of no taxation without representation. The Bush administration's reaction to climate change has been to study it and then to announce that the United States would find a technological fix. But if you are living in Bangladesh, that's not very comforting. The Chinese, on the other hand, are building a coal plant every week big enough to serve the entire population of Dallas.[25] If you are living in Miami, you should be very worried.

Bangladeshis could try lobbying in the halls of Washington; Americans could try petitioning in the halls of Beijing. Bangladeshis and Americans and anyone else could go to the U.N. Security Council, but they would find that the great powers of 1945—France, England, Russia, the United States, and China—have a veto on whatever the council decides. Moreover, no country from Latin America, Africa, the Middle East, or Southeast Asia even has permanent representation. At this point, Bangladesh has few other options. But the United States can and must insist that all the nations of the world come together and meet the challenge of doing the best that humankind can do to stop global climate change with today's technologies. The nations of the world can sign a treaty undertaking a comprehensive set of national obligations, can design an ongoing global decision-making process, can pour money from all nations into researching solutions. But whatever we citizens of the world do, all nations must have meaningful representation, enough so that they genuinely have a say in what happens to their citizens.

Guaranteeing meaningful representation is difficult—should Nauru, a tiny island state in the South Pacific, have the same voice as China or India, the world's most populous nations? Or the same voice as the United States, the world's most powerful nation? Or Russia, the world's largest? And how can we ensure that people living under authoritarian governments, people who are not represented in their own domestic politics, are represented globally? Answering these questions is difficult, but doable, just as it was for the Founders trying to ensure that the people of tiny Rhode Island had an equal voice with populous Virginia. The framers ultimately came up with a bicameral scheme: the U.S. Senate, with two votes for each state, coexists with the House of Representatives, in which a state's political power varies from census to census, depending on the size of its population. Similarly, in some global or regional institutions, the rule is one state, one vote, while others have employed various systems to address the representation issue: weighted voting, different classes of members, and rotating membership of states within the region.

What matters is the principle of meaningful representation. If we truly believe that all human beings have an equal right to institute governments to protect their rights, then those governments must have the ability to do just that at the global level. The United States must take the lead in applying this principle in international and regional institutions across the board, including in the Security Council itself. We should embrace the principle because it is the right thing to do. But as with all our values, over the long term, it is also the smart thing to do—serving both our ideals and our interests. What goes around comes around, and as other nations grow in power, size, and economic weight, their decisions will increasingly affect us.

Principles that could constrain us today may well guarantee our freedom tomorrow.

———————

As we have seen, the American concept of equality allows for plenty of inequality. Equality of opportunity gives everyone an equal chance at the starting line, but natural differences, hard work, determination, ambition, personality, resilience, social pressures, family pressures, and blind luck, among other factors, determine the order at the finish. If we were seeking equality of result, we would have many different starting lines for many different people, and some people would not have to race at all. Globally, we cannot equalize the life chances of individuals born in New York or New Delhi, Los Angeles or Lagos, Chicago or Caracas. But we can work to provide all those babies with a minimum package of birthrights: to guarantee that they will not starve; that they will have access to basic vaccines and other health care sufficient to make it past their fifth birthday; that they will have shelter and schooling and a chance to make more than a subsistence living.

These basic birthrights are achievable. In 2000, at the Millennium Summit of the United Nations, 189 nations came together and committed to just that. They adopted a set of millennium development goals (MDGs) that, by 2015, aim to achieve specific development results: halving the proportion of people living on less than one dollar per day; making primary education universal and eliminating the education gap between boys and girls; reducing the incidence of child mortality by two-thirds; and halting and beginning to reverse the spread of diseases like HIV/AIDS, malaria, and tuberculosis, amongst others.

Progress on these goals has been mixed at best. For example, the percentage of people living in extreme poverty in the developing world has gone from 27.9 percent in 1990 to 19.4 percent in 2002. Most of these gains, however, have come from Asia; sub-Saharan African poverty rates remain stubbornly high and extreme poverty has actually increased in some parts of the former USSR. On other goals, like halving the number of people suffering from hunger, the world is actually worse off today than it was in the mid-1990s, thanks to wars, drought, and floods.[26]

The United States and other wealthy countries can do much more to achieve the MDGs. Most Americans believe that the United States gives far more in aid than it actually does. We currently give a bit more than 0.1 percent of our GDP in official development assistance, about $15 billion per year. Increasing that number to 0.7 percent—the target set by the United Nations—would increase U.S. contributions to about $90 billion and challenge other developed nations to raise their commitments as well.

Many Americans, perhaps most, would embrace these goals altruistically if they knew the real facts. But we need not rely on altruism. Achieving these basic but universal birthrights will be as good for us as for the people we are trying to help. Providing global equality of opportunity, at the most basic level, means providing an opportunity for billions of people to become productive members of society—buying, selling, thinking, building, serving, and caring. Those are the activities that fuel economic growth, for their countries and for ours. These activities also provide societies with the essential infrastructure to address problems of disease, crime, environmental degradation—all the problems that spill across borders and ultimately hurt us. Again, living up to our values also serves our interests, both at home and all around the world.

And we can do more. In absolute dollars, trade is a far more effective way to improve the life chances of billions of people around the world than straight aid. As it stands, our agricultural subsidies and protective tariffs make it impossible for many farmers in poor countries to sell their wares, rewarding American agribusiness at the expense of poor farmers abroad and consumers and taxpayers at home. (Europe and Japan have even worse policies, but America, the rhetorical champion of free trade, has no cause for satisfaction.) Every year, the U.S. government spends billions of taxpayers' money on propping up the American agriculture industry. Much of this money goes to the largest corporate farms, which account for the lion's share of American agricultural production. This makes American agriculture products artificially cheap and thus competitive with products from countries with much lower production costs.

For example, cotton, which America used to grow with slave labor, continues to be a source of inequality. In 2001–2002, some 7,500 American cotton farmers received $3.9 billion in federal subsidies, more than the annual GDP of the West African nation of Burkina Faso, whose two million people depend on cotton as their primary export crop. American subsidies cost the neighboring country of Mali $43 million in lost exports in 2001, more than the $37 million Mali received in aid from the United States.[27]

The debate in Congress, of course, is not about helping the farmers of West Africa. Congress represents the American people, so the debate is about the costs of leveling the playing field between American cotton growers and African cotton growers by removing U.S. subsidies to growers in North Carolina, Alabama, and Texas. Labor in West Africa costs a small fraction of labor in the American South, where the cost of living is much higher. Why shouldn't the American government protect American farmers?

Part of the answer is that protecting some groups at the expense of others in our society breeds inequalities. Cheaper cotton may harm domestic cotton producers, but it benefits American consumers who buy cotton clothes and sheets. Different groups scrambling for protection in the halls of Congress ultimately make us all worse off. A better way would be to remove subsidies and transfer part of the savings back to the farmers by way of programs that, through new training and research, make them truly—not artificially—more competitive on the global market. This is just common sense. According to the Federal Reserve Bank of Dallas, protecting a job in the American sugar industry costs American consumers $826,000 a year in higher prices. A dairy job costs us $685,000 per year, and a job making women's purses $263,000. And these numbers do not even include the subsidies coming directly out of taxpayers' pockets.[28] Getting rid of welfare programs that *increase* inequality should be a no-brainer.

Ending handouts to corporate farms would also help West African economies get on their feet, which is good for them *and* for us. Growth in West Africa—twenty-one of Africa's least developed countries grow cotton—creates new customers for a whole host of consumer products. Those customers may still not be purchasing things produced by American workers; they may be buying from China or India. But if so, then more than two billion people in China and India are becoming steadily better off, and as they do, they start watching American movies, using American computers, purchasing American medical technology, and investing with American financial services.

In other words, we may be at the top of the global economic food chain, but like the natural food chain, it all starts with the krill, or cotton or corn or coal, at the bottom. We have a direct stake in providing much more opportunity to farmers, miners, and factory workers in the poorest countries in the world—the countries that have precisely the most room to grow. A smart trade policy can do that, while at the same time reducing hidden inequalities at home. We can help others to help themselves and help ourselves at the same time. Imagine, the African states from which slaves were taken to grow American cotton in the eighteenth and nineteenth centuries could be selling us cotton in the twenty-first century, and making us all better off.

EQUALITY, LIBERTY, AND DEMOCRACY are all deeply intertwined in our pantheon of values. The claim that all are created equal was the foundation of our bid for liberty from England and the founding premise of our democracy. But equality has also been the value most difficult to achieve, one that we continue to struggle with today.

We have made great progress in two hundred years, ending slavery and establishing formal equality for Americans of every skin color, creed, and national origin. Just over half a century after the Supreme Court struck down segregation, the last two secretaries of state have been African American, and a black man is running for president in 2008. Yet not all Americans enjoy equal protection of the laws; most gay Americans, for example, cannot form a permanent legal union with their partners or have a family protected by law.

We have also provided extraordinary opportunities to millions of determined men and women and their families over the course of our history, allowing them to live at least a part of the American dream. But the most pressing issue today is radical and growing economic inequality. It is harder and harder to make it from the bottom to the top, or to guarantee a better life for our children. As the gap between rich and poor increases, so does the gulf between left and right, creating, in John Edwards' phrase, "two Americas." That kind of inequality erodes the foundations of our democracy.

The answer is to restore the American dream, to live up to our label as the land of opportunity. This must be *equal* opportunity, which for millions of Americans must begin with equal access to the education they will need for the jobs they can get. It is no accident that the civil rights movement of the twentieth century started with the desegregation of the nation's schools. The civil rights movement of the twenty-first century must make the nation's schools fit to attend.

Beyond our borders, we face the challenge of simultaneously upholding our values while serving our interests. We can and should stand for the principle of meaningful representation of all the world's peoples in global decision making. And we can and should work to secure for all the world's citizens their minimum birthright: food, shelter, education, health care, and economic opportunity. With this birthright secured, the citizens of the earth can flourish and develop their own capacities as human beings. Such a world would not only be fairer and more prosperous, but would also be a much better world for Americans to live in.

America must stand for a *world* of opportunity. We must live up to the very first line of our very first statement when we came together to forge a new nation. We must look out at our own people and at the world as a whole and say: "We hold this truth to be self-evident, that *all* human beings are created equal, and should have equal rights to life, liberty, and the pursuit of happiness." And if we are successful, a future Walt Whitman will hear the world singing, with all the joy and energy and variety that has long been ours.

Chapter 4

Justice

Justice is the end of government. It is the end of civil society.
It ever has been and ever will be pursued until it be obtained,
or until liberty be lost in the pursuit.

—*James Madison, Federalist No. 51*

Injustice anywhere is a threat to justice everywhere. We are
caught in an inescapable network of mutuality, tied in a single
garment of destiny. Whatever affects one directly, affects all
indirectly.

—*Rev. Martin Luther King, Jr.,*
"Letter from Birmingham Jail," April 16, 1963

FROM SQUABBLING KIDS declaring "it's not fair" to the quest
for accountability by the descendants of decimated peoples, all
human beings seek justice. Justice is the goal of citizens everywhere when they come together and form a government to order
their society. It is the necessary complement to liberty; after all,
the Pledge of Allegiance promises liberty *and* justice for all.

Without justice there can be no peace; without peace there can be no order; without order there can be no liberty.

These are fine words and grand concepts. But what does justice mean, not in abstract terms, but concretely? How can our society make justice a reality? Supreme Court Justice Antonin Scalia put forward one vision of how to administer justice, describing King Louis IX of France—Saint Louis—sitting under a great oak tree after mass and inviting any of his subjects who had a suit to come and present it to him. He would hear the case and give his judgment then and there. His fairness and even-handedness in dispensing justice this way earned him the title of King Louis the Just.[1]

King Louis knew his subjects, and all his subjects knew one another. According to their rank and place in French society, they could all participate in an ongoing conversation about what was a just outcome, a just rule, or a just ordering of society. The answers to those questions change over time; they must be continually debated and adapted to ensure that they reflect the evolving standards of a particular community as to what constitutes good and bad behavior, what is fair and what is not. In thirteenth-century France, that conversation took place mostly at court and more broadly throughout the aristocracy and the clergy, with King Louis at the center.

In America, that conversation takes place in a court of law rather a court of royalty. Often, when I go to Boston, I try to walk by the John Joseph Moakley U.S. Courthouse fronting on the harbor. At regular intervals on the granite facade are tablets carved with ringing quotations about justice from great American lawyers, judges, politicians, and activists. Writing about these inscriptions, *New York Times* columnist Anthony Lewis observed: "They are history. They are passion. Together they form a discussion about what the law can and should do in a free society. They are a democratic conversation."[2]

Conducting that conversation through the courts, or more broadly, through the law, shapes our entire judicial system. It means that courts do not decide cases, at least big cases, only for the litigants. The jurists always know that they are speaking to a broader audience, all the way up to the Supreme Court, which conducts what former Yale Law School Dean Eugene Rostow once called "a vital national seminar."[3]

Individual litigants often sue to start this conversation—as we saw with the NAACP and Rosa Parks or Oliver Brown. Public interest lawyers find a compelling set of facts and turn them into a case, one that will present the issue of racial or gender equality, environmental protection, or a whole host of civil liberties in their very best light. The decisions in these cases, which are often appealed all the way up to the Supreme Court, resolve not only particular disputes but also much larger questions of economic, social, and political justice. Indeed, as early as the 1830s, Alexis de Tocqueville identified this habit of ours as one of the most striking characteristics of American democracy: "There is hardly a political question in the United States which does not sooner or later turn into a judicial one."[4]

Many other countries would resolve these questions through their legislatures, on the grounds that courts are not designed to be centers of democratic debate. Our First Amendment says: "Congress shall make no law abridging freedom of speech." When Congress makes a law that some Americans think abridges their speech, they sue, and the courts decide whether their speech has been abridged. If so, the law is unconstitutional. But in England, the source of American common law tradition, Parliament can and does pass laws that would likely be struck down in the United States, laws like the Official Secrets Act, which prohibits the disclosure of information deemed too sensitive for public release. English courts, however, cannot exercise judicial review over acts of Parliament. So the best an aggrieved citizen can do is to petition Parliament itself to change its mind.

It may seem deeply paradoxical that in a country that prides itself on our democratic traditions as much as the United States does, we nevertheless turn to courts rather than to Congress to decide issues ranging from gun control to birth control, wetlands to welfare, antitrust to affirmative action, and countless others. Yet in many ways, the power we invest in our judges makes our lawmaking *more* democratic. Above all, it protects the minority—any minority—against the majority, guaranteeing that our fundamental liberties can never be taken away by majority rule. That is the core of liberal democracy. If a majority in Congress passes a law abridging any rights secured by the Constitution, the aggrieved party—or an affected organization like the NAACP or the Sierra Club or the National Rifle Association—can turn to the courts and challenge the law directly. Equally important, if the government is exercising its power directly against an individual citizen—arresting, trying, or imprisoning the person—then the arrested party is entitled to a lawyer and, through that lawyer, access to the courts to challenge the circumstances of the detention. Anyone who has seen one of the countless TV shows in which the cops read the perps their Miranda rights knows this by heart. The courts are an essential component of our system of checks and balances—a component triggered by individual citizens.

Another way that the courts make our public conversation more democratic is that they give us something to talk about in a context that we can understand. Article III of the U.S. Constitution provides that "the judicial power" of the government shall extend to cases arising under the Constitution, treaties, or laws of the United States and to controversies between two states or between citizens of different states. Buried in that language is the "case or controversy" requirement. In many democracies, courts can offer advisory opinions, which are designed to pronounce on what a clause in a constitution or a statute means based on an interpretation only of text and legislative history. In the United States, by contrast, judges can only decide an actual "case or controversy," a real dispute with a real plaintiff and a real defendant.

Equally important, we insist that our judges give reasons for their decisions—that they explain to anyone who cares to read their opinions why they chose to decide a particular case the way they did. This means that on any important issue dividing our democracy (racial discrimination, abortion, the death penalty, the scope of privacy rights, free speech, gay marriage, the separation of church and state, and on and on), judges must decide who is right and who is wrong in a specific case where our competing values actually collide (the denial of a seat on a bus, the picketing of a clinic, the funding of a Bible study group in a public high school) and explain why. That decision is then broadcast to other lawyers and interested groups and often reported in the general press. Editorial boards and legal analysts for newspapers and television weigh in. Politicians tell their constituents whether they support or oppose the decision. And the losing party often appeals, starting a whole new round of decision and debate at the appellate level and ultimately, for the most important issues, through the Supreme Court. The result is a democratic debate akin to the conversations happening anywhere in Congress.

Finally, our legal system is both slow and incremental. We want our judges to decide cases one dispute at a time, deciding what needs to be decided but leaving open issues that do not need to be decided for another day and another dispute. In the words of one of our greatest justices, Oliver Wendell Holmes, "the life of the law has not been logic but experience."[5] This gradual approach allows judges to interpret and translate the great words and phrases of our Constitution across decades and even centuries. That process is what judges and politicians typically mean when they say that we have a "living Constitution."

It all sounds great in theory and sometimes measures up in practice. In *Brown v. Board of Education,* for instance, the Court reasoned that in the circumstances of the United States in the 1950s, separate systems of education did not mean equal. In addition to the manifest evidence of lower-quality schools for African Americans, the Court drew on sociological studies showing that segregated education sent negative messages to black students in a predominantly white society.

A court revisiting these reasons today would look at the ways in which our society has changed since the 1950s and at new sociological evidence. It might well conclude that under some circumstances, African American children benefit from an all-black school, just as in some circumstances, girls or boys can benefit from all-girl or all-boy schools. This constant process of evaluating and reevaluating the soundness of the reasons judges give in the context of individual decisions is a vital part of asking and answering what justice means across the generations since our founding.

Just as social attitudes are different a half century after the *Brown v. Board of Education* decision, attitudes were very different a half century before *Brown.* Today's young law students usually don't feel nearly as good about their profession after reading *Plessy v. Ferguson,* a landmark case from 1896, as they do after reading *Brown.* In 1890, Louisiana passed a law requiring separate train cars for whites and blacks. A group of Louisianans formed an association to fight the law and, in 1892, recruited Homer Plessy, who was one-eighth black, to test the law by buying a first-class ticket. He was arrested after refusing to give up his seat. When the case finally reached the Supreme Court, seven of the eight justices decided that Jim Crow segregation requiring blacks and whites to sit in different train cars did not violate the Constitution's guarantee of equal protection of the law on the grounds that segregated facilities were "separate but equal."

It is quite possible to explain the decision in *Plessy* by observing how the Supreme Court was merely reflecting the values of the day, how it was taking account of the need for Southern states, battered both by the Civil War and by Reconstruction, to accommodate overwhelming social change gradually rather than all at once. But the result was that African Americans in the South had to wait another half century to be truly free. The shackles imposed by Jim Crow laws were less visible than the chains of slavery, but no less real.

In short, our judicial system is far from perfect. Judges can perpetrate injustices as well as remedy them. A living constitution that evolves one case at a time can remain a century behind the times. Having every political question turn into a judicial one can result in too many judicial questions being decided according to political considerations—or even according to the politics of individual judges.

Overall, though, Americans genuinely believe, as John Adams wrote into the Massachusetts Constitution, that we are "a government of laws and not of men." Although our courts sometimes fail, they often succeed—speaking truth to power and standing firm against the forces of politics. Our system of judicial review has been adopted in liberal democracies all over the world as a fundamental check on the power of the legislature and the executive. And our system of public interest litigation, whereby individuals and organizations can sue to enforce or overturn laws that help or harm them, has proven attractive to activists around the world.

Even in China today, a country still far from a liberal democracy, the central government is recognizing the value of decentralizing the enforcement of environmental laws by allowing citizens' groups to sue polluters that break the law. Meanwhile, in other countries, individual litigants have managed to obtain important rulings. For example, litigants in Britain succeeded in obtaining a ruling that overturned a ban on gay soldiers. In India, a court ruling required the government to provide water to its citizens.[6] And in South Africa, the government must make material progress on its promise of a right to housing.[7] Suing to enforce individual rights or to restrain the massive fist of governmental power may seem like a quixotic quest in countries riven with violence and poverty, but it allows victims to tell their stories and demand the justice that is their due. And over time, it offers an incremental way to build an edifice of rules and reason. When the fighting is exhausted, that edifice can become the foundation and the structure of a new society.

The impact of the American justice system on other societies around the world, particularly after World War II, highlights the glaring and often inexplicable difference in the way we apply our laws to citizens and aliens. The Constitution's great guarantee of "due process of law" does not even extend to the water's edge; immigrants who cannot make it far enough onto the beach when they land on our shores can be sent back without any process at all. And an American citizen captured fighting with al-Qaeda in Afghanistan cannot be held incommunicado and without a lawyer in Guantánamo, much less be subjected to physical abuse, while the Arab or Pakistani in the next cell, captured in the same place under the same circumstances, has no recourse under American law. This situation may be legal, if the American Congress or American judges choose to make it so. But is that what we mean by "justice for all"?

EVEN AT HOME, our love of the law and obsession with justice have not necessarily made the United States a more just place. More than any other country, the United States uses the language of law (rights) and the tools of law (courts) as the principal instruments of achieving justice. But we do not always get it right. America's failures of justice have been both large, like the *Dred Scott* and the *Plessy* decisions, and small but symbolic, like the 1927 execution of Sacco and Vanzetti, working-class Italian immigrants at a time of anti-immigrant and anticommunist fervor. Judicial failures continue all too frequently today, when competent lawyers charge more than some people can afford and the justice system cannot avoid embodying the prejudices and inequities of society at large.

Like all societies, ours is particularly prone to getting it wrong when we are frightened. In World War I, we scapegoated German Americans, causing many to anglicize their names just as we "de-Teutonized" our language: Presaging "freedom fries," sauerkraut became "liberty cabbage." The horrible excesses of McCarthyism—blacklists and anti-Communist prosecutions— arose at the outset of the Cold War, when suddenly the Soviet Union seemed to stalk Americans throughout the world. And during World War II, our fear seeped into the courts themselves, all the way up to the Supreme Court.

On December 7, 1941, the Japanese Empire launched a surprise attack on the U.S. Navy base at Pearl Harbor, killing thousands of Americans and bringing the United States into the largest armed conflict of American history. As the nation mobilized for war, fear of foreign agents operating in American cities broke out. On the West Coast, this fear was directed mostly against Japanese Americans, long victims of discrimination, living in California, Oregon, and Washington State.

On February 19, 1942, President Roosevelt signed Executive Order 9066, empowering the military to designate parts of the country "military areas" from which anyone might be excluded. A few weeks later, the army declared the entire West Coast a restricted area and ordered all people of Japanese descent—immigrants and native-born Americans alike—into "relocation centers." Under this program 110,000 men, women, and children—none of whom were specifically accused of any wrongdoing—were forced from their homes and made to live in camps. Public reaction to these events, muted by the war, was dominated by virulent anti-Japanese groups publicly calling for internment.

One American, at least, refused to go. Fred Korematsu was born in Oakland, California, in 1919 to Japanese parents. When his family was sent to a race track south of San Francisco for "processing," Korematsu stayed behind and was arrested for failing to obey the relocation order. Later, he was sent to an internment camp in Utah with the other detainees.

With the help of the American Civil Liberties Union, Korematsu fought his sentence all the way to the Supreme Court, claiming equal access to the protections guaranteed in the Fifth Amendment. But in December 1944, the Court decided to uphold Korematsu's conviction.[8]

The Court reasoned that "Korematsu was not excluded from the Military Area because of hostility to him or his race," but rather "because we are at war with the Japanese Empire, because the properly constituted military authorities feared an invasion of our West Coast and felt constrained to take proper security measures." In this context, the military authorities had decided that "the military urgency of the situation demanded that all citizens of Japanese ancestry be segregated from the West Coast temporarily." Importantly, the Court was not prepared to give the president alone the power to make this decision; it at least required the joint authority of the president and Congress acting together.

The military argued that it had found a few specific instances of "disloyalty" on the part of Japanese Americans and could not waste time sorting patriots from traitors. As the Court argued, "the need for action was great, and time was short." Even given "the calm perspective of hindsight," the Court was not prepared to second-guess this decision. Korematsu was sent back to the camp he had been ordered to originally. The six justices who concurred in this opinion thought they had no place questioning military decisions, even though, as the Court noted at the beginning of its decision, under our Constitution, "all legal restrictions which curtail the civil rights of a single racial group are immediately suspect."

While clearer heads did not prevail that day, they did exist. Justice Francis Murphy wrote a scathing dissent in *Korematsu v. United States,* which he thought "goes over 'the very brink of constitutional power' and falls into the ugly abyss of racism." He acknowledged that some Japanese Americans worked against the United States. Even so, "to infer that examples of individual disloyalty prove group disloyalty and justify discriminatory action against the entire group is to deny that under our system of law individual guilt is the sole basis for deprivation of rights." Further, to sanction such discrimination under the Constitution "is to adopt one of the cruelest of the rationales used by our enemies to destroy the dignity of the individual and to encourage and open the door to discriminatory actions against other minority groups in the passions of tomorrow."

With the help of a law professor, Korematsu later found documents proving that the government had misrepresented the facts of his case in court. In 1983, four decades later, his conviction was nullified. The Court, however, never overruled itself. It never declared that relocation of an ethnic group during time of war was illegal (though if forced to decide today, it would surely do so). It was left to Ronald Reagan to recognize the immorality of what had happened when, later that decade, the U.S. government officially apologized for the internment of Japanese Americans and paid over a billion dollars in compensation to the victims. In 1998, President Clinton awarded Korematsu the Medal of Freedom with these words: "In the long history of our country's constant search for justice, some names of ordinary citizens stands for millions of souls—Plessy, Brown, Parks. To that distinguished list today we add the name of Fred Korematsu."

That list will undoubtedly contain still more names in the future. The struggle for justice in America is a constant one. Korematsu took seriously Justice Murphy's warning about the "passions of tomorrow" and recently filed a brief in the case *Rumsfeld v. Padilla.* In the brief, he argued against the indefinite detention of detainees—including American citizens like José Padilla, who was captured during the war on terror. Americans should heed this living link between past and present injustice, lest we turn around one day to find Padilla filing briefs in some future struggle to hold the government to its promise.

The promise is justice not for some, but for all. It is a goal that has guided us, for all our flaws and notwithstanding the parallels between Fred Korematsu and José Padilla, to a better place in our history today than in the past. The ongoing struggle has inspired some of our greatest moments, even as it has uncovered some of our worst failings—moments when our courts have stood up to the most powerful members of our society and ensured that we are in fact a government of laws and not of men. Those moments do not negate our legacy of injustice for many in our society, but they merit our pride and fuel our determination to do better still.

JUSTICE FOR ALL means two things: that nobody is denied justice, and that nobody escapes it. It took Korematsu decades to receive the modicum of justice needed to clear his name, but the perpetrator of injustice in his case, the U.S. government, was never formally held to account. Justice for all must apply to the strong as well as the weak. That is a lesson that President Richard Nixon learned the hard way.

During the early hours of June 17, 1972, five men carrying surveillance equipment were caught breaking into the Democratic National Committee's offices at the Watergate Hotel. It soon emerged that the five intruders had strong ties to the Central Intelligence Agency (CIA) and the Republican Party, connections that became even more suspicious when a check for $25,000 that had been earmarked for President Richard Nixon's reelection campaign appeared in one of the burglar's bank accounts. Though the Nixon campaign and the White House denied any connection to the incident, the FBI launched an investigation and the Washington press corps, led by the *Washington Post,* began digging around.

In September, the *Post* reported that John Mitchell, a former attorney general and the head of Nixon's reelection campaign, controlled a secret Republican group that carried out intelligence-gathering on Democrats while he was attorney general. It was later reported that the Watergate break-in was part of a massive Republican effort to spy on and sabotage Democratic activities throughout the 1972 campaign. Despite these allegations, Nixon trounced his Democratic opponent, George McGovern, in the November 11 election, winning every state but Massachusetts.

But as his second term began, Nixon found himself increasingly beset by the scandal. In January, the Watergate burglars were convicted for spying on the Democrats, and a month later, the Senate formed a special committee to investigate Nixon's campaign activities. Then, in March, one of the burglars, James McCord, who had also served as head of security for Nixon's reelection campaign, wrote a letter to the presiding judge declaring that his codefendants had lied during the trial to hide their connections to the White House. He also claimed that Attorney General John Mitchell and presidential counsel John Dean had encouraged the burglars to lie.

News of the cover-up fueled public outrage, though Nixon continued to deny that he had any knowledge of the break-in or efforts to stymie investigation into the incident. On April 30, the president appeared on national television to announce the dismissal of Dean and other top advisers. Then, on June 25, Dean testified before the Senate committee, outlining the wide range of political espionage the White House had been engaged in and asserting that Nixon had been involved in cover-up operations within days of the Watergate break-in.

Emboldened by this testimony and seeking definitive proof of Nixon's abuse of presidential powers for partisan gain, the Senate committee insisted that the White House turn over documents and tapes of conversations between the president and his advisers. Nixon refused, citing the president's prerogative to hold frank, confidential discussions with his advisers. A protracted legal battle between the Senate and the president ensued, reaching the Supreme Court in 1974.

The Court was faced with a simple but important question: Can the president, simply by virtue of being the president, withhold information from a criminal trial? Nixon gave his opinion in an interview on May 19:

> INTERVIEWER: So what in a sense, you're saying is that there are certain situations . . . where the president can decide that it's in the best interests of the nation or something, and do something illegal.
>
> NIXON: Well, when the president does it that means that it is not illegal.
>
> INTERVIEWER: By definition.
>
> NIXON: Exactly. . . .[9]

The Court unanimously disagreed: "Neither the doctrine of separation of powers, nor the need for confidentiality of high-level communications . . . can sustain an absolute, unqualified Presidential privilege of immunity from judicial process under all circumstances."[10]

Though it agreed that presidential business required some privileged protection, the Court argued that "this presumptive privilege" must be considered "in light of our historic commitment to the rule of law." And when considered in that light, the Court reasoned, the privilege could not stand. On the contrary, "to ensure that justice is done," courts simply must have the power to compel "the production of evidence needed either by the prosecution or by the defense"—even from the president.

By affirming the American belief that no one should be above the law, the Court brought important new evidence into the investigation. Nixon found himself forced to hand over tapes that clearly showed his connection to the Watergate cover-up, a discovery that made impeachment a near certainty. Preempting this possibility, Nixon resigned the presidency on August 8, 1974. However, he never went to jail, as a number of his subordinates did. President Gerald Ford saw to that by issuing him a presidential pardon. Still, it was the courts—the part of government that Hamilton called "the least dangerous branch"—that had forced a president to relinquish the highest office in the land.

Often when I travel abroad, foreigners refer to Watergate as a stain on our history, a time of national scandal like the scandals that we periodically read about in other countries. It was indeed such a time. But it is also, in my view and the view of most Americans I know, a source of great national pride. Our system worked. We certainly demonstrated, as Madison foretold, that our leaders were no angels. But we also proved the greatest strength of our system: not inherent virtue, but the ability to self-correct vice. Watergate's achievement—the spectacle of prosecutors, judges, and members of Congress standing up to the most powerful man in the land—came from a collective desire to see justice done and the presence of institutions that could make it happen.

KOREMATSU AND *NIXON* ARE HISTORY, but the issues they grapple with remain very much alive as the Supreme Court confronts the war on terror. The treatment of enemies, perceived or real, and the scope of executive privilege continue to subvert the

American promise of justice. President Bush claims that the war on terror broadens his powers enormously. Because we face a new threat, he and his lawyers argue, the president can order our military and intelligence agents to treat enemy soldiers and alleged terrorists however he deems fit, regardless of the requirements of domestic and international law.

Sweeping claims of absolute power by any one branch of our government are exactly what our Founders sought to check and balance in designing the Constitution. And in a series of decisions regarding detainees held at Guantánamo Bay, the Supreme Court has begun to push back. The detainees themselves, Muslim men from many countries who were captured on the battlefield in Afghanistan, sued the U.S. government to challenge their confinement. The resulting cases took several years to make it to the Supreme Court, but when the Court finally ruled, it declared to Americans and to the world at large that even at a time of great danger, the rule of law remains our strongest and best hope. Only law can ensure that our government exercises its power in our interests and safeguards our individual rights. If our rights and liberties must be limited for the security of the nation as a whole, then those limits must imposed by law, not by the whim of the executive.

In the first of several related decisions on the rights of detainees, *Rasul v. Bush* (June 2004), a group of Guantánamo inmates sought a writ of habeas corpus—that is, freedom from unlawful imprisonment. To grasp the significance of the case, it is worth understanding the lineage of habeas corpus, a cornerstone of the entire Anglo-American legal system. *Habeas corpus* is Latin for "you have the body," meaning a writ issued by a court to a jailer saying, *You have the prisoner, and you must legally justify why you are holding him. If you cannot, the prisoner must be released.* Habeas corpus predates even the Magna Carta, though the English nobles who came together to draft the great charter recognized and confirmed it as a fundamental common law right. Five centuries later, habeas corpus was one of the few rights that the framers included specifically in the body of the Constitution rather than in the Bill of Rights.

Yet even after four years of holding detainees without charges, without trial, and without any promise of future release, the U.S. government maintained in *Rasul v. Bush* not only that the detention in Guantánamo was lawful, but also that the United States had no responsibility to demonstrate *why* it was lawful. This position meant that a federal or state court could never insist that the detention of any individual prisoner be justified, no matter how long that prisoner was held without trial. Fortunately, the Supreme Court rejected the government's argument, declaring that the federal courts had the power to oversee whatever was happening at Guantánamo, that the detainees, regardless of their alleged crimes, could not be held and tried by the Pentagon without the possibility of appeal to U.S. courts.

In line with the *Rasul* decision, Salim Hamdan, a Yemeni citizen alleged to be Osama Bin Laden's driver, brought a case that, like the *Rasul* case, challenged his four-year detention at Guantánamo and the administration's plan to try him before a military commission. The rules governing these commissions were established only by the executive, without input from Congress. The rules would allow the military to exclude Hamdan and other detainees from their own trials and prevent them from challenging or cross-examining witnesses. What's more, the presiding military officer would have the authority to classify any sources deemed related to national security. Once the proceedings were closed, only military lawyers would have access to the record. The defendant, in short, would not have access to critical evidence against him.

Further, unlike the rules in ordinary courts or in courts-martial under the Uniform Code of Military Justice, the military commission could admit *any* evidence that the presiding officer determined would have "probative value to a reasonable person." That is, the commission would allow anything that a reasonable person would think was relevant to proving the case against the defendant. For example, even hearsay several times removed—"my friend heard his uncle say that the defendant attended an al-Qaeda training session"—could be admitted against the defendant without the defendant's even knowing who the informant was or what he or she said.

In *Hamdan v. Rumsfeld* (June 2006), the Supreme Court held, in Justice Stephen Breyer's view, that "Congress has not issued the Executive a 'blank check'" to prosecute the war on terror. Congress must also have its say, and if Congress and the president disagree, then the president must yield.

The Court also held that the rules governing the military commissions that the president had designed violated both domestic and international law. The right to be present at your own trial, to cross-examine witnesses, and to see the evidence against you are all rights guaranteed in the Manual for Courts-Martial, which would ordinarily apply to all soldiers and prisoners of war. Moreover, in deciding on the procedures for the commissions, the president had to comply with the law of war, which includes the Geneva Conventions signed in 1949. Common Article 3 of the Geneva Conventions specifies the absolute minimum standard that must apply to any combatants who are taken prisoner by any party to a conflict. It requires that a defendant be "tried by a regularly constituted court affording all the judicial guarantees which are recognized as indispensable by civilized peoples." In its decision, the Court reaffirmed that Americans remain a civilized people.

Hamdan v. Rumsfeld was a victory for America, but a fleeting one. The Court had ruled that the president could not hold the detainees in Guantánamo in violation of domestic and international law and without permission from Congress. But with the 2006 midterm elections looming and the administration seeking to depict many legislators as "soft on terror," Congress passed a law essentially giving the president that permission. The Military Commissions Act essentially gives the president the power to lock "enemy combatants" away forever, without even the ability to challenge their detention in court. It also denies prisoners the ability to invoke the Geneva Conventions in their defense.

Fortunately, the new Democratic majority has promised to revisit the issue. And the law has already begun to face another round of challenges in the courts—human-rights lawyer Deborah Pearlstein called the law a "full employment act" for lawyers—and many experts expect such an un-American law to crumble when it comes before the Supreme Court.[11] Indeed, many members of Congress who voted for it were no doubt counting on that likelihood, relying on the judicial branch to clean up their mess.

This is democracy at its lowest. We must now hope that the nine unelected lawyers of the Supreme Court maintain the principles they defended in *Hamdan*. In many ways, *Hamdan* combines the lessons of *Korematsu* with the principle upheld in *United States v. Nixon*. As we have had to learn time and again throughout our history, no individuals, no matter how suspect the group to which they belong, can be punished without an individualized trial, a carefully crafted proceeding in which evidence is presented, arguments can be rebutted, and a neutral decision-maker decides. Justice must be fair, concrete, and blind—even to our enemies. And no one, not even the president, is above the law.

————————

IN THE RUN-UP TO the Military Commissions Act, the White House sought more than just the authority to detain people indefinitely without charge. The president also sought to redefine Common Article 3 of the Geneva Conventions in a way that would explicitly allow U.S. interrogators to delve into what the conventions call "outrages upon personal dignity, in particular, humiliating and degrading treatment." Article 3, which also bans murder, torture, ill treatment of captives, and summary executions, is commonly regarded as the minimal standard of decency for, once again, civilized peoples.

Frighteningly, much of the debate in the public and within our government about the treatment of detainees under U.S. control—in Guantánamo, Iraq, Afghanistan, and secret CIA prisons—has revolved around the precise definition of torture. To an American growing up in the 1970s and 1980s—when the horrors of the dirty war in Argentina and Chile were made public, not to mention countless stories of the Soviet Gulag, Iran's secret police, Iraqi prisons, Turkish jails, the Cambodian killing fields, and the public outcry at the police abuse of Amadou Diallo and Rodney King here in this country—a public discussion among *Americans* of whether and to what extent torture can be justified seems surreal. As the years have passed since 9/11, however, what was once unthinkable has now become daily fare.

Before turning to definitions, it is vital to see—really see and absorb—what all these words actually mean. Begin with the images from Abu Ghraib: a stack of naked prisoners piled on top of one another, a female soldier leading a naked man around on a leash, a man with a hood over his head on a box with electrical wires connected to him, a naked man menaced by dogs.

Do these pictures depict torture? I suspect that most Americans would say no, unless the dogs were allowed actually to attack. But the U.N. Convention against Torture defines torture as "any act by which severe pain or suffering, whether physical or mental, is intentionally inflicted on a person for such purposes as obtaining from him or a third person information or a confession. . . ." Convincing a human being that she or he is about to die is certainly as severe an act of mental duress that we can inflict on a person. And can anyone doubt that these practices are humiliating and degrading treatment, as the Geneva Conventions prohibit? The whole point was to degrade and to humiliate—as a prelude to extracting information.

At Guantánamo, American doctors and psychologists advised members of our military and intelligence branches on how to inflict pain, degradation, or humiliation on individuals in what one observer described as "one giant human experiment."[12] According to a reporter's account of the Pentagon's own interrogation logs, internal investigations, and an e-mail from an FBI agent, U.S. interrogators at Guantánamo engaged in the following practices:

- Sexual humiliation of all kinds, including smearing fake menstrual blood on one prisoner
- Desecrating religious symbols
- Beatings, apparently with medical personnel present
- Force-feeding a prisoner liquids intravenously and forcing him to soil himself

- Exposing a prisoner to such extremes of temperature that he pulled out his own hair
- Keeping prisoners chained hand and foot in a fetal position to the floor with no chair, food, or water for eighteen to twenty-four hours
- Isolation and sleep and food deprivation—all designed to "disrupt a personality"[13]

These activities were formally approved. But there were limits. Personnel overseeing interrogations asked Defense Secretary Donald Rumsfeld for permission to engage in several other activities:

- Waterboarding, a technique in which a prisoner is strapped down to a board and water is forced up his nose until he thinks he is going to drown
- Making the prisoner think that he or a family member is in imminent danger of dying

Rumsfeld, we are told, drew the line and said no. But other members of the Bush administration would have gone further still. John Yoo, Berkeley law professor and former adviser to the Bush Justice Department, took a position that argues that the president himself, like the divine monarchs of old, is not constrained by any law. When Yoo came to Princeton in the spring of 2005 to talk about the scope of the president's power to fight the war on terror, I asked him explicitly if he was saying that the president could, as a legal matter, mutilate someone or kill a family member in front of a detainee to extract information. Yoo replied, "Is there any provision [in the Constitution] that prevents him from doing that?"[14]

The devil's advocate might ask, Why get so upset? After all, someone threatened with the death of a family member, or even convinced of his own imminent death, need only give us the information we seek and then the interrogation will stop. The child will be proven to be still alive and the subject of the interrogation will survive. The same line of thinking would ask, Is waterboarding really so bad? Just a minute or two in which we convince someone he is going to drown?

But if these kinds of torture are acceptable, then why do we rule out Russian roulette? Or fake executions? Imagine it for a moment—*really* imagine it. Imagine someone—a friend, a relative, even yourself—believing that life is about to be blotted out forever. Imagine that person losing control—of his courage, his identity, his dignity, even of his bowels. If he gives in to terror and tells the interrogator what he knows, or what he thinks the interrogator wants to hear, he regains his physical life, but not his identity, his pride, or his manhood. He is broken, just as surely as he might be broken from electroshocks, or branding irons, or cigarette burns. Is it really better to break a human being in a way that does not leave marks?

Those who think physical pain is the litmus test might not balk at the manipulation of fear. Why *not* threaten a prisoner with the death of his child to get him to talk? To any parent, the answer is obvious. No physical pain could be greater than the death of a child. The interrogator might know that it's just a threat, but the whole point of the exercise is that the prisoner doesn't.

In public debate, opponents of mental and physical torture are often derided as soft or weak, or accused of failing to appreciate the realities of war or the necessities of national security. But the public leader who has fought the hardest to insist that the United States abide by the prohibitions against torture in the

Geneva Conventions is Senator John McCain, a former POW who spent five years in a North Vietnamese dungeon. General Colin Powell, the former secretary of state, wrote, in support of Senator McCain, that "the world is beginning to doubt the moral basis of our fight against terrorism."[15] Twenty-eight former generals and admirals argued publicly that the "abuse of prisoners . . . is anathema to the values Americans have held dear for generations."[16] And the title of this book, *The Idea That Is America,* comes from a letter written by a young military officer who saw the worst that Iraq could dish out and still could not countenance the abuses perpetrated by his fellow soldiers. These are men tested by war and violence, who know where true strength lies.

If we were so horrified at the pictures from Abu Ghraib, then it is difficult to explain how Congress can now openly countenance the humiliation and degradation of prisoners by American interrogators. We should have simply explained to the world when the pictures were released that this kind of treatment is necessary to save American lives from terrorist attack. On the other hand, if we reject what we saw in those pictures, then it seems a bit tricky to claim today that this humiliating and degrading treatment is permissible. The only way out of this conundrum is that humiliating and degrading treatment is permissible as long as it is out of sight. But if we are ashamed to speak of it, then we should be ashamed to do it.

I can argue why ruling out torture and humiliating and degrading treatment is strongly in American interests, how interrogation of this sort rarely works. I can explain how the damage it does to us in the world far outweighs any specific information that we get. Indeed, even if we get information that actually succeeds in stopping a particular attack today, we are breeding legions of new terrorists tomorrow. I can also point out how seriously we endanger our own soldiers when they are captured abroad. I can talk about how fundamentally we degrade ourselves, beginning with the young men and women ordered to carry out such treatment and ending with our very identity as a nation. As President Theodore Roosevelt said in his 1906 State of the Union address, "No man can take part in the torture of a human being without having his own moral nature permanently lowered."

I can make those arguments. I believe them. But what I really want is an America that will simply stand up and say, as President Bush did when he saw the Abu Ghraib photographs, that this is *not who we are*. I want a president, and a country, who means it.

———

KEEPING FAITH WITH JUSTICE in the world means genuinely committing to justice *for all*. Not just for Americans. Not just for combatants who fight in traditional armies wearing traditional uniforms. Not just for alleged terrorists who have the relative good fortune to be captured by American police officers on U.S. soil, rather than by military or CIA officers operating beyond our borders.

We should begin by publicly embracing both the letter and the spirit of the Geneva Conventions—conventions that we helped negotiate and have championed for decades as fundamental bulwarks of civilized warfare. Again, our own military officers make the case best. In September 2006, in another letter to Congress, forty-five retired generals and admirals wrote to Senators John Warner and Carl Levin, then the majority and minority leaders of the Senate Armed Services Committee, to urge them to reject any effort to water down the Geneva Conventions:

> Common Article 3 of the Geneva Conventions provides the minimum standards for humane treatment and fair justice that apply to anyone captured in armed conflict. . . . The United States military has abided by the basic requirements of Common Article 3 in every conflict since the Conventions were adopted. In each case, we applied the Geneva Conventions—including, at a minimum, Common Article 3—even to enemies that systematically violated the Conventions themselves.[17]

The signatories were at particular pains to reject the administration's view that the Geneva Conventions did not apply to "unlawful combatants" like members of al-Qaeda, arguing that, on the contrary, the negotiators of the Conventions, including the American representatives, wanted to ensure that Common Article 3 covered both regular and irregular forces.

If the signatories to this letter were to petition Congress in person, rather than by letter, we would see a phalanx of the top brass, stars and bars and medals shining and representing thousands of hours of service to our country. They would stand in the tradition of our first great general, George Washington himself. During the Revolutionary War, American soldiers were taken prisoner by the British, and Americans succeeded in capturing British soldiers in return. The British treated captured American soldiers abominably. But when British soldiers surrendered to our troops after the Battle of Princeton, Washington ordered one of his lieutenants: "Treat them with humanity, and Let them have no reason to Complain of our Copying the brutal example of the British Army."[18] Congress and the Continental army generally adopted what became known as a policy of humanity: "Their moral choices in the War of Independence enlarged the meaning of the American Revolution."[19]

Another of our greatest presidents, Abraham Lincoln, followed this example. He signed the Lieber Code in 1863, setting forth the minimum standards governing the treatment of captured Confederate soldiers—soldiers guilty of nothing less than treason in the eyes of most Union troops (incidentally the same charge the British leveled at American revolutionaries). The code, which was distributed to Union soldiers on the battlefield, noted that even military necessity "does not admit of cruelty—that is, the infliction of suffering for the sake of suffering or for revenge, nor of maiming or wounding except in fight, nor of torture to extort confessions." Furthermore, the code reminds us that "Men who take up arms against one another in public war do not cease on this account to be moral beings, responsible to one another and to God." The code was followed by the Confederate soldiers as well, and its principles were adopted a year later in the first Geneva Convention, of 1864, requiring humane treatment of soldiers wounded in battle.[20]

From our very first days as a country, then, we have tried to define and hold the moral high ground in the conduct of war. The laws we and other countries have created to restrain the conduct of war have still allowed for horrors like the firebombing of Dresden and Tokyo in World War II, to say nothing of Hiroshima and Nagasaki. But we helped to create and pass the Geneva Conventions of 1949 precisely to tighten those laws and steadily increase the protection of prisoners and civilians alike. By Vietnam, horrible pictures of dead and maimed civilians roiled the nation. The revelations from Abu Ghraib and Guantánamo should have had a similar effect, and for many people, they did. But Abu Ghraib should have led not simply to the prosecutions of a few individual soldiers, but also to firings or resignations higher up the chain of command. And all these incidents should have produced a president determined to reclaim our traditions of warfare and restore our nation's and soldiers' pride.

However, we must also recognize the reality that war has changed significantly since the last time the Geneva Conventions were updated, in 1977. We should not throw them out entirely and start over, as some have argued. Rather, in the tradition of war presidents like Washington and Lincoln, we need to work with other nations to adapt the laws of war to fit the twenty-first century.

The modern laws of war began with the Brussels Declaration of 1874, incorporating the lessons of the Napoleonic Wars in Europe and the U.S. Civil War. The law gradually developed over time with the inclusion of treaties that prohibited certain armaments, provided for the humanitarian treatment of wounded or imprisoned soldiers, and created protections for noncombatants. The four Geneva Conventions are the most recent and comprehensive list of safeguards. But the law of war has always been a step behind the practice of war. The massed troop formations of the Napoleonic Wars gave way to the trench warfare of World War I, which was replaced by the blitzkrieg and aerial bombardment of World War II, which in turn gave way to the guerrilla warfare of Vietnam and, now, to global terrorism perpetrated by nonstate actors.

The nature of warfare has changed since Vietnam, but the Geneva Conventions have not. International law must keep pace with the changing face of war, just as the interpretation of our own Constitution has had to evolve over the centuries. We must accept the Geneva Conventions as expressing the current law of war regarding prisoners of war and interrogation standards. But those conventions did not anticipate the retention and interrogation of individuals with no loyalty to an army or even an insurgent group, but rather to a shadowy, global network of individuals determined to commit acts that by their very nature are war crimes and even crimes against humanity. Above all, in earlier wars, the interrogation of prisoners might have revealed immediate battle plans, but could not be essential to stopping the next attack before it started. Today, finding out what prisoners know could be the key to preventing thousands of civilian deaths.

We face a world of old rules and new threats. The right response is not to throw out the old rules or to unilaterally reinterpret them. It is instead to work with other nations to establish a new consensus around the rules that apply to war in its contemporary form. We are not alone in this challenge. Many countries, including those with constitutional traditions we can draw from, like Britain, Spain, or Israel, to name only a few, have struggled with terrorism. We must work with these and other nations to amend the Geneva Conventions or to draft new standards for detaining and interrogating individuals who are acting on behalf of no state but who have nevertheless declared war on multiple nations and indeed on an entire civilization.

The way is slow and cumbersome and difficult. International negotiations often are. And lines dividing permissible from impermissible behavior are notoriously hard to draw. Is sleep deprivation permissible? Loud noise? Bright lights? Stress positions? National courts in many countries have been and will be grappling with these questions. So will citizens around the world. Specific judgments drawing sharp lines or setting forth new standards will trigger debate within and across countries. This debate will in turn inform negotiations between governments, just as domestic judicial decisions and the debate they trigger inform negotiations between the political branches of government.

In the end, the result will be worth it: a set of clear rules that will justify our actions under law in the eyes of the world and of our own people. The rules will protect our soldiers and special forces around the world. If indeed, as President Bush says, the war on terror is likely to last for many decades, then surely it is worth taking a few years at the outset to ensure that we fight the war on the right side of the law.

———————

LIBERTY AND JUSTICE FOR ALL. Justice is intertwined with liberty, because the social and political order necessary for liberty can only survive if a nation can respond to its citizens' demand for justice. African Americans and the white Americans who stood alongside them understood the fight for equal rights as a fight for justice, a fight against the *injustice* of blighted lives and blighted hopes determined not by worth or merit, but by shades of skin. Martin Luther King simply refused to believe that "the bank of justice is bankrupt." Today, when the struggle against formal discrimination is largely won, the fight continues for social and economic justice.

The inscription above the great marble columns of the Supreme Court in Washington offers another link between justice and liberty. It reads "Equal Justice under Law"—the promise of our democracy and the prerequisite of our liberty. In Watergate, our elected representatives stood up against our elected president because he sought to exercise his power unconstrained by law. Demanding that he account for his behavior under law, like any other citizen, ultimately brought him down. As it was, Nixon created an "imperial presidency" that our founders would have recognized as a grave threat to our liberty.[21]

Injustice can destroy liberty as surely and swiftly as any tyrant can. "No person . . . shall be compelled in any criminal case to be a witness against himself." Those are the words of the Fifth Amendment to the Constitution. They protect Americans from torture, from lesser forms of police abuse, and even from talking to police or prosecutors without a lawyer present. But they also protect the core of our identity as a nation by safeguarding the very concept of personhood that underlies all our rights—the right to speak freely, to worship, to be safe in our houses and other private spaces, to be who we want to be.

Andrew Sullivan described precisely what torture does: "Torture uses a person's body to remove from his own control his conscience, his thoughts, his faith, his selfhood." How then can the tortured person ever again be free? "If the state has the power to reach that deep into a person's soul and can do that much damage to a human being's person, then the state has extinguished all oxygen necessary for freedom to survive."[22] The only possible way that we, as free Americans, could accept such a state is if we accept that the subjects of torture are somehow less than human or, at any rate, less human than we are.

That was precisely how so many Americans viewed African Americans, for centuries. This view was the wellspring of injustice and oppression—of the hatred that Lorraine Hansberry and her family endured for daring simply to live side by side with white neighbors. It made a mockery of our claim of equal justice under law and undermined our moral worth and standing in our own eyes and the eyes of the world.

Yet today we are openly saying to that same world, through our president and our legislators: We come from a country where we are willing to smear fake menstrual blood on a Muslim because we understand that sexual degradation is a particularly effective way of humiliating a faithful Muslim, and we are quite willing to violate and manipulate faith as a way of destroying dignity and ultimately dissolving a personality to extract information. In our actions against an enemy, we are prepared to do things sufficiently hideous to cause captives to pull out their own hair. We are prepared to do such things because we are trying to protect the lives of our people—lives that, contrary to everything we believe as Americans, are suddenly more important than our values.

The great U.S. senator and orator Daniel Webster once wrote, "Justice is the great interest of man on earth. It is the ligament which holds civilized beings and civilized nations together."[23] We are losing that ligament, and with it, our own moral compass. We must somehow find our way back, and push our way forward, to liberty and justice for all.

Chapter 5

Tolerance

To kill the Americans and their allies—civilians and military—
is an individual duty for every Muslim who can do it in any
country in which it is possible to do it, in order to liberate the
al-Aqsa Mosque [Jerusalem] and the holy mosque [Mecca] from
their grip, and in order for their armies to move out of all the
lands of Islam, defeated and unable to threaten any Muslim.

> —*Osama bin Laden, fatwa entitled "Jihad Against Jews and*
> *Crusaders World Islamic Front Statement," February 28, 1998*

Against fanaticism, genuine democracy wields an irresistible
weapon—it is *toleration.*

> —*Carl Schurz, German immigrant turned Republican politician,*
> *addressing the Massachusetts legislature, April 18, 1859*

THE PILGRIMS, America's best-known early European settlers,
came to this continent because England had become intolerant of
their way of life. In the wilderness of North America, they could
worship as they saw fit, free of religious controls. But they were
equally intolerant in their turn. The New England Puritans were

not seeking to establish a community of free worship but rather a safe haven for their particular brand of rigorous Protestantism. They cast out dissidents like Anne Hutchinson for troubling the peace simply by daring to speak "diverse things . . . prejudicial to the honour of the churches and ministers."[1]

Their intolerance and rigidity could have spelled their doom. But the harsh North American winter soon taught them at least a measure of tolerance, not as a virtue but as a necessity. Only half of the settlers who survived the passage from England on the *Mayflower* lived to see spring in their new home. Many more might have perished but for the food and furs provided by the local American Indian tribes, who showed great tolerance for the strange people who had come into their midst. When the weather turned warm, these same locals taught the newcomers how to grow and hunt for food in the strange land. By autumn of that first year, the Pilgrim community had learned to sustain itself, and the settlers celebrated their first harvest by inviting their neighbors to feast and give thanks for the year's bounty.

This story, though exaggerated and mythologized over the centuries, contains several essential truths about tolerance as a bedrock American value. Tolerance was not a luxury, but a *necessity.* The Puritans could not survive without the American Indians. Even though they thought they could be rid of free-thinkers like Anne Hutchinson, when Massachusetts joined together with Roger Williams' community of free worship in Rhode Island, the Quakers in Pennsylvania, and the Catholics in Maryland, to name a few, only a national doctrine of tolerance could hold the nation together as a democracy.

Great thinkers and statesmen have long recognized the importance of tolerance in a free society. For the English philosopher John Stuart Mill, the father of modern liberal thought, tolerance was crucial. In his famous 1869 tract *On Liberty,* Mill speaks of this important value: "A man cannot get a coat or a pair of boots to fit him, unless they are either made to his measure, or he has a whole warehouseful to choose from. . . . [A]re human beings more like one another in their whole physical and spiritual conformation than in the shape of their feet?"[2] Tolerance of diversity, Mill goes on to say, benefits society not only because people can find what suits them best, but also because allowing individuals to pursue different paths generates new ideas and innovations.

Mill's views on tolerance were directly relevant to the American experience, precisely because America depended on tolerance for its very survival as an enormously diverse democracy. Consider the views of the great turn-of-the-century American public servant Elihu Root, who served as senator, secretary of war, and secretary of state, and who won the Nobel Peace Prize in 1912. Root took the idea of popular *self*-government seriously, meaning self-government in the sense of ingrained habits of restraint and self-control. Tolerance played a prominent role. "Democratic government," he wrote, requires people to seek facts, discuss them with their fellow citizens, "have a kindly consideration for opposing opinions, and a tolerant attitude for those who differ."[3] As we found out with the Puritans, if we cannot respect others' opinions, then our pluralist political system has little hope of success.

Tolerance is not just conducive to democracy; it also, as the Pilgrims found out, makes us strong. Consider one of the most famous early affirmations of tolerance as part of the American creed: George Washington's letter to the Touro Synagogue in Newport, Rhode Island, the first synagogue on American soil. In 1790, the synagogue's warden, Moses Seixas, had written Washington on the occasion of the president's visit to Newport, thanking him for the "blessings of civil and religious liberty which we enjoy under . . . a benign administration." In his reply,

Washington observed that all Americans "possess alike liberty of conscience and immunities of citizenship." In particular, "It is now no more that toleration is spoken of, as if it was by the indulgence of one class of people, that another enjoyed the exercise of their inherent national gifts."[4] Washington was proclaiming, only shortly after the birth of the nation, that tolerance was a fundamental American value.

Today, as America grows more diverse than ever, that birthright becomes ever more important. On the rostrum of the Chamber of the House of Representatives, where the Speaker of the House sits, is carved "Union, Justice, Tolerance, Liberty, Peace." Above the rostrum, over the flag that hangs down behind the Speaker, is the more familiar "E Pluribus Unum"—out of many, one. It is no accident that tolerance is the central value. As Walter Lippman wrote in 1914, "the great social adventure of America is no longer the conquest of the wilderness but the absorption of fifty different peoples."[5]

We are a diverse people. We come from the generations of immigrants who poured into the country bringing their sweat, hope, and know-how. We are the descendants of slaves brought here against their will and denied the most basic rights of citizenship for generations. We are American Indians who still struggle with the generations of wrongdoing and sheer ignorance on the part of European-heritage Americans. And we are mostly mixed-heritage Americans who have evolved into various homegrown groups—everything from Mormons to hippies. This diversity can bitterly divide us. But, when we are united through tolerance, it can also fuel our collective strength.

It is important to remember that tolerance is not the same as approval or liking. A person can certainly disapprove or actively dislike another's behavior and yet tolerate it. As parents, my husband and I have strong views about the desirability of manners and the undesirability of too many video games for our children (which, admittedly, probably simply means that our kids are video fiends at their friends' houses). Many of our friends have different views on both these subjects. We do not agree, but we continue the friendship and would not dream of trying to impose our views. This tolerance has limits, of course—we would probably not continue a friendship with parents who allowed their children to lie, steal, or do hard drugs. But as a general matter, we remind ourselves that we do not necessarily know best, even if we claim so in front of our own kids, and we try to have the forbearance to bite our tongues when we see behavior we don't like.

In our public debates today, tolerance is far too often equated with weakness, irresolution, or lack of conviction. Yet the tolerance that made us a nation requires strength and self-restraint. Individuals who accept that others may believe and behave differently in deciding how to live their lives have sufficient security and confidence in their own choices not to fear that those choices will be eroded when they themselves are exposed to those differences. They also have enough self-discipline not to rush to judgment, not to condemn out of ignorance or anxiety.

Of course, tolerance must have its limits, just as my husband and I must decide the limits of what we will tolerate in our friends' child-rearing practices or indeed what behavior we will tolerate from our kids themselves (an ongoing process). As a society, we similarly engage in an ongoing process of deciding what we want these limits to be. These debates have been going on for a long time in our courts and legislatures, for example, over the right of Jehovah's Witnesses not to salute the flag (allowed), the right of some American Indian groups to use traditional hallucinogenic mushrooms in religious ceremonies (allowed), or the right of a religious group to practice polygamy (denied). While

our diversity as a nation requires us to err on the side of tolerance, it also requires us continually to discuss what our commitment to tolerance requires and what it does not.

In the twenty-first century, this commitment faces the
strongest challenge yet: planting and sustaining tolerance not
only within and among nations, but also among civilizations. In
1992, the political scientist Francis Fukuyama published *The
End of History and the Last Man,* in which he argued that free
markets and liberal democracy had decisively displaced all other
forms of political and social organization.[6] The following year,
Harvard professor Samuel Huntington published "The Clash of
Civilizations?" predicting a new set of global fault lines based
not on political and economic ideology but on faith, ethnicity,
and culture.[7] Both authors offered far more subtle analyses than
reviewers or the reading public generally gave them credit for,
but Fukuyama and Huntington have come to stand for two
competing positions in a broad debate. Fukuyama is identified
with the view that liberal democracy transcends, or at least can
transcend, all cultural or civilizational difficulties, making tolerance at best a second-order concern. Huntington, on the other
hand, is seen to stand for the proposition that we are destined to
compete against those who are different than us, making tolerance unachievable.

The American experience suggests that we need to aim somewhere between these views. Liberal democracy *requires* tolerance,
and tolerance is hard. It is not the inevitable by-product of ever-
expanding democracy and liberalism; it must be continually in-
stilled and practiced. On the other hand, America's own
experience as a nation melding together the people of many nations demonstrates that civilizations need not necessarily clash.
Tolerance may be hard, but it is not impossible.

AMERICA LEARNED MANY of its most important lessons about tolerance back in the nineteenth century. Between 1845 and 1854, nearly three million immigrants entered the United States, accounting for about 15 percent of the country's total population. Most of the newcomers were from Ireland, Germany, and Scandinavia, and many, unlike the existing American population, were Catholic. They came to America seeking to escape war and famine in Europe, but the reception they found was often less than welcoming.

The existing residents of the United States were taken aback by the new immigrants' customs and Catholicism, and worried about their numbers. Catholics, especially the Irish, were blamed for poverty and crime and were generally believed to be lazier and more inebriated than the so-called native Americans (i.e., the Europeans who had arrived earlier).

Americans also charged Catholics with endangering American democracy. Many feared that the Catholic immigrants' first loyalty was not to Washington but to Rome. The belief was that the newcomers swore allegiance to Pius IX, the conservative pope who opposed the failed European democratic revolutions of 1848, and that they were therefore unsuited to American democracy. As the *Philadelphia Sun* wrote in 1855, Catholicism was "a desolating curse . . . antagonistical to human rights and republican institutions."[8] These fears increased as the new immigrants became naturalized and exercised their right to vote, often supporting ethnic party machines.

In the North, hostility toward Catholics also became curiously wedded to antislavery movements. Many American somehow came to believe that because Catholics were subservient to Rome, they must also support human bondage. Protestant abolitionists tended to view both slavery and Catholicism as hierarchical systems inimical to freedom. On July 4, 1855, the radical Cincinnati preacher C. B. Boynton told his congregation that "there are two dangers which threaten our noble Republic. Between these two co-operating foes, the Papacy and Slavery, stands Young America sorely beset."[9]

As the number of Catholic immigrants, and, consequently, their voting power, increased, nativists became increasingly hostile. In 1849, Charles Allen founded the secretive Order of the Star-Spangled Banner in New York City. The group was dedicated to limiting immigration, restricting political office to native-born Americans, prohibiting Catholic schooling, and other such measures. Order members swore an oath of secrecy and were told to answer all questions about the organization with the words, "I know nothing." This phrase became a shibboleth for the order as it spread around the country, and members soon became known as Know-Nothings.

As their numbers grew, the Know-Nothings emerged from the shadows to form a public political party called the American Party. In 1852 and 1854 they won significant victories in Congress and at the state level, coming to control forty-three seats in Congress in 1855. They also made their presence known outside the halls of power, forming street gangs in cities like New York and Chicago to harass and intimidate Catholics. Going by names like Wide Awakes, Black Snakes, Rough Skins, Red Necks, Rip Raps, Rip Saws, Screw Boats, Drips, Plug Uglies, and Blood Tubs, nativists scuffled with immigrants, who formed their own gangs, like the Dead Rabbits, Double Pumps, Pealers, Pluckers, Shad Rows, and Butt Enders.[10] In 1854,

American Party toughs even stole and destroyed a granite block that Pius IX had contributed to the Washington Monument.

In 1859, the Massachusetts legislature was considering a proposal to delay naturalized immigrants' voting rights. This measure, the kind of legislation supported by the American Party and its sympathizers, would have reduced new Americans' political power. It garnered national attention and attracted the interest of Carl Schurz, a German-born Wisconsin politician who made a fiery speech against the proposal in Boston's Faneuil Hall.

Schurz had come to America in the wake of the failed democratic revolutions in Europe in 1848. He quickly rose through the ranks of the Republican Party, eventually becoming a U.S. senator, President Lincoln's ambassador to Spain, a Union general during the Civil War, and, later, secretary of the interior. A self-described freethinker, Schurz had little patience for religious bigotry. In Boston, he called on the legislators to remember the "true Americanism" that had brought him across the Atlantic. It was true, he acknowledged, that not every immigrant who arrived on American shores was as educated or experienced in democracy as American-born citizens.

Yet, Schurz continued, "with all this, our democratic system gives rights to the ignorant and power to the inexperienced." Why would the Founders have created such a system? Schurz asked. Only with confidence in American institutions. "Has the present generation forgotten," he asked, "that true democracy bears in itself the remedy for all the difficulties that may grow out of it?" He went on to refute the idea that Irish immigrants and Catholics generally were unfit for American democracy: "True Americanism, toleration . . . has absorbed their prejudices"—that is, any undemocratic traditions newcomers might bring or that natives might hold—"and will peaceably absorb everything that is not consistent with the victorious spirit of our institutions."[11]

His speech was not quite what we would today call politically correct. But it proved decisive. The Massachusetts legislature rejected the voting restrictions, a sign that the nativist agenda was in trouble. Indeed, in the run-up to the Civil War in the second half of the 1850s, the Know-Nothings faded as quickly as they had arisen. At a party meeting in Philadelphia in 1855, Southerners took control and passed a resolution calling for the continuation of slavery. Almost the entire Northern faction stalked out of the meeting immediately, many joining the newly formed antislavery Republican Party. The American Party did poorly in the 1856 elections, when its presidential candidate, Millard Fillmore, carried only Maryland and the party's congressional representation dropped to just twelve seats. By 1860, the party was almost entirely defunct, its candidate coming in fourth out of four in that year's presidential election.

Why did anti-immigrant and anti-Catholic feeling become such a powerful force in American political life, only to wither so quickly? Most historians agree that Know-Nothingism was swept aside, along with many other political concerns, by the all-consuming debate over slavery and partition that gripped the nation in the years before the Civil War. As Americans faced up to their "peculiar institution," perhaps they found themselves forced to reflect on their other failings and hypocrisies. Slavery made a mockery of the American rhetoric of freedom and equality; anti-Catholicism sought to extend a national system of apartheid to yet another class of citizens.

The winner of the 1860 election, Abraham Lincoln, perfectly captured this truth in a letter he wrote in 1865:

I am not a Know-Nothing. That is certain. How could I be? How can any one who abhors the oppression of negroes, be in favor of degrading classes of white people? Our progress in degeneracy appears to me to be pretty rapid. As a nation, we begin by declaring that "all men are created equal." We now practically read it "all men are created equal, except negroes." When the Know-Nothings get control, it will read "all men are created equal, except negroes, and foreigners, and catholics." When it comes to this, I should prefer emigrating to some country where they make no pretence of loving liberty—to Russia, for instance, where despotism can be taken pure, and without the base alloy of hypocracy [sic].[12]

The Know-Nothings garbed themselves in the trappings of America, organizing groups with names like the Order of the Star-Spangled Banner, and the American Party. They made their anti-immigrant case with American rhetoric, talking about the need to protect freedom and equality from foreign encroachment. But in the end, the country was not fooled. Intolerance may call itself American, but it can never be American.

ALTHOUGH THE KNOW-NOTHINGS have disappeared, intolerance has not. In the 1870s, a group also calling itself the American Party organized in California on a platform of excluding Chinese and other Asians from industrial jobs. In 1968, Governor George Wallace of Alabama ran for president on the American Independent Party ticket with a segregationist agenda. And today, groups calling themselves Minutemen—named for the heroes of Concord and Lexington—harass undocumented workers along our southern border and advocate sharp reductions in immigration from Latin America.

It seems that every group to arrive in America must face a torrent of intolerance before being grudgingly accepted—and then still not completely. How ironic that a country of mostly immigrants so quickly forgets the struggles of our forebears to take an equal place in American society. More ironic still is that we would dress such sentiments up as patriotism. Fortunately, successive generations of newcomers have managed to prevail and find their places in American society, affirming the value of tolerance even when those who have already been here a while disregard it. Intolerant elements in this country are always quick to paint themselves red, white, and blue, but so far, at least, they have not been able to get those colors to stick.

WE USUALLY THINK of tolerance as racial or religious tolerance. But a liberal democracy equally requires political tolerance, that is, tolerance of viewpoints different from our own. That principle may seem more than a little idealistic in the poisoned, partisan climate in which we now live, but tolerance has helped our nation before.

In March 1928, a young newspaper publisher named Arthur Vandenberg found himself appointed to represent Michigan in the U.S. Senate after the elected senator suddenly died. Vandenberg, a Republican, later became a fierce critic of Democratic President Franklin D. Roosevelt and his social policies; the senator described the New Deal as "congressional surrender to alphabetical commissars who deeply believe the American people need to be regimented by powerful overlords in order to be saved."[13] A staunch believer in free markets and local government, he led the congressional Republicans' charge against Roosevelt's plans to restore the nation's economy after the Great Depression through federal spending programs.

Vandenberg was also an isolationist. As World War II began in Europe and Asia, he advocated a strict policy of neutrality for the United States and a firm arms embargo on Axis and Allied powers alike. Pearl Harbor forced him to reconsider this stance, though he continued to refer to the most horrendous conflict in history as "Roosevelt's private war," and attributed American involvement to what he called the president's "secret diplomacy," diplomacy that he thought deliberately led us into war.[14]

As the war drew to a close, Vandenberg led congressional Republicans in their attack on Roosevelt's postwar strategy. The president was arguing for a broad, collective security organization—what would eventually become the United Nations—while conservatives opposed the idea. They believed that any international peace organization would tie U.S. hands, particularly if it were to include the Soviet Union.

Vandenberg was proud; a correspondent for the *New York Times* called him "a big, loud, vain, and self-important man, who could strut sitting down."[15] It was thus all the more surprising when Vandenberg rose on the Senate floor on January 10, 1945, and gave what immediately became known as "the speech heard round the world":

> Mr. President, there are critical moments in the life of every nation which call for the straightest, plainest, and the most courageous thinking of which we are capable. We confront such a moment now. . . .
>
> No man in his right senses will be dogmatic in his viewpoint at such an hour. . . . Each of us can only speak according to his little

lights—and pray for a composite wisdom that shall lead us to high, safe ground. It is only in this spirit of anxious humility that I speak today.[16]

Vandenberg went on to announce what he later called his "dramatic conversion," declaring that although he had always believed in self-reliance, the shock of Pearl Harbor and the ensuing horrors of the war had convinced him that America could no longer defend itself alone. His humility led him to a complete reversal of position, from isolationist to champion of the collective security organization then under negotiation. President Roosevelt was at first taken aback, but ultimately he was so impressed by his former foe that in 1945, he appointed him to represent the United States at the San Francisco conference where the United Nations Charter was drafted. Later, as chairman of the Senate Foreign Relations Committee, Vandenberg joined with Roosevelt's successor, Democrat Harry Truman, to promote the Truman Doctrine, the Marshall Plan, the NATO alliance, and other elements of the bipartisan Cold War consensus that defined American foreign policy for the next four decades.

Today, Vandenberg's portrait is one of the few chosen to hang in the Senate Reception Room as a reminder that, in Truman's words, "Partisanship must end at the water's edge." Perhaps the portrait should be taken out and hung in the Senate chamber itself. Vandenberg's successors and the broader political community today seem to have forgotten the idea that tolerance for other views and those who hold them must underpin democratic debate. In Vandenberg's time, political battles were no less fiercely fought than they are today; back then, Democrats and Republicans, liberals and conservatives, had sharply different views on how to build the postwar world. Yet today it is almost impossible to imagine anyone taking the Senate floor in a "spirit of anxious humility." Intolerance and partisanship go hand in hand.

And yet the circumstances facing Vandenberg, Roosevelt, and their peers were not so different from those facing America's political leaders after September 11, 2001. Once again, as Vandenberg said about Pearl Harbor, a surprise attack "put the gory science of mass murder into new and sinister perspective," forcing Americans to recognize that "our oceans have ceased to be moats that automatically protect our ramparts."[17] Americans, Republican and Democrat alike, came together in grief and anger to seek the composite wisdom that would lead to high, safe ground.

But the spirit of unity proved all too short-lived. The years following the September 11 attacks have been some of the most partisan in memory, embittered by opposing views of the Iraq war and by the 2004 presidential election. The presidential contest looked less like a policy debate and more like a shouting match between the "Bush is a dangerous idiot" camp and the "John Kerry is a traitor" camp. Conservative talking head Ann Coulter topped the bestseller lists with a book entitled *Treason*, in which she bluntly argues that anyone who disagrees with her is guilty of high crimes against the nation. Liberal filmmaker Michael Moore found a box-office hit with his documentary *Fahrenheit 9/11*, which cast President Bush as a pawn of Saudi princes.

When people believe strongly in their ideas and defend them fiercely in the public square, democracies prosper. But for that kind of dialogue to occur, the participants on both sides must actually be prepared not only to persuade but to be persuaded, to accept the possibility of actually shifting position or even, like Vandenberg, completely changing their minds. When is the last time anyone in Congress, or any president, for that matter, admitted being persuaded not simply to compromise, but actually to think differently about an issue?

In the current political climate, intolerance masquerades as conviction, while tolerance is ridiculed as relativism. Yet tolerance is the indispensable first step toward even the possibility of persuasion. As in our earliest days, it is a vital source of strength, both as the precondition for unity and for the innovation and energy that results from the clash of ideas. Where are the Vandenbergs of today?

AFTER THE FALL of the Berlin Wall, Francis Fukuyama was not alone in imagining "the end of history," the possibility that empires had been destroyed, nationalism conquered, and Communism vanquished.[18] Peoples all over the world aspired to free markets and liberal democracy; surely, the future would usher in the final triumph of the West. History, however, has returned with a vengeance.

Today Iran rises as Persia reborn, the great civilization that once stretched from Macedonia to India. China reminds the world of its nearly millennium-long head start even on Europe. India recalls the glories of the third-century Gupta empire and the sixteenth-century Mughal empire, which built the Taj Mahal. And some extreme avatars of fundamentalist Islam wish to return the world to a fourteenth-century caliphate, when cities like Baghdad and Constantinople reigned as sparkling centers of culture and learning (whose diversity and openness the fundamentalists ignore).

Merchants in the Middle East today talk of a new Silk Road—the storied overland trade route that once linked the Mediterranean to the Yellow Sea through ancient cities like Tyre, Samarkand, Kashgar, and Chang'an. As of 2006, the Persian Gulf was China's eighth-largest trading partner, with Chinese banks setting up business in Dubai to help deepen and widen Chinese ties across the region. As Europe turns east and Asia turns west, the old world revives. The Middle East—the cradle of civilizations—threatens continually to become the cradle of global conflict. Yet it is also again becoming a crossroads of civilizations from east to west and north to south.

This emerging world appears to confirm Huntington's vision of the clash of civilizations.[19] His thesis is very simple: The world is largely divided into distinct cultures—which Huntington categorizes as Western, Eastern Orthodox, Latin American, Islamic, Japanese, Chinese, Hindu, and African—that compete for resources and power. In this world, the primordial divisions of blood, race, and soil cannot be tamed by tolerance. And where intolerance reigns, liberty, democracy, equality and justice cannot survive.

A world of clashing civilizations is the world that our ancestors came from and that our very existence as a nation seeks to deny. It is a world that Americans reject, never more powerfully than immediately after September 11. As a nation, we understood that we had not been attacked by Islam itself—either the religion or the civilization—but by individual extremists. Addressing a special session of the U.N. General Assembly in the weeks after the September 11 attacks, Rudolph Giuliani—then mayor of a city that is home to one of the greatest mix of races, religions, and cultures in the world—reminded the world that the fight against extremism was not a fight between cultures, but between values.

> The strength of America's response [to the attacks], please under-
> stand, flows from the principles upon which we stand. Americans
> are not a single ethnic group.
>
> Americans are not of one race or one religion. Americans emerge
> from all your nations.

Giuliani continued with what is essentially a statement of the
American creed:

> We are defined as Americans by our beliefs—not by our ethnic ori-
> gins, our race or our religion. Our beliefs in religious freedom, po-
> litical freedom, and economic freedom—that's what makes an
> American. Our belief in democracy, the rule of law, and respect for
> human life—that's how you become an American.[20]

In his joint address to Congress nine days after September 11,
2001, President Bush expressed his agreement with these sentiments: "I also want to speak tonight directly to Muslims
throughout the world. We respect your faith. . . . The enemy of
America is not our many Muslim friends; it is not our many
Arab friends. Our enemy is a radical network of terrorists, and
every government that supports them."[21]

Think about these responses. They portray al-Qaeda's attack
precisely as an attempt to divide us along religious and civilizational lines—Muslim versus Christian, Arab versus American.
In standing firm against this attack, Americans not only tolerate
but embrace difference, arguing for the values that unite us
across civilizations. A theology of tolerance is our strongest
weapon against preachers of hate.

Five years later, however, many Americans both in the administration and out were singing a different tune. By Septem-

ber 2006, President Bush had identified the new enemy of the American people as "Islamo-Fascism," described as the twenty-first-century successor to Communism and Nazism. Far from celebrating our tolerance of multiple faiths, ethnicities, and cultures and focusing on how universal values can unite people across civilizations, we are now identifying an entire religion with a totalitarian ideology.

This approach to fighting terrorism is dangerous and deeply counterproductive. It is a self-fulfilling prophecy, in the sense that by continually coupling Islam with fascism or terrorism, we are in fact communicating to the Muslim world that we are engaged in a war on Islam. This is exactly the message that al-Qaeda uses to whip up supporters and new recruits. Though not the message that President Bush wants to send, it is the message that Muslims hear. The result is that we are playing right into al-Qaeda's hands. A war on terror against Islamo-Fascists transforms Muslim mass murderers into Islamic warriors, which is exactly how they want to see themselves.

We must return to our initial instincts immediately after September 11 and again make clear that our enemy is not *Islamic* anything. The threat to our security comes from individual terrorists organized in global networks capable of attacking in the United States itself, Europe, Indonesia, Africa, and the Middle East. These individuals are plotters, aiders, abetters, and perpetrators of the deliberate mass murder of innocents. We should go after the terrorists with everything we have—intelligence, law enforcement, and special operations. And at every turn, we should emphasize that they violate the commandments of every religion and every great civilization. They are not warriors, but outlaws; not avatars of a great civilization, but barbarians attacking civilization itself.

WE KNOW IN OUR DOMESTIC POLITICS that tolerance in a democracy, or indeed in any community, must have defined limits. Upholding tolerance as a universal value, then, also requires us to identify precisely what we *cannot* tolerate. We start by making clear, with the peoples of all nations, that we cannot tolerate terrorism. But we must also condemn the values that make terrorism thinkable.

Recasting the clash of civilizations as a clash of values means that we condemn the intolerance of a sect so narrow that it consigns co-religionists to death. We celebrate liberty as the freedom to worship any god in any way and condemn the forced imposition of any faith. We celebrate democracy as the right of *all* citizens to choose their government, and we condemn the rule of the self-proclaimed elect of any God. We celebrate equality as the equality of all men and all women, all believers of any faith, all believers and unbelievers, and all ethnic backgrounds and nations. We celebrate justice as the rule of law and condemn murder and destruction by any group for any cause. And we celebrate humility as the command of all religions and condemn the arrogance of any one group of believers who claim to speak for an entire faith.

As an expression of our values and in recognition of our common humanity, we should join with other civilizations to lead a dialogue based on finding and celebrating the values that crosscut all civilizations. Some efforts are already under way. In September 2004, the Spanish prime minister, José Luis Rodriguez Zapatero, called for the creation of an Alliance of Civilizations to strengthen cultural linkages, primarily between the Arab and Muslim world and the West. The idea was met with broad approval, and the initiative was launched by the U.N. secretary-general and cosponsored by the governments of Spain and Turkey, two great cultures that owe much to the cross-fertilization of East and West. In November 2006, a group of experts produced a report that recommended a host of policies to further cross-cultural understanding, ranging from increasing efforts to resolve the Israeli-Palestinian conflict to improving the quality of education in the Muslim world.[22] America has much to gain from being engaged in, and being seen to be actively engaged in, this dialogue.

One of the most important ways that we can promote cultural linkages is to celebrate the contributions of other cultures to what are still portrayed as Western values in many parts of the world. A great example of this approach comes from our own Capitol. Over the gallery doors of the House Chamber, where our own lawmakers meet, are twenty-three marble relief portraits of lawgivers—which the Architect of the Capitol describes as figures throughout history who have established the principles underlying our own legal system.[23] The selection of individual lawgivers must surprise many Americans and is likely to please our foreign visitors.

Some of the figures depicted are predictable: Thomas Jefferson, George Mason, and Sir William Blackstone, the great English jurist whose *Commentaries on the Laws of England* was a bible for early American courts. Others, however, are more surprising. Hammurabi, the great Babylonian king who is said to have handed down the first legal code—a man whom today we would call an Iraqi. Maimonides, the great twelfth-century Jewish philosopher of Cordova, Spain, who compiled Talmudic law. Pope Gregory IX, during the same period, authored a series of authoritative interpretations on canon law. Saint Louis, the great French king and jurist described in the chapter on justice. Justinian I, the Byzantine emperor who compiled Roman law into the Justinian code. Solon, the Athenian statesmen who contributed much to the constitution and laws of the world's first democracy. And Suleiman the Magnificent, the sixteenth-century sultan of the Ottoman empire and the ruler who made what we now know as Turkey the center of one of the greatest empires of its day.

Together, these figures reflect the great legal traditions of civilizations other than our own. Each of these civilizations has spawned radical intolerance at times: the fanaticism of the Spanish Inquisition, the Roman persecution of Christians, the Turkish massacre of Armenians, the American system of slavery and segregation of African Americans, the Greek dehumanization of barbarians, the Israeli extremists who oppose any peace with the Palestinians, and radical Islamic sects who would visit death on all unbelievers. The hall of lawgivers stands against all such excrescences. It symbolizes a zone of legitimate difference defined by the overlap of all civilizations, a zone of tolerance and mutual respect. That zone also marks the boundaries of the universal civilization we must unite to defend.

DIALOGUE IS ESSENTIAL, but in the end, it is not enough. In a globalized world, tolerance cannot be a passive value. It is not enough for America to say to other countries, "We respect the way you are, so let's all just go about our business." Tolerance is an active process of engaging, listening, and responding. We cannot just agree to respect each other; we have to work at it.

Consider how the United States promotes itself in the Arab and Muslim world. We Americans are often shocked when we see polls about how people in those countries perceive us. Our response is typically to think that the citizens of other countries don't truly know us or understand what we are trying to do in the world. And so we ratchet up so-called public diplomacy by trying to better explain ourselves and our policies abroad through media and "strategic communications." Most of these efforts have been ham-handed. Years under authoritarian regimes have made Arab and Muslim audiences adept at taking the spin off official communications. It is unlikely that pop-music-laced, pro-American news like the broadcasts that Arabs can hear on the American-funded Radio Sawa will change many minds about the events Middle Easterners see on Al Jazeera and other channels.

Perhaps the answer is not to do a better job of explaining American positions to the Islamic world, but to help people there reclaim their hope and dignity, which many feel the West has taken from them. Osama Bin Laden attracts respect because, for all his horrors, he taps Muslims' need to assert themselves against what they see as a powerful external aggressor. The sense of humiliation on which al-Qaeda feeds is both poison to democratic reform and fuel for extremism.

America should strive to build a positive image of the Arab and the broader Muslim world. The image should de-emphasize militarism (the history of Islam is no more bloody than that of Christianity). Instead, we should emphasize the greatness of Islam's past, the strength of its values and traditions, and our hope for a future Muslim world that is a prosperous, respected part of the international community. Instead of just "tolerating" Islam, we should help Arabs and other Muslims remember the greatness that a once-tolerant Islam achieved and could achieve again.

Islamic civilization has a very strong tradition of tolerance. In Spain under the Umayyads and in Baghdad under the Abbasid Khalifas, Jews and Christians enjoyed many of the same privileges as Muslims did, including education and the right to maintain their own beliefs. Compare that with the extremes of the Spanish Inquisition, which, after Christians retook control over the Iberian Peninsula, drove many Jews south to take refuge in Muslim lands.

This vision of a peaceful, prosperous, and tolerant Islam is important to reinforce in American minds, to counter the creeping intolerance that inevitably results from the continual bombardment of images of Muslim terrorists. Equally important, this vision can be a powerful antidote to Bin Ladenism, rallying Muslims around progress and reform in the name of Islamic civilization. American public diplomacy could help progressive elements in the Arab and Muslim world build such a vision in a number of ways. We could sponsor traveling exhibitions that highlight the achievements of Islamic civilization. We could give more support to universities, rights groups, and other elements of civil society. We could hold a national year-long celebration of Islamic culture, the kind of cultural diplomacy that countries like China and France do so well. Such measures can set an important tone that would reinforce ongoing efforts like the Middle Eastern Partnership Initiative, which strives to promote democratic reform and economic development in the region.

America has never been particularly serious about this kind of cultural diplomacy, but think about what we do at home. Almost every American town of any size holds its own ethnic celebrations. There are Puerto Rican parades, Greek festivals, Polish sausage-fests, Italian feasts, Chinese New Year celebrations, and West Indian parades. In big, diverse cities like New York and Chicago, it seems that some ethnic group is parading, feasting, or performing every day. These celebrations are a rich part of the American cultural fabric, a chance for communities to celebrate and share their traditions. Why not share the fun with the world by supporting more cultural exchanges and celebrations across borders? This is one aspect of American foreign policy that individual states, cities, and private groups can lead, ideally with strong federal support.

Ultimately, American public diplomacy might be more successful if we talk less about ourselves, about how well-intentioned and tolerant we are, and more about how much we would welcome a world in which Islamic countries had regained their place as representatives of a great and forward-thinking civilization. It is not enough for Americans to tolerate Muslims; we must also help the Arab states and the rest of the Muslim world reclaim the confidence to tolerate us.

TOLERANCE IS NOT MORAL RELATIVISM. It stands firm against people and behavior that cannot be tolerated. It is not harmony, or even agreement, but rather a necessary, and often testy, coexistence. In our own history, tolerance was essential to allow diverse groups of Americans to live together in relative peace and to grow stronger together as a nation. Today, the realities of globalization require diverse cultural, ethnic, religious, and national groups from every corner of the global to coexist. As in America in our earliest days, tolerance is the key to survival.

Terrorists now seek to make the clash of civilizations a reality, to engulf us in a global war of competing faiths. Tolerance cannot exist in this world; it is equated with the sin of unbelief. We must respond by making clear that we cannot and will not tolerate terrorism itself, nor any creed that celebrates and encourages it. Yet at the same time, we stand for a world in which *all* Muslims—Sunni, Shiite, Sufi, Wahabi, and any other sect—can peacefully coexist as long as they tolerate one another and believers in all other faiths, as well as those who choose not to believe at all.

Confronting Americans afraid of immigration in the 1850s, Carl Schurz reminded Americans to remember the strength of one of our most important values: "Religious fanaticism . . . is powerless against genuine democracy. . . . Against fanaticism, genuine democracy wields an irresistible weapon—it is *toleration*. Toleration will not strike down the fanatic but it will quietly and gently disarm him."[24]

America can join with nations around the world to use tolerance to disarm today's fanatics. We can provide an alternative vision of human development and embrace the great contributions of all civilizations to human progress. We can prove that tolerance is a sign of strength, a mark of confidence, and a test of national character. And in our own enormous diversity, melding immigrants from all nations, we can stand for a vision of a world in which the clash of civilizations is a memory of the past rather than a map of the future.

Chapter 6

Humility

When in the course of Human events, it becomes necessary for
one people to dissolve the political bands which have connected
them with another, . . . a decent respect to the opinions of
mankind requires that they should declare the causes which
impel them to the separation.

    —*Declaration of Independence*

It's a huge honor to be the greatest—to be the President of the
greatest country in the world.

    —*George W. Bush, speaking in Orlando, December 4, 2001*

LIBERTY, DEMOCRACY, EQUALITY, justice, and tolerance all
rest comfortably in the pantheon of American values, but humility? The rest of the world certainly does not see us as humble. Indeed, I suspect, *humble* is not exactly the word that comes
to mind when most Americans are asked to describe themselves.
A 1955 Gallup survey found that 66 percent of Americans believed that "The United States is better than all other countries
in every possible way."[1] Globalization, if anything, has simply

strengthened this view; more recent surveys find that a good 60 percent of Americans agree with the statement "Our culture is superior to others."[2]

Yet humility is just as much a core American value as its more traditional counterparts. To find this American value, we must first define it. Humility does not mean false modesty or self-abasement. It is not the same as meekness or timidity. Humility is the quality of being humble: the recognition that others may know more than we do, that others may have skills, talents, and abilities that we lack, and that others may be right when we are wrong. It is the awareness of how small and insignificant we are in the face of larger forces—of nature, of God, even of humankind. And it is the willingness to listen, to learn, and to grow.

To understand the meaning of humility more fully, consider its opposite. The closest antonym of humility is *hubris,* the Greek term for the deluded heroes who thought they knew better and could do better than the gods. The Greek myths and epics—the founding texts of Western literature—tell stories of those who rose too high in their own self-esteem and were soon humbled by larger forces. Remember Icarus, who soared too close to the sun on his wings of wax and tumbled helplessly into the sea. Or Odysseus's crew, who thought they could help themselves to the sun god's cattle—which the vengeful deity quickly ensured was the last steak of their lives. Or even Oedipus, whose vain quest to avoid the fate the gods laid for him makes him the unwitting agent of his own downfall.

In English, the opposite of humility is not pride, a justified recognition of achievement, but arrogance—*excessive* pride and certainty of superiority to others. Arrogant people snub others by dismissing the possibility that they could learn anything of value by listening or consulting. Their behavior often induces a fierce desire in others to see them humbled; think of the phrase "Lo how the mighty have fallen." And although American myths are much more likely to be tall tales than stories of hubris, many of us remember our parents telling us not to get "too big for our britches." This attitude underlies Americans' love for the underdog and our celebration of common, decent folk.

Like tolerance, humility is a virtue for the strong, not the weak. It requires strength and honesty to recognize our imperfections and to try to see ourselves as others see us. Our best role model is none other than George Washington, who started and ended every presidential address by acknowledging the enormous, and, in his view, undeserved, honor of his compatriots' electing him president. Looking back on his presidency at its end, he told his fellow citizens: "I am . . . too sensible of my defects not to think it probable that I may have committed many errors. Whatever they may be, I fervently beseech the Almighty to avert or mitigate the evils to which they may tend."[3] Dwight Eisenhower, another general-president, knew why leaders like Washington were so aware of their own faults. As he explained a century and a half later in a speech at London's Guildhall at the close of World War II: "Humility must always be the portion of any man who receives acclaim earned in the blood of his followers and the sacrifices of his friends."[4]

Humility's role as a core value in American history has multiple sources. It is a fundamental tenet of the religious faith of many Americans. It is the unavoidable flip side of our secular faith: our unshakable belief in progress and self-improvement. Finally, humility is an essential component of liberty, democracy, equality, justice, and tolerance.

Like our other values, humility has often been neglected— perhaps more now than ever before. A 2005 Pew survey found that 67 percent of Americans think our country listens to others when making policy.[5] This view perhaps reflects our *desire* to be humble, but other nations see us as overwhelmingly—breathtakingly—arrogant. The same survey found that only 13–19 percent of Polish, Turkish, French, and Canadian respondents, and 32 percent of the British, think that the United States takes other countries' opinions into consideration when acting abroad.

Other countries are responding in part to our actions. The United States has bucked international opinion on a series of issues: the Kyoto protocol on limiting carbon emissions, Guantánamo Bay, and, most centrally, the war in Iraq. But we also offend with our words. We are quick to point out the failings of other countries, and often rightly so: China should be held to account for its human rights abuses, Nigeria for its corruption, and Russia for rolling back media and civil society.

But we are painfully slow to recognize the failings of our own society. American politicians like to say that we enjoy the best health care in the world, but our child mortality rate is higher than Cuba's. Our educational system produces many skilled workers, but also leaves large swaths of the population behind; we have a higher percentage of illiterate adults than many countries, including Poland, Barbados, Uzbekistan, and Russia.[6] We jail a higher percentage of our population than does any other country in the world, a number certainly related to our above-average rates of violent crime. And this burden falls most heavily on our minorities. A white American male stands a one-in-seventeen chance of going to prison in his lifetime; an African American male, a one-in-three chance.[7]

Finding and recognizing the value of humility in our past will make it easier to recover and embrace it for our future, a vital step toward reestablishing our ability to lead in the world. We cannot lead by coercion—at least not for long. We must instead rely on persuasion and *soft power,* the power of convincing other people to want what we want, rather than forcing them to do what we want.[8] Great leaders lead by motivation rather than imposition.

Today, however, fewer and fewer nations are motivated to follow us. Only 29 percent of people around the world—less than a third—think that America plays a positive role in the world. The single biggest reason for our slide is not our policy in Iraq, although that is certainly not helping. It is a pervasive global perception of American hypocrisy, that we say one thing and do another and that we make our own rules while accusing other nations of being rule-breakers.[9]

It is hard to be humble and hypocritical at the same time. In other words, the best cure for our present plight is to eat some humble pie and then work hard to bring our actions back into line with our words. We must recognize our flaws at home and work much harder to fix them. We must understand that we do not lead in the world by right, or even by power, but by the consent, and at the request, of other nations. And we must again learn to respect the views of others if we expect to earn their respect in turn.

HUMILITY RUNS THROUGH THE VEINS of most Americans primarily through their faith. America is a deeply religious society, at least by the standards of most other industrialized countries. In every religion, God and humility sit back to back—a fact believers, including many Americans, sometimes forget.

We can start with the Bible, as our forebears did. In his famous 1630 address, John Winthrop, the governor of the Massachusetts Bay Colony, exhorted his fellow colonists to consider themselves a "City upon a hill," with the eyes of the world upon them. Too often, this phrase is taken out of context and understood as an expression of American arrogance. But Winthrop did not see it this way. He meant it as a caution, warning the colonists that if they did not live up to the teachings of their faith, "we shall be made a story and a by-word through the world. We shall open the mouths of enemies to speak evil of the ways of God and all professors for God's sake. We shall shame the faces of many of God's worthy servants, and cause their prayers to be turned into curses upon us."[10]

To avoid this fate, Winthrop continued, the colonists must strive "to do justly, to love mercy, to walk humbly with our God." He was quoting the book of Micah from the Old Testament: "Act justly, love mercy, and walk humbly with God." This text turns up in all corners from American life—in countless sermons, in blogs, on bumper stickers, and carved in stone on the side of the former Union of American Hebrew Congregations at Madison Avenue and East 65th Street in New York.

But it is not merely a Judeo-Christian sentiment. Similar injunctions spring from virtually all the religions that make up the American mosaic of faiths. The Koran tells Muslims "The true servants of the Gracious God are those who walk on the earth humbly" (25:64). In the *Analects,* Confucius reminds us that "the firm, the enduring, the simple, and the modest are near to virtue." And the Hindu Bhagavad Gita says directly, "Be humble, be harmless, have no pretension" (13.7–13.8).

The scriptures of all faiths demand humility because humility is the reflection of true faith. Believers who truly accept the enormity and infinity of God must be humbled, understanding the enormity of their own imperfections and the infinity of the path to be traveled to overcome them. Humility is the under-

standing that any individual's life plays out on a stage overshadowed by much larger forces.

In the Declaration of Independence, Thomas Jefferson wrote
of "the Laws of Nature and of Nature's God." He was prescient;
for countless Americans who subscribe to no specific religion,
nature is the towering force that humbles humanity. But
whether the cathedral is a soaring structure carved by humans or
the towering redwoods of the California forest, humility is
Americans' natural and national response. Americans need
travel no farther than their place of worship or stand before the
purple mountains' majesty to recall and affirm the place of humility in our pantheon of national values.

Recognizing and honoring humility, of course, is not the
same as practicing it. That humility is demanded before God or
nature does not mean that it is given. Hearing Sunday sermons
or Saturday services or Friday prayers does not necessarily dictate our actions during the week. And as we master and despoil
our natural environment, the wonder that attends the awareness
of our own insignificance before a landscape hundreds of millions of years old is increasingly lost to us.

HUMILITY IS NOT ONLY a product of America's religious
faiths; it is equally ingrained in our secular faith in progress. As
individuals, we are always striving for self-improvement—just
look at the bestseller list! Self-help books, from diets to time
management, occupy a permanent place at the top. And as a nation, we believe not only that we *can* be better, but that we *will*
be better. This process of seeking but never fully attaining is one
of the engines that drive the continuing transformation of
American society.

When Americans write about a national belief in progress, they often link it to the optimism and self-confidence that underpin the American can-do spirit. This combination can easily shade into arrogance. But a faith in progress is equally consistent with humility and sobriety at how far we have to go. Believing that we will get better requires believing that we can continually improve, which in turn means acknowledging our current imperfections.

Our Founders were indeed both humbled and sobered by the immensity of the task we set ourselves as a nation. In his 1825 speech at Bunker Hill, Daniel Webster explained that if America succeeded in self-government, it would prove that democracy *could* succeed for all the world. If the nation failed, on the other hand, the failure would also have much larger consequences—just as Governor Winthrop warned the Puritans that if they failed to live up to their faith, they would discredit their creed before all the world.

Webster spoke at one of the moments in our history when we felt that we were realizing our creed. At such times, our optimism and pride break through in claims about American exceptionalism that seem anything but humble. In the 1830s and 1840s we were riding high; our economy bounded ahead on a mix of industrialization and westward expansion fueled by surging numbers of immigrants. All across America, factories were built, fields cleared, bricks laid, and harvests reaped. It was hardly surprising that the French aristocrat Alexis de Tocqueville, touring the country during this period, came away struck by Americans' deep optimism rooted in opportunity and progress.[11]

Then came the cataclysm of the Civil War, in which we tore ourselves apart. We could no longer claim to be immune from the ills of violence and faction that beset other nations. Half our country fought to preserve the right to enslave some of our fellow human beings. Although the Union won, our ideals had to be recaptured for the nation as a whole. In calling for a "new birth of freedom" at the end of the Gettysburg Address, Lincoln certainly knew and recognized our failings. He stood on the bloody ground where some fifty thousand American soldiers— Union and Confederate—had been wounded or killed over three days. He believed that rebirth and renewed progress toward our ideals was possible. But his tone was one of profound humility: of the living before the dead, of the present before the past and the future, and of individual lives and cares before a great collective cause. When he called on all Americans to dedicate themselves to "the great task" of ensuring "that government of the people, by the people, for the people, shall not perish from the earth," he again portrayed America as a country charged with demonstrating the potential of all humankind.

This link between humility and destiny—humility at the greatness of what we perceive to be our destiny and at the magnitude of what is needed even to come close to achieving it—is a recurrent theme in our history, even as we became a great power in the twentieth century. In 1944, with Americans fighting hard in both the Atlantic and the Pacific, the 78th Congress dedicated a memorial to Samuel Morse, the inventor of the telegraph. The plaque hangs in the Capitol today. Headlined "What God Hath Wrought!"—the words of one of the first messages ever sent by telegraphy—it salutes "the humility and vision which enabled this inventor to be the conveyor of this universal blessing to mankind."[12] Congress undoubtedly sought, above all, to salute the value of Morse code in wartime. But the message remains: To be an instrument of greatness requires humility.

This message bears learning and relearning. Notwithstanding our often rosy view of our own history, our progress as a nation has been anything but linear. It might be better understood in terms of cycles of humility, surging national confidence, arrogance, and come-uppance. At each turn of the wheel, after the Civil War, the Gilded Age, the crash of 1929 and the Great Depression, Vietnam, we have rediscovered the value of humility as the prerequisite to true progress. As we examine the consequences of our hubris in Iraq, humility's turn is coming round again.

WE ALSO FIND HUMILITY woven through our other American values. To begin with, it is built into our conception of democracy. Condoleezza Rice made exactly this point in a 2006 speech to the Southern Baptist Convention: "America will lead the cause of freedom in our world, not because we think ourselves perfect. To the contrary, we cherish democracy and champion its ideals because we know ourselves to be imperfect."[13]

Rice was alluding to an essential truth about American history: The structure of our government is predicated on humility, on the recognition of human fallibility. As James Madison explained in Federalist No. 51, "If men were angels, no government would be necessary." But he knew, and we know, that we are not angels. And so government is necessary, in large part to save us from ourselves. We look to our institutions to align bad incentives with good outcomes—recognizing, as Madison also put it, that "ambition must be made to counteract ambition. The interest of the man must be connected with the constitutional rights of the place."[14]

Democracy is also premised on tolerance, which is closely bound up with humility. Tolerance of the views of others requires a recognition that no matter how perfectly right our opinions may seem to us, they may not be right for others. This sense of tolerance is the minimum humility necessary for life in a democracy. As discussed earlier, tolerance does not mean denying the possibility of truth. It just means denying that any one of us possesses the monopoly on truth.[15]

Humility equally underpins justice; think of the presumption of innocence. Our forebears learned the hard way that guilt requires proof, not intuition. Our senses, our biases, our associations and inferences and conclusions—all are too likely to be wrong. To presume that someone is innocent until proven guilty is to suspend judgment, which is precisely to admit the fallibility of first impressions, hunches, or presuppositions.

Finally, both liberty and equality assume that very different individuals can live side by side and exercise the same guaranteed rights. The proposition cannot hold if the individuals are each certain of their own superiority, even less so if each of us presumes to know what is best not only for ourselves but for others. My rights end where yours begin; my certainty of my rightness must also.

In sum, even if humility is not blazoned in our monuments and anthems nearly as often as are other American values, it is nonetheless essential to our nation. Humility runs like a hidden thread through our history, emphasizing perfectibility but not perfection, truth-seeking but not certainty, and hope but not naïveté. It is the value that we are perhaps most often condemned to relearn. But when we do rediscover humility, we are a far better people.

WHAT WOULD A FOREIGN POLICY grounded in humility look like? Think of the characteristics of someone you would define as humble. The hallmarks of humility are not prostration before others or self-deprecation, but rather sincere respect for the opinions of others and a willingness to learn and listen. Those are precisely the hallmarks of a foreign policy guided by humility, especially a foreign policy implemented by a leader among nations.

Humility on the part of a nation, rather than an individual, also includes a healthy respect for the unintended consequences of ill-considered actions. With such awareness comes a strong measure of prudence. Finally, humility does not shy from admitting error and changing course when necessary. Leadership requires not only resolve, but also the flexibility to redirect that resolve when previous judgments and decisions prove to be mistaken.

Again, the Founders offer an excellent place to start. It was "a decent respect to the opinions of mankind" that *required* the colonists to explain the causes leading them to declare independence from the mother country. The body of the Declaration—the parts that are read far less often than the immortal words of the Preamble—is a bill of particulars, a precise list of charges against the king that are designed to prove the colonists' case before "a candid world."

The Declaration of Independence also makes clear that the colonists expected their new nation to receive the respect that was its due—the "separate and equal station" among "the powers of the earth." The idea that nations deserve respect to manage their own affairs—the modern notion of sovereignty—seems natural enough to us today, but was not always considered a fundamental principle of international relations. Between 1618 and 1648, the nations of Europe fought an exceptionally brutal war, known simply as the Thirty Years' War, largely over religion. Catholic states wanted Protestant states to become Catholic and to treat Catholics in their territory well, and vice versa. After horrible massacres of Protestants and Catholics on both sides, the major European powers decided that the best hope of keeping the peace was to establish a system of sovereignty that entitled each state to respect and noninterference from all other states. They enshrined this principle in the peace agreement that ended the Thirty Years' War: the Treaty of Westphalia. All states, large or small, Catholic or Protestant, monarchy or—as the Americans hoped—republic, were entitled to run their internal affairs without interference from their neighbors. This system has provided the basic backbone of relations between nations for almost four centuries—although with plenty of violations, exceptions, and modifications.

By and large, when we have premised our relations with other nations on mutual respect, we have reaped the benefits. One of the best examples of a concrete American foreign policy based on respect comes from Franklin Delano Roosevelt. In relations with Latin America, FDR launched the Good Neighbor policy, which for perhaps the first time in history accepted our neighbors as equal partners of the United States. This policy contrasted sharply with the interventionist approach taken around the turn of the century by his distant cousin and great-uncle, Teddy Roosevelt. TR's treatment of the countries south of the Rio Grande, like that of most American presidents, was anything but humble.

THE UNITED STATES has a long and tangled history with the nations to our south—a history characterized more by hubris than humility. In 1823, the United States issued the Monroe Doctrine, warning European nations not to interfere in the affairs of the Americas. What we really meant, though, was that Europe should stay out of Latin America so that we could have a free hand to intervene there as we liked. Theodore Roosevelt later made this understanding explicit in his 1904 corollary to the Monroe Doctrine, in which he posited the U.S. right to intervene in the region to preserve stability and enforce contracts. Despite our pious claims against European imperialism, the United States intervened militarily in Latin America thirty-seven times in the forty-two years between 1890 and 1932, a policy we called *gunboat diplomacy.*

Our interventions reached deep into the internal affairs of Latin American countries. We invaded Panama in 1856 to protect the Atlantic-Pacific railroad from Panamanian nationalists seeking self-determination. In 1903, we forced Cuba to write a measure into its constitution allowing the United States to intervene in that nation whenever we desired. A year later, we forced the Dominican Republic to give American customs agents control over its finances in order to ensure the payment of its debts. We sent marines to Mexico in 1905 to help the dictator Porfirio Díaz put down a strike. In 1909, when the justly elected president of Nicaragua suggested that American mining and banana companies pay taxes, we forced him out and installed a new president so illegitimate that we would later have to invade Nicaragua to back his government. The list goes on.

Not surprisingly, these measures brought just the opposite of peace and stability. The countries of Latin America suffered numerous domestic problems in the nineteenth century. Many were relatively new countries struggling to establish viable political systems in the face of gross social inequality, the legacy of colonialism, and underdevelopment. Adding American interventions to that mix—interventions almost invariably aimed at preserving U.S. economic interests rather than those of the country in question—did little to help. Indeed, it was a major cause of the very instability the United States purported to quell.

In 1928, both the Republican president, Herbert Hoover, and his Democratic challenger, Franklin Delano Roosevelt, realized that our cavalier policy in Latin America was producing neither peace nor stability and was jeopardizing long-term U.S. interests. It was a pragmatic assessment of the virtues of humility. FDR made his case in *Foreign Affairs* in 1928. He argued that with the "cooperation of others we shall have more order in this hemisphere and less dislike."[16] Hoover won the election and afterward made a goodwill tour of Latin America. In Honduras, he declared, "We have a desire to maintain not only the cordial relations of governments with each other but also the relations of good neighbors."[17] Hoover followed up on this sentiment by beginning to withdraw U.S. troops from Haiti and Nicaragua—where they had been posted to bolster regimes friendly to the United States—and officially retracting the Roosevelt Corollary to the Monroe Doctrine.

This bipartisan reorientation of U.S. policy in Latin America, which became known as the Good Neighbor policy, continued when FDR assumed the presidency in 1933. At the start of his term, Roosevelt announced, "In the field of world policy, I dedicate this nation to the policy of the good neighbor—the neighbor who resolutely respects himself and, because he does so, respects the rights of others."[18] The reaction was skeptical. The Mexican diplomat Luis Quintanilla asked, "How could one speak of . . . Good Neighborliness when the stumbling block in the path of good relations was nothing less than the most powerful republic in the Hemisphere?"[19] But Roosevelt's words were soon backed with actions.

In December of that year, at the Pan-American Conference in Montevideo, Secretary of State Cordell Hull supported a resolution prohibiting the armed intervention of one American republic in another. In 1934, the United States renounced its constitutional right to intervene in Cuba and withdrew its troops from Haiti earlier than planned. During its entire twelve years, the Roosevelt administration never once intervened in Latin America, even when Bolivia and Mexico expropriated the assets of U.S. oil companies. When the oil companies called on America for troops, the State Department answered in a way perhaps strange to our ears today: "Our national interests as a whole outweigh those of our petroleum companies."[20]

Under Roosevelt, the United States also radically increased economic partnership with Latin America, lowering the protective tariffs and quotas that had prevented Latin American goods from being sold in U.S. markets. Such a move could not have been easy for the Roosevelt administration, which was battling the Great Depression at home and did not overly trust in free markets. But Roosevelt was convinced that equal and reciprocal economic relations with Latin America—as opposed to the mercantilism of previous decades, when American firms tried to squeeze as much benefit from Latin America while offering little in return—were essential for hemispheric peace. He argued that trade agreements would not only create new destinations for American goods, but would also ease the pressures on nations with no natural resources or other means of producing wealth to go to war to gain them.[21] His view was prescient: When the Japanese attacked Pearl Harbor in 1941, no small part of their motive was the drive to secure the natural resources of Southeast Asia for their own use and to block America preemptively from stopping them.

Neighborliness worked. In 1936, the Argentine foreign minister wrote in a Buenos Aires newspaper that the Good Neighbor policy was "the most wise, the most prudent and the most sagacious that the great Republic of the North has ever followed" and had "gained the confidence of the twenty-one American republics."[22] In the lead-up to World War II, the United States and the Axis powers competed for influence in Latin America, each seeking to control the raw materials and other resources needed for war. Latin America largely sided with the United States, despite the pro-Axis sentiments of the authoritarian elite across the region. After the war, this solidarity led to the creation of the Organization of American States, which guaranteed peace and promoted representative democracy across the Americas.

"The [good neighbor is the] neighbor who resolutely respects himself and, because he does so, respects the rights of others."[23] These words were Roosevelt's mantra. Self-respect did not translate into superiority, but into an equal regard for others. This is another face of humility, the face that FDR understood was essential for democracy itself. At his second inauguration, in January 1937, when the American economy was stirring but millions of Americans were still reeling from the Depression, he rallied the nation with a wonderful speech. Toward the end, he spoke of the difficulty of maintaining unity in a time of such adversity, of listening to all sides and formulating a common goal: "To maintain a democracy of effort requires a vast amount of patience in dealing with differing methods, a vast amount of humility. But out of the confusion of many voices rises an understanding of dominant public need."[24]

An equally vast humility is required when a nation is dealing with different nations and trying to bridge political, economic, and cultural divides. Yet the effort is usually worth it. Relations based on mutual respect make for a far better neighborhood.

TODAY WE NEED a global good neighbor policy. This means having the humility to accept that America does not have all the answers to national and international problems, that global leadership is earned rather than assumed, and that collective problems require genuinely collective solutions. It means respecting other nations as we respect ourselves and would have them respect us.

What a global good neighbor policy does *not* mean, at least in the twenty-first century, is that we automatically put governments before their citizens. Many people around the world, particularly authoritarian regimes, insist that this is what sovereignty requires: respecting whatever government happens to control a particular nation. As Americans, we face continual tension between the requirement under international law that we respect *nations,* meaning governments, and our own democratic value of respecting all *peoples.* We founded our nation at a time of tyranny and unjust monarchies in many nations, so we respected the opinion not of governments but of their citizens— of all humankind. At the same time, however, we must operate in a world of 192 nations under rules and within institutions that we have helped to create and in which we have an important stake. So we must continually balance respect for nations, which are represented by whatever government is in power, with respect for their citizens.

Practically speaking, that balance means working with other nations to adapt the system of sovereignty we inherited from the Treaty of Westphalia. We now face a world in which many of the greatest dangers posed to individual citizens come not from the threat of war from an outside power, but from their own governments. Where governments massacre, dispossess, or ethnically cleanse their own citizens on a massive scale, they forfeit their right to respect from other nations. But a global good neighbor policy would mean that America would work to forge a collective response through regional or global institutions, accepting that our perceptions of a particular situation could be biased or inaccurate, and that our assessment of the costs and benefits of intervention could be wrong.

The best place to begin a global good neighbor policy is by cleaning up our global environment, an area in which the competing claims of citizen versus government are far less complicated. Climate change threatens all people worldwide, potentially altering the conditions of life itself. Remember, a dramatic shift in climate killed the dinosaurs through no fault of their own. They had no control over their fate, because their brains were the size of walnuts. But we humans are actively courting disaster by pumping gases into the atmosphere. Will our developed craniums be enough to save us from ourselves?

As carbon emissions continue to rise, imagine large parts of Florida, Calcutta, Shanghai, and Manhattan—the World Trade Center memorial site—under water. Imagine more violent storms like Hurricane Katrina; we cannot say where any one storm comes from, but the number of category 4 and 5 storms has already doubled since the 1970s. Imagine malaria, dengue fever, and other tropical diseases creeping toward our southern border. Imagine a new dust bowl rising in the heartland. And if you can't imagine, just look at the evidence already in front of us: By the end of the decade, Mount Kilimanjaro in Tanzania will have lost its snow.

Arrogance in the face of these forces could wipe humans from the face of the earth. Yet arrogant we humans have been. As the evidence of man-made climate change has steadily grown since the 1980s, the U.S. government has obstinately refused first to do anything about it and, more recently, even to acknowledge it as fact. As recently as 2004, the Bush administration denied the mounting evidence—now deemed unequivocal by the world's most distinguished scientists—that human behavior was even contributing to the steady warming of temperatures across the earth.

The world's best response to climate change to date has been the 1996 Kyoto Protocol, which commits developed countries to reduce their carbon emissions by a meager average of 5.2 percent below 1990 levels. Developing countries, even rapidly growing countries like China, India, and Brazil, are part of the agreement, but were not required to reduce their emissions. The logic was that their per-capita emissions are far lower than those of the developed world, particularly the United States, and that these countries have the right to industrialize today in the same way that wealthy nations did one hundred years ago. The Clinton administration lobbied hard to bring other countries closer to its position, which advocated mandatory caps for both developed and developing countries. Ultimately, however, the administration failed to convince either its negotiating partners or a highly skeptical Congress at home. In 1997, the U.S. Senate passed a resolution, ninety-five to zero, rejecting the protocol on the grounds that it excluded some of the biggest carbon emitters in the developing world and would be too costly to implement.

The senators were partly right about the first point; by 2030, the increase in China's coal use alone will surpass Kyoto's savings five times over.[25] Because the whole world needs to tackle climate change if the global community is going to win this fight, the world will have to think about how to bring the developing countries in fairly. But the Senate was dead wrong about the second point. It is hard to calculate exactly how much it would cost the United States to implement Kyoto; the government's own estimates range from $7–10 billion a year to up to $400 billion by 2010, depending on what assumptions are made and who is making them.[26] But we do know for certain that whatever the cost of action today, the cost of *inaction* will be far greater for our children tomorrow.[27]

The Bush administration has highlighted Kyoto's flaws and compromises to avoid taking any responsibility for climate change. It has created a partnership between the United States, Japan, China, Australia, and other Asia-Pacific countries to promote the transfer of clean technology, but has refused even to consider the serious action needed to head off disastrous damage to the planet and our way of life. Whatever Kyoto's problems, the United States—the world's largest emitter—cannot expect to lead from behind.

The time has come for the United States to lead the fight to stop and reverse the behaviors that are imperiling our planet. We must begin, like Senator Arthur Vandenberg in 1945, by reversing our current position and seeking a new policy in "a spirit of anxious humility," humility in the face of nature itself. A global good neighbor policy focused on combating climate change would demand the reassertion of the public interest over competing private interests; respect for the needs of developing countries over developed countries in return for an agreement on the part of developing countries to develop in more climate-friendly ways; and a willingness to sacrifice now to save future generations.

America is presently the world's single largest carbon emitter, but that will change. In China today, fewer than ten people in one thousand own a car, compared with six hundred out of every thousand Americans. If the Chinese lived like us, imagine the effect of the exhaust from those additional 780 million cars on the global atmosphere. Yet the Chinese have every right to aspire to live like us, just as we Americans rushed to develop the natural resources of our great continent and to gobble energy to attain our current standard of living. As a result, the chance that

New Orleans, and Miami, and even New York will remain above sea level increasingly depends on the ability of China—and of India, Brazil, and other developing countries—to rein in their own carbon emissions.

Up to now, the American position has been "if you're not going to cut your emissions, then we're not going to cut ours"—a very convenient position for an administration that does not want to do anything to confront this problem. It is also a position that allows China and other developing countries to continue to get away with doing nothing. If the richest country in the world cannot be bothered to do anything, why should poorer countries, which contribute less to the problem, make sacrifices on behalf of the rich? But the American people, the Chinese people, and everyone else on this planet deserve better. And we in the United States, because we emit more than anyone else, have the responsibility to take the lead.

We need to craft an international deal that fully respects the needs of developing countries to bring their people from often abject poverty to a world of heat or cooling, light, and transport. Our respect for their needs must come from our understanding and respect for our own needs, past and present. We should first accept restrictions on our own emissions along the lines called for in the Kyoto Protocol. This step will send a powerful signal to the world and give us the credibility we will need to negotiate a new climate change treaty. The new treaty must impose restrictions on greenhouse gases wherever they arise—in countries rich and poor—but in a way that takes different levels of development into account. Various mechanisms—technology transfer, emissions trading schemes, financial assistance to help poor countries implement the necessary changes—will be needed to make such an international agreement work. But work it must, or someday far in the future the skeletal remains of the human species may resemble the dinosaur records of today.

BEATING GLOBAL WARMING will require genuine sacrifice on the part of all Americans, as indeed will a responsible national energy policy. We will all have to do our part—conservation, public transport, higher energy prices, higher car prices, and even higher taxes if they are necessary to create more efficient energy-saving infrastructure to benefit the public. President Bush asked no sacrifice of the American public as a whole after 9/11; indeed, the only price paid by American citizens in the war on terror has been by our soldiers and their families. This situation must change.

When confronted with national crises, our greatest leaders have demanded sacrifice rather than promise glory. Our nation has always risen to the challenge, most notably in World War II, but also in Vietnam, when tens of thousands of young American men and their families accepted the draft. And in the 1970s, after the first energy crisis, we lowered our thermostats and increased our fuel mileage. Sacrifice for a common cause can create a strong common bond, both by convincing ordinary citizens that they can actually make a difference on the most momentous issues of the day and by submerging normal differences in the service of a higher goal. Today we feel this unity when we honor the soldiers serving in Iraq—whether or not we support the war—but their sacrifice is not one that most of us share directly.

Awareness of sacrifice—above all, the ultimate sacrifice of giving a life—also inspires humility. In the Gettysburg Address, Lincoln is humbled by the enormity of the sacrifice made by soldiers on both sides. Similarly, when the guns of World

War II were finally silent, Truman exemplified a humble national attitude in his 1945 Thanksgiving proclamation:

> We give thanks with the humility of free men, each knowing it was the might of no one arm but of all together by which we were saved. Liberty knows no race, creed, or class in our country or in the world. In unity we found our first weapon, for without it, both here and abroad, we were doomed. None have known this better than our very gallant dead. . . . Our thanksgiving has the humility of our deep mourning for them, our vast gratitude to them.[28]

Fighting global climate change does not have the same immediacy as facing bullets from enemy lines or risking a roadside explosion planted by an unseen foe. But hurricanes, floods, droughts, and diseases can take hundreds of thousands if not millions of lives, a fate that can only be averted by collective sacrifice.

Finally, and most generally, we must understand our own limits in addressing all the world's problems. That understanding is the definition of humility and the wellspring of sustained respect for others. If we can build on this foundation and lead the way in becoming global good neighbors, the global neighborhood will become a better place to live for the citizens of all nations.

NOT TOO LONG AGO, an American presidential candidate called for "an American foreign policy that reflects American character. The modesty of true strength. The humility of real greatness." Moreover, that candidate's party platform had harsh words for the presidential administration in power: "The arrogance, inconsistency, and unreliability of the administration's diplomacy have undermined American alliances, alienated friends, and emboldened our adversaries." These were the words of Governor George W. Bush and the position of the Republican Party platform in the 2000 presidential campaign.

I could not agree more with these sentiments. But as we move toward the presidential campaign of 2008, our present policies are a long way from the "humility of real greatness." On the contrary, international perceptions of American arrogance are greater than perhaps at any other time in history.

Still, President Bush was right to say that an American foreign policy that truly reflects American character would include a healthy dose of humility. He was right because humility before God is demanded by the many faiths that interlace American life. Humility is the foundation of our continual striving to improve ourselves, to advance, to live up to our own ideals. And humility is an essential component of liberty, democracy, equality, tolerance, and justice. In all these ways, humility rightly takes its place as a core American value.

Humility as we define it is not self-flagellation. It is not humiliation. Nor is it an admission of weakness. Rather, it is an absence of conceit, of a particular kind of pride that says we know better and are better than everyone else. Humility can accompany both confidence and strength; it is the essential characteristic that allows strong, confident leaders to hear and correct their inevitable mistakes.

Such a demonstration of humility has been almost nonexistent of late. If we are honest with ourselves and examine the record of our deeds since the Cold War and, overwhelmingly, since the turn of the millennium, we must admit that we have come much closer to hubris than humility. Yet precisely in the spirit of humility, we should be perfectly willing to be hard on ourselves and scrutinize our failings. We should continually challenge ourselves to live up to our ideals.

In a century in which human conduct risks tipping the balance of nature itself, the importance of becoming global good neighbors cannot be underestimated. By practicing national humility, America can work better with other nations to address problems that are no longer confined to national borders but threaten all humans as inhabitants of a common planet. We must find a way with all the citizens of the world to do justice, love mercy, and walk humbly with our gods.

Chapter 7

Faith

Our fathers' God, to Thee,
Author of liberty,
To Thee we sing;
Long may our land be bright
With freedom's holy light;
protect us by Thy might,
Great God, our King.

> —*Samuel Francis Smith,*
> *"America (My Country, 'Tis of Thee)," 1832*

Democracy's most powerful weapon is not a gun, tank, or bomb. It is faith—faith in the brotherhood and dignity of man under God.

> —*Harry Truman, Christmas radio address, December 24, 1950*

PRINCETON UNIVERSITY opens every year with Opening Exercises and closes with Baccalaureate Sunday. And every year, I leave those services deeply moved and with a sense that I understand something profound about contemporary American life.

The faculty march in, in full academic regalia, behind an African drum band beating out rhythms that quicken the step and lighten the heart. We open with a Christian hymn, "O God, Our Help in Ages Past," and hear an invocation from a Christian minister. But then comes the call to worship—from the opening chapter of the Koran, chanted in Arabic and then recited in English by two Muslim students. The first reading, from another student, is a Buddhist Bodhisattva vow. Then a psalm read by another student, an address from the university president calling incoming freshmen or outgoing seniors to be true to the principles that the university seeks to embody, and blessings from four more students—a Muslim, a Catholic, a Hindu, and a Jew, each reading from their holy texts.

As I emerge from the cool shadows of the chapel into the fall or spring afternoon, I face the statue of John Witherspoon—the stern Presbyterian divine who signed the Declaration of Independence and who served as the sixth president of Princeton—and I imagine his astonishment at the service. Princeton was founded by "new light" Presbyterians in 1746 primarily to train ministers. Most other early colleges had religious roots—Harvard University was founded to produce ministers for the Massachusetts Bay Colony, the College of William and Mary was Anglican, and Yale University was the creation of Congregationalist ministers. Faith and learning were intertwined for our nation's Founders, as they remain so today for the vast majority of American students, but Witherspoon's students followed only one faith.

Today Princeton educates students in every discipline, from every state in the country and from abroad, from every income level and walk of life, and from every faith. Across America, the variety of faiths has expanded from Anglicanism to Zoroastrianism. And Americans are more religious than anyone else in the developed world. Fifty-nine percent of Americans think religion plays an important role in their lives, compared to 30 percent in Canada, 33 percent in Britain, 29 percent in Italy, 21 percent in Germany, and 11 percent in France.[1] More Americans go to church every week than to all sports events combined![2]

For many if not most Americans, then, the idea of faith as an American value summons first an image of religious faith: the body of beliefs between each individual and his or her God, a vision of the origins of life and the nature of death. These are the faiths that prescribe principles for daily behavior, binding communities and cultures in churches, temples, mosques, and other places of worship. Indeed, in many cases faith is synonymous with religion: When President Bush talks about faith-based charities, he means charities connected to religious denominations.

But the faith that is part of the idea that is America is more than religious faith. It is faith not only in God, but also in man—in humanity itself. The Enlightenment philosophers that the Founders read—Locke, Montesquieu, Rousseau, Hume—celebrated human capacity. This capacity was inherent in human nature itself—the properties that separated us from animals—and hence belonged to *all* human beings, regardless of race, creed, geography, or any other accident of birth.

The capacity in question was the capacity of human beings to take charge of their own lives and to be authors of their own happiness. They could create their own beauty, through literature, art, and music. They could cultivate their own virtues, through philosophy, law, and history. They could discover and shape their world, through the natural sciences. And they could devise institutions to govern themselves without divine authority and enrich themselves without divine providence.

In this human-centered world, a set of ideals came to the fore, many of them closely overlapping religious precepts. They are the values celebrated in this book: liberty, democracy, equality, justice, and tolerance. They are instrumental and intertwined: Democracy is the best instrument we have found to safeguard liberty; liberty, equality, justice, and tolerance are necessary for a sustained and successful democracy; equality requires equal justice; justice requires the equal protection of the laws. At the same time, these ideals represent the best of the human condition, a vision of perfect fulfillment for all humankind. It is a vision that can never be fully attained but that can inspire humans to try. And in the trying, they can come closer to the ideal, creating a better if never perfect world.

This last assumption requires faith. Faith is "belief in the unknown or the unknowable," anything that we cannot pin down and precisely explain.[3] In the great religions, the unknown is the divine. In the humanism of the Enlightenment, the unknown—the part taken on faith—is the human capacity to overcome the vicissitudes of nature, accident, and the darker side of our own nature. The Enlightenment was part of the age of reason, yet it spawned a faith of its own—a faith in the ability of reason to solve all problems.

For some, religious faith and Enlightenment faith necessarily conflict. Think of our debates in this country over the role of religion in public life. Think of the debates in Muslim countries over similar issues. The religious right tell us that anyone who believes in evolution is going to hell, while too many intellectuals dismiss anyone who goes to church as intellectually defective. Some of these debates are the healthy and necessary workings of an open political system that must reconcile competing worldviews, but many arise more from a holier-than-thou mentality than from a true desire for public dialogue.

For the Founders and probably for most Americans and most other people around the world, religious faith and humanist faith fit together in many ways. From the religious point of view, all humans are equal because all are created in God's image. And if all are equal, then all must have equal rights, including the right to self-government. Indeed, many spiritual leaders have stood at the forefront of the struggle for racial equality, from Henry Ward Beecher leading the abolitionists to Martin Luther King, Jr., leading the civil rights movement. From the humanist point of view, the morality, discipline, and spiritual commitment taught through religious faith can prove essential to liberty, democracy, justice, and the other values we cherish. Although many American intellectuals see religion through an anti-civil-liberties lens, citing the role of the religious right in crusades against abortion, gay rights, and the separation of church and state, religious radicals have also fought for women's rights, for disarmament, and for sanctuary for asylum seekers.[4]

Our two faiths fit together best when both religion and Enlightenment humanism are strongly leavened by humility. Religion without humility becomes righteousness and rigidity. Humanism without humility becomes a belief in the transcendent virtue of a particular people—a belief that Americans can far too readily identify with American exceptionalism.[5] The best of our democratic traditions, by contrast, rest on a Madisonian understanding of the inevitable vices of human nature and the resulting need to design institutions to check and balance individual vices in ways that serve the larger public good.

At its best, American faith fuses our religious traditions with our secular principles. The American faith that emerges is powerful, greater than the sum of its parts. It combines a spiritual connection to something larger than ourselves with a belief that our destiny rests in our own hands. It demands commitment to ideas so big and so challenging that we cannot see precisely how to realize them, so we suspend reason and proceed on faith. Indeed, Abraham Lincoln called our commitment to the Constitution and its principles our "political religion."[6]

Seemingly more sophisticated societies in other parts of the world often deride American faith as nothing more than naïveté. At its best, however, our faith is self-conscious armor against cynicism, against the world-weariness that has seen it all before and that saps the will even to try to help, to change, or to persist. We could not believe as strongly as we do in progress, opportunity, and the very idea of the American dream without a strong dose of faith. We could not embrace ideals as distant as universal liberty, democracy, equality, justice, tolerance, and humility without faith in our ability to achieve them. This faith is the engine that has driven the stories I have told in this book.

OUR BEDROCK CONVICTIONS grew on the North American continent at least a century before Washington, Jefferson, Madison, or the other Founders were born or the United States freed itself from Great Britain. Early settlers like Anne Hutchinson arrived with great hopes for the lives they sought to build anew. When these hopes ran up against obstacles—in Hutchinson's case, the persecution she faced for worshipping as she wished— religious faith allowed American idealists to stubbornly hold to their principles. Few women or men would have left the relative comfort of the Massachusetts Bay Colony to forge a new life in the wilderness, but Hutchinson's beliefs would not allow her to recant, giving her an imprudent but principled courage: "But now having seen him which is invisible I fear not what man can do unto me."[7]

Later, faith in a universal cause—a cause common to all human beings—gave Americans the courage to separate themselves from Britain. Though the revolutionaries faced improbable odds in going up against a European superpower, their principles would brook no other course. Patrick Henry spoke of "the holy cause of liberty"; Thomas Paine called on his fellow citizens to endure "the times that try men's souls."[8] Indeed these principles inspired the patriotic determination that proved decisive against a foe that, for all its military superiority, ultimately had less of a stake in victory.

The heady atmosphere of victory reinforced the Founders' humanist faith, giving them the confidence to write what was at the time a radically idealist Constitution. For the first time in history, a country decided to see what would happen when principles like liberty, democracy, and equality were put at the center of the political system. This was not done casually; the serious and pragmatic men of the founding could only undertake such a grand experiment when girded with the confidence engendered by a faith in both their values and their God. They knew that they were launching into the unknown, on behalf of themselves and all humanity, on a journey that would require faith. But they believed that they were building a nation that would secure to all its citizens the rights given to them by their creator, according to the laws of a nation created before nature and nature's God.

Of course, the government that these men set up was not entirely faithful to the principles that inspired it. But even as our government broke faith with women, blacks, landless white men, and others, these groups did not lose faith in the country's ideals. Rather, each group believed in the ideals strongly enough to struggle for their fulfillment against odds often just as great as those the Founders had faced in the fight against Britain. Again, it was the courage found in their convictions that allowed these Americans to succeed.

For Martin Luther King, Jr., preaching on the Washington Mall in 1963, the strength of the civil rights movement came from faith in the promise of America:

> With this faith, we will be able to hew out of the mountain of despair a stone of hope. With this faith, we will be able to transform the jangling discords of our nation into a beautiful symphony of brotherhood. With this faith, we will be able to work together, to pray together, to struggle together, to go to jail together, to stand up for freedom together, knowing that we will be free one day.[9]

King's was perhaps the quintessential American faith, fusing deep religious convictions with an understanding of the Constitution as secular scripture and an unshakable confidence in the capacity of Americans to live up to their ideals.

A century earlier, a similar faith had given immigrant groups the strength to demand inclusion. As discussed above, the Know-Nothing movement sought to deny the American dream to would-be Americans who left their homes all over the world believing in the promise of a better life. Anti-immigrant groups sought to limit the reach of the American promise, to shut the doors behind those who were already here. This time, it was Carl Schurz, the German-born, Republican politician who demanded of Massachusetts legislators, "'Where is your faith?' Aye, where is the faith that led the fathers of this republic to invite the weary and burdened of all nations to the enjoyment of equal rights? Where is that broad and generous confidence in the efficiency of true democratic institutions?"[10]

Breaches of faith also came in the internment of Japanese Americans during World War II and in the political corruption of the Nixon White House. Yet in both these cases Madison's system of checks and balances ultimately worked. Fred Korematsu was denied justice by the Supreme Court but ultimately attained it from President Clinton; President Nixon set the executive branch against the judicial branch and lost, although he was ultimately pardoned by another president. The larger lesson is the vindication of the Founders' recognition that government cannot be based on faith alone—either religious or humanist faith. Both must be tempered by a humble recognition of our own failings—here the excesses of fear and the temptations of power. A government built on the premise that humans are *not* angels can ultimately be strong enough to vindicate the faith of its people.

AMERICAN FAITH has given us a sense of purpose that has allowed us to achieve great things. But the same sense of mission, of purpose, even of destiny, can also lead us astray. All grand destinies carry this danger. It can blind us to realities that we must see and accept—that progress is not guaranteed, that not all Americans have access to opportunity, that the American dream can be a mirage, that we can work against our principles as easily as we can fulfill them. Abroad, those realities multiply—we must face the complexities of foreign cultures and politics, the misunderstanding of motives and goals, the mistrust of power. In Iraq, for instance, faith that the Iraqi people would rise up and welcome American troops as liberators and immediately embrace the institutions and practices of liberal democracy led to an almost criminal negligence in the failure to plan for the postconflict phase of the war.

President Bush says, rightly in my view, that "freedom is not America's gift to the world, it is the almighty God's gift to every man and woman in this world."[11] But his faith that people around the world will hear and believe him at a time when they see America invading countries to deliver this gift is foolhardy and blind. And when he claims that God is on his side, and on America's side, the world has reason to tremble. After all, it was Lincoln who reminded the nation toward the close of the Civil War that both the Union and the Confederacy "read the same Bible, and pray to the same God, and each invokes His aid against the other."[12] Faith alone does not make us right; it only makes us certain of our rectitude. That combination—faith and arrogance—has killed millions.

Faith combined with humility, on the other hand, can help put us on the path to wisdom. America had a glimpse of that wisdom in New York City one spring day in 1944. Toward the end of World War II, when Americans' faith in their values was strengthening as the dark years of war gave way to the glimmer of victory on the horizon, citizens gathered in Central Park to hold a vast "I Am an American" celebration. One of our greatest jurists, Judge Learned Hand, was asked to speak. He asked, "What is the spirit of liberty?" His answer is striking and worth quoting at length. It is not the answer of a righteously triumphant nation, but instead a call to question ourselves. He began with faith—his faith in America itself:

> I cannot define it; I can only tell you my own faith. The spirit of liberty is the spirit which is not too sure that it is right; the spirit of liberty is the spirit which seeks to understand the mind of other men and women; the spirit of liberty is the spirit which weighs their interests alongside its own without bias; the spirit of liberty remembers that not even a sparrow falls to earth unheeded; the spirit of liberty is the spirit of Him who, near two thousand years ago, taught mankind that lesson it has never learned but never

quite forgotten; that there may be a kingdom where the least shall be heard and considered side by side with the greatest.[13]

Like Martin Luther King and so many other great Americans of various faiths, Hand fused faith in America with faith in his religious beliefs, calling on the Bible to bolster the spirit of both liberty and humility.

A humble faith is the wellspring not of certainty but of hope. Senator Barack Obama first burst onto the national political scene with his speech at the 2004 Democratic Convention and later with his bestseller, *The Audacity of Hope*. He talked about the "genius of America," which he said was nothing other than faith:

> a faith in simple dreams, an insistence on small miracles; that we can tuck in our children at night and know that they are fed and clothed and safe from harm; that we can say what we think, write what we think, without hearing a sudden knock on the door; that we can have an idea and start our own business without paying a bribe; that we can participate in the political process without fear of retribution, and that our votes will be counted—or at least, most of the time.[14]

The larger point of his speech was to ask voters whether they wanted to participate in a "politics of cynicism or a politics of hope." The politics of hope is a politics of believing that things can get better, that Americans can come together again and meet the challenges we face even in the face of difficulty and uncertainty. The difficulties we face make hope audacious, but our underlying faith makes hope possible.

Senator Obama's determination to transcend partisanship follows in the footsteps of the historian Arthur Schlesinger, Jr., who issued a passionate call in 1948 for members of the non-Fascist right and the non-Communist left to come together as "the vital center," a center united by a common commitment to a free political society.[15] In such a society, differences over economic and social policy could be worked out not by revolution or the definitive triumph of one party over the other, but by reasoned deliberation under law. All such differences disappear, however, in a common fight against totalitarianism, whether of the right or the left. To win this fight, Schlesinger argued, democracy must be reborn as "a fighting faith."

In foreign policy today, we must again embrace our values as a fighting faith.[16] But we cannot take up the fight with mortars and bombs and tanks, or at least not primarily. Fighting instead means demonstrating *why* our faith is justified, how in fact a liberal democracy can deliver on its promises for all citizens better than any other form of government can. We must fight back by fixing America first.

———————

AMERICANS' FAITH in our values, universal values, should be a bridge to the world. But unless we can be clearer about the role of faith in our society and our politics, we cannot communicate it to others. That is why we face the paradox of being the most religious society among advanced industrial democracies and yet being pilloried in the Muslim world and elsewhere as the apotheosis of godless materialism. Fifty-eight percent of Americans think our country is not religious enough. But this is nothing compared with the 95 percent of Jordanians who think we Americans should be more religious. Around the Muslim world, the Jordanians are joined by other majorities who, instead of hating our beliefs, think we Americans should take them more seriously.[17]

The most visible face of America, after all, is not sermons but Hollywood movies, MTV videos, Super Bowl halftime shows, Madison Avenue advertising, and Wall Street finance. It is hardly surprising, then, that most people around the world think of us as a country not of faith or values but of markets—of an endless stream of material goods. The freedoms they see on display are not the freedom to vote or to worship or to speak truth to power, but rather the freedom to slip the bonds of any moral restraints, to break the ties of family and community, and to forge a life of money and material pleasure. This image is certainly not all of America, but it is some of America, and it is the America that we overwhelmingly project to the rest of the world.

These perceptions pose a direct threat to us today. Many violent Islamic fundamentalists today read the writings of Sayyid Qutb. As Lawrence Wright explains in his acclaimed *Looming Tower: Al-Qaeda and the Road to 9/11,* Qutb was a midlevel Egyptian civil servant and literary and social critic whose writing went one step too far for the Egyptian monarch. Threatened with arrest, Qutb instead chose self-exile. His friends and family paid his passage to New York, where he arrived in December 1948, to a city flush with the post–World War II economic boom and bursting with goods and people of every description. Lonely and homesick, Qutb felt himself to be living in a spiritual wasteland. "What I need most here is someone to talk to, to talk about topics other than dollars, movie stars, brands of cars—a real conversation on the issues of man, philosophy, and soul."[18]

Qutb also saw New York as a deeply unequal place, where rich and ambitious strivers jostled side by side with street people, alcoholics, and prostitutes. He traveled from New York to

Washington and later to Colorado, where he completed a master's degree in education and witnessed a deep racism even among American progressives. He came to see America as a country without a soul, a society where capitalism was the true god and Christianity nothing more than an illusion. In America and after he returned to Egypt, Qutb's faith became a dark and twisted thing. He saw American capitalism and Soviet communism as two sides of the same materialist coin, a materialism he came to identify with modernism itself and the domination of the West. He sought instead to recover a "pure, primitive Islam," an absolute unity of faith and life. To achieve such a state, all unbelievers, including Muslims who had strayed from the pure faith, must be destroyed.

Qutb's writings and radicalism today inspire thousands and perhaps tens of thousands of young Muslim men—and women—to seek our destruction. The Muslim brotherhood, the Taliban, al-Qaeda, and still other less organized groups see America much as Qutb did. But instead of going to America, as Qutb did, they have had America brought to them through the powerful forces of globalization. Looking at our country and the West as a whole, they form a vision as alienating as Qutb found America itself. On the other side, they see the comforting anchor of a pure and traditional Islam, a code of conduct, a set of strict disciplines, a cause larger than life. In the words of former Secretary of State Madeleine Albright, who was writing on America, religion, and world affairs, "Al Qaeda's leaders do not speak factually, but neither do they speak trivially. They concern themselves with transcendent issues of history, identity, and faith. To be heard, the rest of us must address matters equally profound."[19]

This conversation would do us good. Many of us perceive that our culture and our politics are skewed far too much toward the securing and safeguarding of material comforts, toward a harsh and unbridled individualism, and toward an ethic of greed rather than of care. Voices from across the political spectrum are calling for a renewal in this country: a renewal of values, a renewal of faith, a renewal of hope. Far too many Americans look in the mirror every morning and are no longer exactly sure of what they see.

A renewal in our domestic politics is indispensable for our foreign policy. In 1955, Senator John F. Kennedy, a leader who as president succeeded in inspiring an entire generation with renewed faith in American values, gave a commencement speech at Assumption College. He spoke of the Cold War, warning his listeners that Americans focused too much on the physical and material aspects of the struggle, on the brute violence of actual war rather than the slower, internal hollowing of human souls. "We tend to forget," he reflected, "those ideals and faiths and philosophical needs which drive men far more intensely than military and economic objectives."[20]

So too today. Broadcasting bromides about the purity of our intentions will not advance our cause in the world. We need first to recover our faith as a people in our own ability to live up to and implement our values. This recovery should draw on the best and deepest traditions in America's many religions and retrace the connections between religious faith and Enlightenment faith. It will also require a frank look at our failings, an open acknowledgment that in many ways our society has lost its way. We must be able to diagnose our ills as readily as the travelers in our midst or the watchers from far away.

As Americans, we are blessed to be citizens of a country built on many kinds of faith. We must recognize how religious faith and Enlightenment faith have intertwined to support all our values: liberty, democracy, equality, justice, tolerance, and humility. Whether we respect the rights and dignity of our fellow humans because we believe that we are all created in God's image or because we simply see no moral basis for elevating some of our kind above others, we can find a common creed. And we can celebrate the power of faith itself, as the light that illumines and commits us to something larger than ourselves.

Conclusion:
Stars to Steer By

When an American says that he loves his country, he means
not only that he loves the New England hills, the prairies
glistening in the sun, the wide and rising plains, the great
mountains, and the sea. He means that he loves an inner air,
an inner light in which freedom lives and in which a man can
draw the breath of self-respect.

—*Adlai Stevenson*

AMERICAN PATRIOTISM IS GROUNDED not only in our love
for our country itself, but also in our love for the values our
country stands for—of the *idea* that is America, no matter how
far short we may fall in practice. It is the idea that knits us together in our vast diversity. It is the idea that our soldiers fight
for. It is the idea that all patriotic citizens stand for, even against
our own government. And it is an idea that ultimately belongs
to all the world's peoples.

Americans are hardly unique in having forged a national
identity based on a set of fundamental principles. The French

glory in their country's heritage as the source of the Declaration of the Rights of Man and of "Liberty, Equality, and Fraternity." The English rightly love their tradition of individual rights and restrained rule begun with the Magna Carta. The Chinese venerate many of the principles of Confucianism as part of the essence of being Chinese. South Africans celebrate *ubuntu,* the belief in a universal bond of sharing that connects humanity. Indeed, a journalist's story about the near destruction of a fabled Baghdad street of booksellers in the late summer of 2006 closed with a heart-wrenching description of the last bookseller to remain open breaking down in tears. "Iraq," he said, as he wiped his eyes, "it is the first country. It set the laws of Hammurabi."[1]

But values play a particularly important role in the American national psyche for a unique reason: Although we inhabit a common land that we love, we do not share a common race, creed, or national origin. Liberty, democracy, equality, justice, tolerance, humility, and faith bind us together more powerfully than do blood or soil. But here's the paradox. It is the vigorous and impassioned debates we have about the practical meaning of those values and the trade-offs between them that bind us most strongly. The tone of those debates is often fierce and divisive, but the disagreement and dissent that fuel them is an essential part of American life.

Debates and struggles over the meaning of our values have driven our history forward. Democracy once meant suffrage only for propertied white men. At the dawn of the Revolution, liberty meant slavery for 20 percent of the population. Equality once meant segregated schools. And justice has often not been for all. Successive groups and generations of Americans have challenged the meaning and the implementation of these values—calling on our government to make good its promises and also disputing precisely what was promised.

We are a strong and vibrant nation because we have different views about what our values mean in practice. Our disagreements generate extraordinary political energy and fuel our social and civic engagement. These debates have propelled us forward through nearly four centuries of American history, and they will animate our nation for centuries to come. And as we have done in the past, we will undoubtedly reverse ourselves periodically in the future. The balance between order and liberty, for instance, is continually being redrawn as we face new internal and external threats.

The sum of all these debates is the great American debate, the essence of our politics, the secret of our historic success, and the source of our strength as a vibrant, open society. But to safeguard and build on that strength, we must be mindful. We must conduct our debate within both substantive and procedural limits. As broad and deep as our national debate is, our values do not have limitless meanings. Substantively, our values can mean many things, but our history shows they cannot mean all things. Liberty cannot mean slavery; democracy cannot mean disenfranchisement; justice cannot mean the denial of habeas corpus or one's right to see the evidence against oneself. Somewhere along the spectrum of grays, black becomes white. The exact location of that point is itself a matter of debate, and as every lawyer knows, drawing lines in these circumstances is always an imperfect exercise. But lines must be and can be drawn, by our courts, our legislators, and we ourselves as participants in shaping public opinion. The lines we draw define the zone of legitimate difference, of tolerance, of robust debate.

We must also conduct our great national debates within procedural limits—above all, with respect and civility. Debate in our present political culture all too often gives way to demonization—literally. Consider the following examples. Musing on the 2008 elections, the Reverend Jerry Falwell said that he hoped Hillary Clinton would be the Democratic nominee. No one, he said, would energize his conservative evangelical constituency as she would: "If Lucifer ran, he wouldn't."[2] Or take Grover Norquist, the powerful conservative activist who heads the antitax group Americans for Tax Reform. He has described bipartisanship as "date rape," and he likes to talk about reducing the federal government so much that he could "drown it in the bathtub."[3]

The Democrats can be just as vitriolic. Liberal commentator Lewis Lapham has called the Bush administration a "rapacious oligarchy" led by a "criminal—known to be armed and dangerous."[4] The *I Hate* series of books features such titles as *The I Hate George W. Bush Reader: Why Dubya Is Absolutely Wrong About Everything; The I Hate Dick Cheney, John Ashcroft, Donald Rumsfeld, Condi Rice . . . Reader: Behind the Bush Cabal's War on America;* and *The I Hate Republicans Reader: Why the GOP Is Totally Wrong About Everything.*[5] You know partisanship is out of control when you can buy a George W. Bush voodoo doll, complete with pins, on Amazon.com.

This kind of overheated rhetoric and intense partisanship has replaced genuine debate in contemporary America. We have created an invidious political culture that is not only unpleasant but also dangerous. It distracts us from the real issues at stake in our politics and prevents us from coming together to solve them. George Washington himself once warned Americans about this danger. He devoted part of his 1796 farewell address to the dangers of "faction," arguing that it sidetracks deliberation over important questions, weakens the government, and "agitates the community with ill-founded jealousies and false alarms."[6]

The debate over Iraq and the war on terror is a perfect example of what President Washington warned against. Partisanship in our nation's capital is so intense that after the 2006 election, in which voters made clear that the country must change course on Iraq, the Senate could not even manage to *debate* the president's plan for a surge of troops, much less actually decide anything. The Senate is supposed to be a deliberative body, able to hear and respond to evidence and arguments. When political gamesmanship becomes so intense that it creates stalemate, the country suffers. Voters cannot hold their leaders accountable, because the citizens cannot figure out where politicians truly stand.

In other areas, our first responders are only barely better equipped today across the country than they were on 9/11. Countless measures that would deter terrorists have failed to find bipartisan support. As a result, we have failed to fortify potential terrorism targets. In industrial plants, we still use chemicals that could cause toxic clouds if the facilities were blown up. We have barely improved our ability to identify and treat diseases that could result from biological attacks. Instead our presidential elections are dominated by aptly named wedge issues—designed precisely to split us off into factions and drive us apart—like gay marriage and school prayer, rather than by the national crises in health care and education that we simply must address as a nation.

It is up to voters across the spectrum to demand a change. One place to start is to reject the notion that the members of any one political party or any one group of voters within a party are "values voters," a term today applied to the religious right. We are *all* values voters; we just disagree on the nature of the values at stake and the right trade-offs among them. Again, that disagreement itself is healthy; the ability to debate important issues and the core values that underlie those issues has made our democracy strong and vibrant. When our system is working properly, the results of those debates are sounder policies, policies supported not along party lines but on their merits, policies that have made America strong, safe, prosperous, and free.

We must also expand national debates beyond the politicians and pundits (including me!). These debates must genuinely engage the American people. Particularly at a time of rising threats, new challenges, and rapidly changing technology in the world, we need to engage our entire society—public sector, private sector, and nonprofit sector. If two heads are better than one, then we need as many participants as possible; we also need to hear the widest possible spectrum of views before making critical decisions.

In 1991, the famed television journalist Bill Moyers gave a speech to a group of legislators. He described his travels across the country, among a restless, dissatisfied electorate: "But beneath the general buzz, you can, by listening intently, hear people say that it's not just new legislation or more programs that will make the difference. What they want is to be invited into the conversation of democracy."[7] Moyers went on to describe a letter he had received in the wake of a series of televised interviews he had conducted with the philosopher Mortimer Adler, author of *Six Great Ideas*. The letter was from a plumber, who addressed Adler on behalf of a group of construction workers: "While we cannot all agree whether or not we would hire you as an apprentice, we can all agree that we would love to listen to you during our lunch breaks." The series, said the plumber, "has completely turned around our impression of education. . . . We have grown to love the ideas behind our country's compositions, and . . . we have all become devout Constitutionalists."[8] From this experience and others like it, Moyers called for "a new political compact—to reconnect the citizens and politics, government and the people."[9]

Easier said than done. But voters hold the ultimate lever in politics—the vote itself. Accepted political wisdom among campaign consultants, for instance, is that although voters profess not to like negative campaigning, it works—meaning that candidates who use nasty partisan ads tearing down their opponent are more likely to win than candidates who stick to the issues. If voters really want to be reconnected to the system, to have representatives who will debate the issues and show political courage, then we must consciously punish the partisan behavior that has become politics as usual. We must reward leaders who are willing to tackle hard issues and who will make the compromises necessary for bipartisan support. We must elect politicians who will not always tell us what we want to hear, but who will actively challenge the received wisdom, who will admit to changing their minds from time to time, and who will be prepared, if necessary, to ask individual citizens to sacrifice for the common good.

The "conversation of democracy" is only as lively, valuable, and productive as we make it. We can reject the role of money in politics by electing members of Congress who promise to clean it up, and then holding them to their word. We can change the tone of the conversation by punishing partisan sniping and rewarding representatives who prove themselves most adept at working across party lines. And we can insist on fair representation by demanding that our voting districts actually represent a cross-section of the local population in a specific area, rather than a carefully selected group of partisans within gerrymandered lines.

We have overhauled our political system before. At the end of the nineteenth century, machine politics, in which nominally elected politicians ruled with impunity through a system of corruption and patronage, dominated many states and most major cities. The Progressive movement that swept the country cleaned out many of the machines and ended entrenched systems of patronage and political spoils. The result was a new era of trust busting, laws regulating child labor and dramatically improving working conditions across the board, the adoption of the federal income tax, the creation of the Federal Reserve, and a host of other reforms. We've done it once. If we are determined enough, we can do it again.

SINCERE AND OPEN DEBATE is more important now than ever. When we are under threat, our instinct is to close ranks, to stifle dissent, to insist on a particular version of our values as the patriotic line. But our instincts are wrong. We live in an age in which we face new threats, new enemies, new technologies, and new global powers. In these circumstances, any government, right or left, will make mistakes. Indeed, as discussed in the chapter on justice, our whole nation committed serious errors and injustices during World War II; similarly, the nation plunged into the nightmare of McCarthyism at the outset of the Cold War. When we witness such injustices perpetrated by our own government, it is our duty to speak out and engage one another in open debate.

As we debate the great issues of our age, we must be prepared to change our minds. After three years of battling in Iraq, the Pentagon came to realize that many of its rules and tactics were deeply counterproductive. In a manual issued in the fall of 2006, soldiers were advised to do essentially the opposite of what they had been doing. In fighting an insurgency, unlike a traditional enemy, the new rules advised, "The more force used, the less effective it is."[10]

On homeland security, it turns out that spreading information about threats rather than hoarding it under more and more layers of classification is more likely to protect us. After all, the passengers on Flight 93 were able to block an intended attack on the Capitol or the White House because they knew from their cell phones what terrorist pilots had done with the other planes. The passengers sacrificed their own lives, but saved countless others. On the other hand, the passengers on the planes that were crashed into the Twin Towers had never been warned about terrorist plans to use planes as flying bombs, something U.S. intelligence services already knew. If our government had publicized that information, instead of guarding it so tightly that it was hidden even from other parts of the government, the fate of all of the planes on 9/11 might have been different.[11]

In each of these cases, our initial instincts were wrong. Today we continue to follow many policies that may well do us more harm than good. The transformation of our embassies into protective bunkers abroad may increase the perception of the United States as a militarist society and may make effective public diplomacy almost impossible. The tightening of our visa requirements may mean that smart students and businesspeople, who might have come to America to learn about us, instead go to Canada, Australia, or England. And the rejection of any limits on our sovereignty in areas such as testing nuclear weapons and the preventive use of force may prevent us from imposing those limits elsewhere, making the world ultimately a more dangerous place. In these and other policies that ultimately prove to be faulty, we can learn from experience and from testing competing ideas. Admitting error is a sign not of weakness, but of wisdom.

Different Americans have different views on all these issues, as do our friends and allies abroad. The point here is the elementary value of keeping an open mind, the very thing that screechy, partisan pundits discourage and that so many of our politicians seem to equate with flip-flopping or weakness of character. These attitudes are particularly counterproductive in debates about our values, where they routinely lead to accusations of moral relativism. We must instead embrace a broad, generous understanding of American values that includes a tradition of active debate about their practical application and their theoretical limits.

WE NEED NOT ONLY to embrace a vigorous national debate on what we stand for, but also to launch a global debate about the meanings and trade-offs of *universal* values. Liberty, democracy, equality, justice, tolerance, humility, and faith bind Americans together, but these values do not stop at the shores of the Atlantic and Pacific or the banks of the Rio Grande and Saint Lawrence. We have always insisted that our values are universal values. Indeed, part of what we think makes us distinctively American is that we hold to a set of values that apply around the world.

Today, other countries, by and large, do not believe us. When we say, "We want to promote universal values," they increasingly hear, "We want to impose American values." We have enemies in the world—from terrorist groups to governments trying to keep a hold on power by demonizing us—who deliberately amplify this message. But even many of our friends in the world think that we no longer listen or learn, but that we instead insist that the American way is the only way. To change these perceptions and to get our foreign policy back on track, we have to face and answer hard questions about why we make the trade-offs we do, and when and whether we are practicing what we preach. We must also accept that other nations might have equally valid understandings and applications of values that they understand to be theirs just as much as we see them as ours. That is the meaning of universal values.

Engaging in this debate means asking ourselves some tough questions. The countries of the European Union do not practice the death penalty. Do they have the right to lecture us on the death penalty? If not, do we have the right to lecture Islamic countries on the practice of cutting off a hand for thievery? What if a majority of citizens in a particular Muslim country support the practice?

Under French law, Muslim girls may not wear head scarves in schools. Is that a violation of freedom of expression or freedom of religion, an infringement of the core value of liberty? If not, then why it is permissible for us to insist that Amish children attend school until at least eighth grade? Or for us to ban prayer in schools? Citizens of other countries looking at America could offer many other examples.

If we sincerely believe that our values are genuinely universal, that it is "self-evident" that all humans have the same basic endowments and all are entitled to self-government, then we must learn much more about how other nations implement our shared values. We need to learn much more about the idea that is Japan, France, South Korea, India, South Africa, Germany, Botswana, Ghana, Brazil, Turkey, the United Kingdom, Chile, Mexico, Costa Rica, Canada, Italy, Australia and a great many other liberal democracies. Genuinely engaging the citizens of these countries in a global debate will help us see ourselves as others see us—an easy way to gain both friends and humility, not necessarily in that order.

A concrete example of this kind of dialogue is occurring in courtrooms around the world toady. When judges decide cases today they increasingly look at similar cases from other countries, sometimes even referencing them in their opinions. Traditionally, courts in countries with young legal systems have looked to more established countries, and none more than the United States, in their deliberations. But as constitutional traditions have solidified in a range of democracies around the world—not just the United States and Europe, but in Brazil, Argentina, South Africa, India, and Japan—judges are able to draw from a wide range of experiences to arrive at just conclusions. Foreign decisions do not bind us, and we may certainly decide that what works in Israel or England or South Korea is not appropriate for us. But it is important at least to look.

What we find may well surprise us. Just as different opinions and positions overshadow common values domestically, cultural differences can obscure values that span the entire globe. Consider the Universal Declaration of Human Rights, which enumerates thirty specific articles of international human rights law, everything from the right "to life, liberty and security of person" to the right to choose how one's children are educated. When it was adopted in 1948, forty-eight of the fifty-eight then members of the United Nations signed on, and the others merely abstained (of the abstaining parties—the Soviet Bloc, Saudi Arabia, and apartheid South Africa—only one remains today). Already by the late 1940s, most countries—from all parts of the world, representing all its major cultures—could agree on thirty fundamental principles.

At the same time, we can learn a great deal by engaging other nations on how they practice and prioritize their values regard-

ing specific issues. Consider, for instance, the debate raging today within the United States about how far we must compromise our ideals and our values to ensure our security. Many
other democracies have wrestled with the same issues. England
faced the Irish Republican Army (IRA). France faced Algerian
terrorist groups. And today Israel is facing Palestinian terrorists.

None of these nations has covered itself with glory as it wrestled with these threats. The British government sowed the seeds
of generations of hatred by suspending normal judicial processes
and human rights guarantees regarding IRA prisoners before it
finally reversed course as the result of a national inquiry. The
French fought a hideously brutal war against Algerian insur-
gents before finally accepting defeat.

In Israel, Israeli human rights groups have led campaigns
against their government's treatment of accused Palestinian
terrorists much like the cases brought by American human
rights groups against the Bush administration's treatment of
the detainees at Guantánamo. In a key decision, the Israeli
supreme court rejected the use of torture against Palestinian
detainees unless the practices used were explicitly and directly
authorized by the Israeli legislature (which it has not done). In
the words of Justice Aharon Barak, then the president of the
Israeli supreme court, "A democracy must sometimes fight
with one hand tied behind its back. Even so, a democracy has
the upper hand."[12]

Israel makes the trade-off between liberty and security one
way; other liberal democracies will make it another way—just
as they will differ on how much equality to trade for justice,
how much democracy to trade for equality—and on and on. The
universality of all humanity must necessarily include a universe
of diversity, of many different ways to achieve the same great
goals.

Just as at home in the United States, however, these choices must be made within a zone of legitimate difference. National constitutions and international human rights treaties establish a threshold of absolute minimum guarantees. It is never permissible to deliberately trade an innocent life for greater security. Nor can a nation vote democratically to deny minorities their civil rights. And governments can never simply confiscate the legitimately earned property of others.

Above this threshold, however, we should be prepared to tolerate national differences with strength and self-confidence. We must be secure enough to listen and learn, to invite other nations and peoples to challenge our versions of universal values just as we question theirs. We must insist on tolerance itself as part of the pantheon of universal values. We should insist that other nations respect the decision of a majority of the American people and of American courts on the legality of the death penalty—a position that we share with Japan, among other liberal democracies. Conversely, we must respect the decision of many other nations to impose limits on hate speech, libel, and the leaking of official secrets; to have an established state religion; or to deny or limit the right of abortion.

Launching and helping to lead such a global debate will make us stronger and safer. We should begin with the stories recounted in this book. We must acknowledge how long it has taken us to make our values a reality for all Americans and recognize that, in many areas, we still have a long way to go. By admitting our own limitations as a nation, we will communicate immediately that we are willing to engage in a real debate about what these values mean and how they can best be achieved. We will signal that for us, democracy is not some kind of template to be imposed on others, but is instead a system of government that depends on debate and difference. And in the end, we will be a far more effective advocate for our own values if we invite questions rather than dictate answers.

AFTER SIX YEARS of the war on terror, four years of the war in Iraq, decades of seemingly endless and intractable conflict in the Middle East, and new threats of nuclear proliferation, collapsed states, and religious conflict seemingly mounting on all sides, the temptation of many Americans is not to engage, but to withdraw. Our reaction is not to debate our values, but to clutch them close and hole up. We have been here before.

The history of America in the world is ambivalent, reflecting cycles of missionary engagement and determined isolation. In its earliest days, America was a retreat from the world for millions of immigrants, not only a chance to make a better life in a new world but also to leave the old world behind. Thomas Smith, a Massachusetts Puritan and artist, articulated in a poem the longing of early colonists to escape the worldly intrigue of Europe to lead a more spiritual existence in the New World:

Why why should I the World be minding
therin a World of Evils Finding.
Then Farewell World: Farewell thy Jarres
thy Joies thy Toies thy Wiles thy Warrs
Truth Sounds Retreat: I am not Sorye.
The Eternall Drawes to him my heart
By Faith (which can thy Force Subvert)
To Crown me (after Grace) with Glory.[13]

Retreat from the joies, toies, wiles, and warrs of the old world has tempted us at regular intervals throughout our history. The strongest and most recent surge of this isolationist sentiment was in the decades between World War I and World War II, the age of "Fortress America." Exhausted by World War I and distracted by the Great Depression, Americans turned inward in the 1920s and 1930s, confident in the security of the Atlantic to the east and the Pacific to the west. It took Pearl Harbor to disabuse Americans of their false sense of security.

Isolationism has taken other forms as well. In one version, isolationists have insisted that we have a duty to lead the world—but by example only. We will try to live up to our values at home and hope that our experience inspires others. This was Jefferson's vision of American foreign policy, revived most recently in calls for a policy of "exemplarism." Such a policy would cast American values as universally desirable while rejecting our ability to promote them actively.[14]

At other periods in our history, we have embraced engagement with missionary fervor, setting out to remake the world anew in our own image. This is at least the widespread understanding, or misunderstanding, of Woodrow Wilson's call to defend democracy, or more recently of George W. Bush's proclamation of a global mission to make the world safe from tyranny. In our own view, we leave our shores not only to defend ourselves and our own interests, but also to set things aright where they have gone badly wrong elsewhere in the world—to dislodge dictators and fight for human rights and democracy. Over two centuries, many on the receiving end of our mission—including the French in World Wars I and II, Bosnian Muslims and Albanian Kosovars after the Cold War, and even many Iraqis—have in fact greeted us as liberators and saviors. But over time, and for many bystanders, our motives seem much less pure.

Today, isolation is simply not an option. We can avoid sending our soldiers abroad in wars of choice, certainly. But we cannot avoid attacks such as 9/11 or the bombings of our embassies, ships, and barracks around the world. We cannot build a wall of tariffs without crippling our own economy. And we surely cannot build a physical wall the length of our borders—on land, at sea, and in the air. We cannot block pathogens from traveling across continents and oceans any more than we can stop hurricanes and floods from intensifying due to global warming. Nor can we stop the millions of Americans whose families and friends live scattered across the globe—and other Americans, who are simply moved by the suffering they see on television or on trips abroad—from caring deeply about what happens to the global community. How can we expect American citizens not to urge our government to respond to humanitarian, political, and economic crises?

We must engage the world and do so in the way our values demand. We must work with other nations to define and promote a concept of ordered liberty. We must evaluate ourselves and others according to a PAR index: popular, accountable, and rights-regarding government. We must reform international institutions to provide meaningful representation for all the peoples of the worlds and commit ourselves fully to achieving the Millennium Development Goals to equalize at least minimum life chances around the world. We must reject torture and cruel and degrading treatment unequivocally and absolutely and again embrace the Geneva Conventions as essential protections for our own soldiers and combatants captured anywhere in the world. We must reject the clash of civilizations and instead develop and embrace a vision of a peaceful, prosperous, and tolerant Islam. We must launch a global good neighbor policy based on respect for other nations, for their citizens, and for the forces of nature. And we must affirm both religious faith and Enlightenment faith as an essential part of the American creed and as a bridge to other nations.

These specific policies would reflect and project our values. But they are certainly not the only way. Debates over the policies that would keep faith with our values have been the catalysts for progressive change throughout our history, as we have seen time and again. Engaging in those same debates about our foreign policy will be similarly valuable. And the global extension of those debates about how we and other nations understand and implement our shared values itself affirms those values as universal.

This engagement with the world is built into the very core of who we are as a nation. It is not the engagement of self-appointed missionaries, much less of conquerors or crusaders. It is the engagement of seekers in a collective quest, and it requires tolerance of the many possible paths in pursuit of that quest. It is an engagement borne of a conviction that liberty, democracy, equality, and justice are birthrights for *all*—not just all Americans. And, finally, it is a form of engagement that demands humility—a frank acknowledgment of the immense challenges we confront in making those concepts real for actual human beings around the globe.

"Ideals are like stars," wrote Carl Schurz, the soldier, statesman, immigrant, and author whose words have recurred in these pages. "You will not succeed in touching them with your hands. But like the seafaring man on the desert of waters, you choose them as your guides, and following them you will reach your destiny."[15]

Liberty, democracy, equality, justice, tolerance, humility, and faith—these are America's fixed stars. If we think of ourselves as a city on a hill, we suggest to the rest of the world that *we* are the beacon spreading light to other nations. But if we think less of ourselves and more of our ideals, we can join with other nations in seeing them shine above us all. If we aspire continually to the *idea* that is America, rather than contenting ourselves with the reality, we must look to those stars to steer by. If we stay the course, they will lead us to a better and safer world.

Notes

PREFACE

1. William Harlan Hale, *The March of Freedom: A Layman's History of the American People* (New York: Harper and Brothers, 1947), 1. All the quotes in my preface are either from Hale's preface, pp. ix–x, or from pp. 1–2.

INTRODUCTION

1. Abraham Lincoln, Speech at Springfield, Ill., June 26, 1857, in *Collected Works of Abraham Lincoln* (Rutgers University Press, 1953, 1990), 2:405.

2. Woodrow Wilson, quoted in John Pullen, *Patriotism in America* (New York: American Heritage Press, 1971), 21.

3. William Harlan Hale, *The March of Freedom: A Layman's History of the American People* (New York: Harper and Brothers, 1947), 27–28.

4. J. K. Rowling, *Harry Potter and the Half-Blood Prince* (New York: Arthur A. Levine Books, 2005), 644–645.

5. Daniel Webster, Speech at Bunker Hill, June 17, 1825, available at www.dartmouth.edu/~dwebster/speeches/bunker-hill.html.

6. George Washington, Farewell Address, 1796, available at www.yale.edu/lawweb/avalon/washing.htm.

7. Thomas Jefferson to Tench Coxe, June 1, 1795, manuscript letter in the Manuscript Division of the Library of Congress (181), available at www.loc.gov/exhibits/jefferson/jeffworld.html.

8. Jimmy Carter, Inaugural Address, Washington, D.C., January 20, 1977, available at www.yale.edu/lawweb/avalon/presiden/inaug/carter.htm.

9. Jimmy Carter, Farewell Address, Washington, D.C., January 14, 1981, from "Selected Speeches of Jimmy Carter," Jimmy Carter Library and Museum Web page, www.jimmycarterlibrary.org/documents/speeches/farewell.phtml.

10. Osama Bin Laden, quoted in Peter Bergen, *Holy War, Inc.: Inside the Secret World of Osama Bin Laden* (New York: Free Press, 2002), 20.

11. Abraham Lincoln, first debate with Stephen A. Douglas at Ottawa, Illinois, August 21, 1858, available at www.nps.gov/archive/liho/debate1.htm.

12. Mark Twain, "Papers of the Adams Family," in *Letters from the Earth* (New York: Crest, 1964), 109.

13. Carl Schurz, remarks in the U.S. Senate, February 29, 1872, *Congressional Globe,* Senate, 42nd Cong., 2nd sess., 1287.

14. Louis Brandeis, in *Whitney v. People of State of California,* 274 U.S. 357 (1927).

15. James Baldwin, *Notes of a Native Son* (Boston: Beacon Press, 1955), 9.

16. "United States! the ages plead, — / Present and Past in undersong, — / Go put your creed into your deed, / Nor speak with double tongue." From Ralph Waldo Emerson, "Ode," poem sung in the Town Hall, Concord, N.H., July 4, 1857, available at www.potw.org/archive/potw369.html.

CHAPTER 1: LIBERTY

1. This passage in fact comes from the Bible, Leviticus 25:10.

2. Thomas Jefferson to Admantios Coray, October 31, 1823, Manuscript letter, Manuscript Division (204), Library of Congress Web site www.loc.gov/exhibits/jefferson/jeffworld.html.

3. George Washington, First Inaugural Address, available at www.yale.edu/lawweb/avalon/presiden/inaug/wash1.htm.

4. "Mrs. Hutchinson, you are called here as one of those that have troubled the peace of the commonwealth and the churches here; you are known to be a woman that hath had a great share in the promoting and divulging of those opinions that are causes of this trouble . . . you have spoken diverse things as we have been informed very prejudicial to the honour of the churches and ministers thereof, and you have maintained a meeting and an assembly in your house that hath been condemned by the general assembly as a thing not tolerable nor comely in the sight of God nor fitting for your sex." From "The Examination of Mrs. Anne Hutchinson at the Court at Newton, 1637," available at Commonwealth of Massachusetts Web site www.mass.gov/statehouse/statues/hutch_transcript.htm.

5. "We, whose names are hereunder written, being desirous to inhabit

in the town of Providence, do promise to submit ourselves, in active or passive obedience, to all such orders or agreements as shall be made for public good by the body in an orderly way, by the major consent of the inhabitants, masters of families, incorporated together into a township, and such others as they shall admit into the same, only in civil things." From John Russell Bartlett, ed., *Records of the Colony of Rhode Island and Providence Plantations* (Providence, R.I.: A. C. Greene & Bros., 1856–1865), 1:14.

6. Thomas Jefferson, First Inaugural Address, March 4, 1801, available at www.yale.edu/lawweb/avalon/presiden/inaug/jefinau1.htm.

7. U.S. Constitution, art. 1, sec. 2, clause 3. Italics added.

8. Thomas Jefferson, *Notes on the State of Virginia,* Query XVIII, 1787, available at www.yale.edu/lawweb/avalon/jevifram.htm.

9. An estimated 6 percent of the 10–15 million Africans who were brought to the New World ended up in North America, with most of the remainder going to South America and the Caribbean. Later, however, many more were born into slavery in the United States, so that by 1860, approximately two-thirds of all New World slaves, some 4 million human beings, lived in the American South. S. Mintz, "American Slavery in Comparative Perspective," Digital History (2003), available at www.digitalhistory.uh.edu/black_voices/voices_display.cfm?id=24.

10. *"Fellow Citizens:* Pardon me, and allow me to ask, why am I called upon to speak here today? What have I or those I represent to do with your national independence? Are the great principles of political freedom and of national justice, embodied in that Declaration of Independence, extended to us?

". . . The blessings in which you this day rejoice are not enjoyed in common. The rich inheritance of justice, liberty, prosperity, and independence bequeathed by your fathers is shared by you, not by me. The sunlight that brought life and healing to you has brought stripes and death to me. This Fourth of July is *yours,* not *mine. . . .*

"America is false to the past, false to the present, and solemnly binds herself to be false in the future. Standing with God and the crushed and bleeding slave on this occasion, I will, in the name of humanity, which is outraged, in the name of liberty, which is fettered, in the name of the Constitution and the Bible, which are disregarded, and trampled upon, dare to call in question to denounce, with all emphasis I can command, everything that serves to perpetuate slavery—the great sin and shame of America." From Frederick Douglass, "What to the Slave Is the Fourth of July?" speech at Rochester, N.Y., July 5, 1852, available at http://douglass archives.org/doug_a10.htm.

11. W. Joseph Campbell, *Yellow Journalism: Puncturing the Myths, Defining the Legacies* (New York: Praeger, 2003), 76.

12. The first quote comes from Lincoln's speech on the Kansas-Nebraska Act of 1854 and was given at Peoria, Ill., on October 16, 1854. The second comes from his letter to H. L. Pierce of April 6, 1859. Both sources are from American Anti-Imperialist League, "Platform of the American Anti-Imperialist League," in *Speeches, Correspondence, and Political Papers of Carl Schurz,* ed. Frederick Bancroft (New York: G. P. Putnam's Sons, 1913), 6: 77, n. 1.

13. Patrick Henry's response to English loyalists who labeled his May 30, 1765, speech to the Virginia House of Burgesses treasonous.

14. Woodrow Wilson, "War Message," address to Congress, April 2, 1917. Available at http://net.lib.byu.edu/~rdh7/wwi/1917/wilswarm. html.

15. http://net.lib.byu.edu/~rdh7/wwi/1918/14points.html.

16. See G. John Ikenberry, *After Victory: Institutions, Strategic Restraint, and the Rebuilding of Order After Major Wars* (Princeton, N.J.: Princeton University Press, 2000), whose author I am indebted to for this discussion.

17. Harry Truman, address to the U.N. Conference on International Organization, San Francisco, June 26, 1945.

18. Jefferson to George Rogers Clark, December 25, 1780, in *Papers of Thomas Jefferson,* ed. Julian P. Boyd (Princeton, N.J.: Princeton University Press, 1951), 4:237–238.

19. Andrew Kohut, "Anti-Americanism: Causes and Characteristics" (December 10, 2003), Pew Global Attitudes Project, available at http://pewglobal.org/commentary/print.php?analysisID=77.

CHAPTER 2: DEMOCRACY

1. Douglas O. Linder, "The Trial of Susan B. Anthony for Illegal Voting" (Kansas City, Mo.: University of Missouri–Kansas City Law School, 2001), Famous Trials Web site, www.law.umkc.edu/faculty/projects/ftrials/anthony/sbaaccount.html.

2. Susan B. Anthony, "Is It a Crime for a Citizen of the United States to Vote?" speech given at various towns in Monroe and Ontario counties, N.Y., 1872, in Famous Trials Web site, ed. Douglas O. Linder (Kansas

City, Mo.: University of Missouri–Kansas City Law School, 2007), www. law.umkc.edu/faculty/projects/ftrials/anthony/anthonyaddress.html.

3. Various accounts of the trial are given on the Web site of the Elizabeth Cady Stanton and Susan B. Anthony Papers Project, Rutgers University, New Brunswick, N.J., at http://ecssba.rutgers.edu/docs/ sbatrial.html.

4. Ibid.

5. Demos: A Network for Ideas and Action, "Voting Rights for Citizens with Felony Convictions," www.demos.org/page15.cfm.

6. James Madison, "Federalist No. 57," in *The Federalist Papers*, ed. Isaac Kramnick (Harmondsworth, England: Smith, 1987), 345.

7. James Madison, "Federalist No. 51," in *The Federalist Papers*, ed. Isaac Kramnick (Harmondsworth, England: Smith, 1987), 319–320.

8. Frank Hague, speech to Jersey City Chamber of Commerce, Jersey City, N.J., January 12, 1938, in *The Columbia World of Quotations*, eds. Robert Andrews, Mary Biggs, and Michael Seidel (New York: Columbia University Press, 1996), available at www.bartleby.com/66/98/26498. html.

9. Joseph McCarthy, speech made in Wisconsin in 1952, quoted in *Senator Joe McCarthy*, by Richard Rovere (New York: Harper and Row, 1973), ch. 1.

10. Margaret Chase Smith, "Declaration of Conscience," speech in U.S. Senate, June 1, 1950, available at Margaret Chase Smith Policy Center, University of Maine, Orono, Web site www.umaine.edu/mcsc/About Us/DeclCon.html.

11. *Texas v. Johnson*, 491 U.S. 397, June 21, 1989, available at http:// caselaw.lp.findlaw.com/scripts/getcase.pl?court=US&vol=491&invol=397.

12. *United States v. Eichman*, 496 U.S. 310, 1990, available at http:// caselaw.lp.findlaw.com/scripts/getcase.pl?court=us&vol=496&invol=310.

13. For information on Freedom House (which has offices in New York City and Washington, D.C.), see the organization's Web site, www. freedomhouse.org.

14. Condoleezza Rice, speech at American University in Cairo, June 20, 2005, available at www.state.gov/secretary/rm/2005/48328.htm.

15. Pew Global Attitudes Project, "A Year After Iraq War, Mistrust of America in Europe Ever Higher, Muslim Anger Persists" report (Washington, D.C.: Pew Research Center, March 16, 2004), http://pewglobal. org/reports/display.php?ReportID=206.

CHAPTER 3: EQUALITY

1. This point is well made in Gordon Wood, *The Radicalism of the American Revolution* (New York: Vintage, 1983).

2. Walt Whitman, *Leaves of Grass* (New York: Simon & Schuster, 1900; 2006).

3. Robert Greenstein and Isaac Shapiro, "The New, Definitive CBO Data on Income and Tax Trends," Center on Budget and Policy Priorities report citing Congressional Budget Office data (Washington, D.C.: Center on Budget and Policy Priorities, September 23, 2003).

4. James Lardner and David A. Smith, eds., *Inequality Matters* (New York: New Press, 2007); preview available at www.inequality.org/facts. cfm.

5. Janny Scott and David Leonhardt, "Class in America: Shadowy Lines That Still Divide," *New York Times,* May 15, 2005.

6. Whitman, *Leaves of Grass.*

7. There have been 117 black members of Congress since 1870, and there were 30 from 1869 to 1883. Congressional Research Service, Library of Congress, "Black Members of the United States Congress: 1870–2005," CRS-59.

8. Anthony Lewis, *Portrait of a Decade: The Second American Revolution* (New York: Random House, 1964), 130.

9. The song "Strange Fruit" was written for Holiday by Lewis Allen, a Jewish schoolteacher from the Bronx, in 1940.

10. Lorraine Hansberry, letter to *New York Times,* April 23, 1964, in *To Be Young, Gifted and Black: Lorraine Hansberry in Her Own Words,* ed. Robert Nemiroff (New York: Vintage Book, 1995), 20–21.

11. Langston Hughes, "Harlem(2)," in *The Collected Poems of Langston Hughes,* ed. Arnold Rampersad and David Roessel (New York: Vintage Books, 1995), 426.

12. Jesse McKinnon, "The Black Population in the United States: 2002" (Washington, D.C.: U.S. Census Bureau, March 2003), available at www.census.gov/prod/2003pubs/p20-541.pdf.

13. Among children ages one through four, black children had the highest death rate in 2002, at 47 per 100,000 children. The mortality rate for white children in the same age group was 27–29 per 100,000 children. Forum on Child and Family Statistics, "America's Children in Brief: Key National Indicators of Well-Being, 2006," available at http:// cldstats.ed.gov/americaschildren/hea7.asp.

14. David Satcher, George E. Fryer, Jr., Jessica McCann, Adewale Troutman, Steven H. Woolf, and George Rust, "What If We Were Equal? A Comparison of the Black-White Mortality Gap in 1960 and 2000," *Health Affairs* 24, no. 2 (2005): 459–464.

15. G. William Domhoff, "Power in America: Wealth, Income, and Power" (September 2005; updated December 2006), Who Rules America? Web page, http://sociology.ucsc.edu/whorulesamerica/power/wealth.html.

16. "Inequality in America: The Rich, the Poor and the Growing Gap Between Them," *Economist,* June 15, 2006.

17. Jessica Bennet, "Plastic Predicament," *Newsweek,* August 18, 2006, available at www.msnbc.msn.com/id/14366431/site/newsweek/.

18. Thomas A. Garrett, "The Rise in Personal Bankruptcy," presentation given through Community Affairs Office, Federal Reserve Bank of St. Louis (St. Louis, October 24, 2006), available at http://stlouisfed.org/news/fiyc/assets/bankruptcypresentation.pdf.

19. Lawrence Mishel, "CEO-to-Worker Pay Imbalance Grows," *Economic Policy Institute* (June 21, 2006), available at www.epinet.org/content.cfm/webfeatures_snapshots_20060621.

20. Nolan McCarty, Keith Poole, and Howard Rosenthal, *Polarized America: The Dance of Ideology and Unequal Riches* (Cambridge, Mass.: MIT Press, 2006).

21. Theodore Roosevelt, speech, Chicago, June 17, 1912, in Theodore Roosevelt Association, "In His Own Words: Life of Theodore Roosevelt," Web site, www.theodoreroosevelt.org/life/quotes.htm.

22. Mariann Lemke et al., "International Outcomes of Learning in Mathematics Literacy and Problem Solving: PISA 2003, Results from the U.S. Perspective" (NCES 2005–003) (Washington, D.C.: U.S. Department of Education, National Center for Education Statistics, 2004), available at http://nces.ed.gov/pubs2005/2005003.pdf.

23. Valerie Strauss, "Despite Lessons on King, Some Unaware of His Dream," *Washington Post,* January 15, 2007.

24. Keith Bradsher and David Barboza, "Pollution from Chinese Coal Casts a Global Shadow," *New York Times,* June 11, 2006.

25. Ibid.

26. U.N. Department of Economic and Social Affairs, "The Millennium Development Goals Report 2006" (New York: United Nations, 2006).

27. Oxfam, "Cultivating Poverty: The Impact of US Cotton Subsidies on Africa," Oxfam Briefing Paper 30 (September 2002), summary available at www.oxfam.org.uk/what_we_do/issues/trade/bp30_cotton.htm.

28. Susan Sechler and Ann Tutwiler, "Trading Up," *New York Times,* June 26, 2006.

CHAPTER 4: JUSTICE

1. Antonin Scalia, "The Rule of Law as a Law of Rules," *University of Chicago Law Review* 56, no. 4 (fall 1989): 1175–1781.

2. Anthony Lewis, "Participating in a Democratic Conversation About the Law," in *The Art and Craft of Justice,* guide to the stone carvings and inscriptions of the U.S. Courthouse in Boston (Boston: Boston Bar Association, 1998).

3. Eugene V. Rostow, "The Democratic Character of Judicial Review," *Harvard Law Review* 66 (1952): 193–208.

4. Alexis de Tocqueville, *Democracy in America* (New York: Signet Books, 2001); text originally published in 1835 (volume 1) and 1840 (volume 2).

5. Oliver Wendell Holmes, *The Common Law* (1881). The full text is available at http://www.law.harvard.edu/library/collections/special/online-collections/common_law/Lecture01.php.

6. *Municipal Council Ratlam v. Vardhichand and others,* Indian Supreme Court, AIR 1980 DC 1622194.

7. *South Africa v. Grootboom,* Constitutional Court of South Africa, 2000 (11) BCLR 1169.

8. *Korematsu v. United States,* 323 U.S. 214, decided December 18, 1944.

9. From the third David Frost interview of Richard Nixon, *New York Times,* May 20, 1977, available at www.landmarkcases.org/nixon/nixon view.html.

10. *United States v. Nixon,* 418 U.S. 683 (1974), available at http://case law.lp.findlaw.com/scripts/getcase.pl?court=us&vol=418&invol=683.

11. Pearlstein's comment was quoted in R. Jeffery Smith, "Many Rights in U.S. Legal System Absent in Bill," *Washington Post,* September 29, 2006.

12. See Jane Meyer, "The Experiment," *New Yorker,* July 11, 2006.

13. Ibid.

14. A video of the exchange is available on the Princeton Web site www.wws.princeton.edu/pcpia/2005/webcasts.html.

15. Colin Powell to John McCain, September 13, 2006, available at www.americanprogress.org/ises/2006/09/powell_detainee_letter.pdf.

16. Joseph Hoar et al. to John McCain, October 3, 2005. This letter, signed by twenty-eight former generals and admirals, was originally posted on Senator McCain's Web site and is available at www.global security.org/military/library/news/2005/10/051003-letter-to-sen-mccain.htm.

17. John Shalikashvili et al. to John Warner and Carl Levin, September 12, 2006. This letter, signed by forty-five retired military brass, is available at www.americanprogress.org/issues/2006/09/letter_geneva_threat.pdf.

18. David Hackett Fischer, *Washington's Crossing* (New York: Oxford, 2004), 379.

19. Ibid.

20. The full text of the code can be found at www.civilwarhome.com/liebercode.htm.

21. The phrase was popularized by the historian Arthur Schlesinger, Jr., in *The Imperial Presidency* (New York: Replica Book, 1998).

22. These quotes come from the conservative commentator Andrew Sullivan, "The Abolition of Torture," *New Republic,* December 19, 2005, available at www.tnr.com/user/nregi.mhtml?i=20051219&s=llivan121905.

23. Daniel Webster, "Mr. Justice Story," in Daniel Webster and Edwin Percy Whipple, *The Great Speeches and Orations of Daniel Webster, with an Essay on Daniel Webster as a Master of English Style* (Boston: Little Brown and Co., 1889), 532.

CHAPTER 5: TOLERANCE

1. "The Examination of Mrs. Anne Hutchinson at the Court at Newton, 1637," available at Commonwealth of Massachusetts Web site www.mass.gov/statehouse/statues/hutch_transcript.htm.

2. John Stuart Mill, *On Liberty and Other Essays,* ed. John Gray (Oxford: Oxford University Press, 1991), 75.

3. Elihu Root, *The Effect of Democracy on International Law* (Buffalo: William S. Hein & Co., March 2000), 8.

4. Moses Seixas to George Washington, August 17, 1790, and George

Washington to Moses Seixas, undated. Both letters are available at Touro Synagogue Web pages www.tourosynagogue.org/seixasLtr.php and www.tourosynagogue.org/GWLetter1.php, respectively.

5. Walter Lippman, *A Preface to Politics* (New York: Mitchell Kennerly, 1914), available at www.gutenberg.org/files/20125/20125-h/20125-h.htm.

6. Francis Fukuyama, *The End of History and the Last Man* (New York: Free Press, 1992). Fukuyama first presented this thesis in Francis Fukuyama, "The End of History?" *National Interest,* no. 16 (Summer 1989).

7. Samuel P. Huntington, "The Clash of Civilizations?" *Foreign Affairs* 72, no. 3 (summer 1993): 22–49.

8. *Philadelphia Sun,* 1855, quoted in *Know Nothing Almanac for 1855,* 68, in Stephen E. Maizlish, "The Meaning of Nativism and the Crisis of the Union: The Know-Nothing Movement in the Antebellum North," in *Essays on American Antebellum Politics, 1840–1860,* ed. Stephen E. Maizlish and John J. Kushma (College Station, Tex.: Texas A&M Press, 1982), 176.

9. C. B. Boynton, July 4, 1855, address before the citizens of Cincinnati, quoted in Stephen E. Maizlish, "The Meaning of Nativism and the Crisis of the Union: The Know-Nothing Movement in the Antebellum North," in *Essays on American Antebellum Politics, 1840–1860,* ed. Stephen E. Maizlish and John J. Kushma (College Station, Tex.: Texas A&M Press, 1982), 178.

10. Carleton Beales, *Brass-Knuckle Crusade: The Great Know-Nothing Conspiracy, 1820–1860* (New York: Hastings House, 1960), 17.

11. Carl Schurz, "True Americanism," speech given at Faneuil Hall, Boston, April 18, 1859, in *Speeches, Correspondence and Political Papers of Carl Schurz,* ed. Frederic Bancroft (New York: Putnam, 1913), 60–63.

12. Abraham Lincoln, letter to Joshua F. Speed, August 24, 1855, in *Abraham Lincoln: His Speeches and Writings,* ed. Roy P. Basler (Cleveland: World Publishing, 1946), 332.

13. Senator Arthur H. Vandenberg, *The Evolution of a Modern Republican 1884–1945* (East Lansing: Michigan State University Press, 1970), 121.

14. Ibid., 189–190.

15. James B. Reston, *Deadline: A Memoir* (New York: Random House, 1991), 156.

16. Senator Arthur Vandenberg, *American Foreign Policy,* speech before the Senate, January 10, 1945, 79th Cong., 1st sess., available at www. senate.gov/artandhistory/history/resources/pdf/VandenbergSpeech.pdf.

17. Ibid.

18. Francis Fukuyama, *The End of History and the Last Man* (New York: Free Press, 1992).

19. Huntington's thesis first appeared in his "Clash of Civilizations?" He later expanded the argument in Samuel P. Huntington, *The Clash of Civilizations and the Remaking of World Order* (New York: Simon & Schuster, 1996).

20. Rudolph Giuliani, speech to the U.N. General Assembly, October 1, 2001, transcript, *Washington Post,* available at www.washingtonpost. com/wp-srv/nation/specials/attacked/transcripts/giulianitext_100101. html.

21. George W. Bush, "Address to a Joint Session of Congress and the American People," September 20, 2001, transcript, White House Web page, available at www.whitehouse.gov/news/releases/2001/09/200109 20-8.html.

22. For more information, see the Alliance of Civilizations Web site, www.unaoc.org/index.php.

23. See Architect of the Capital, "Relief Portraits of Lawgivers," www. aoc.gov/cc/art/lawgivers/index.cfm, for more information on the various figures.

24. Schurz, "True Americanism," 60–63.

CHAPTER 6: HUMILITY

1. The poll is cited in M. Shahid Alam, "World's Greatest Country: Do the Facts Lie?" faculty working paper no. 04-001, Department of Economics at Northeastern University, Boston, March 12, 2004, available at www.economics.neu.edu/papers/documents/04-001.doc.

2. Pew Global Attitudes Project, *Views of a Changing World* (Washington, D.C.: Pew Research Center, June 2003), 93, available at www.pew trusts.com/pdf/vf_pew_research_global_attitudes_0603.pdf.

3. George Washington, Farewell Address, 1796, available at www. yale.edu/lawweb/avalon/washing.htm.

4. Dwight Eisenhower, speech at London's Guildhall, June 12, 1945, available at www.eisenhowermemorial.org/speeches/19450612%20guild hall-nolink.htm.

5. Pew Global Attitudes Project, "U.S. Image Up Slightly, but Still Negative: American Character Gets Mixed Reviews," report (Washington, D.C.: Pew Research Center, June 23, 2005), available at http://pew global.org/repts/display.php?ReportID=247.

6. CIA World Factbook, July 28, 2005, available at www.cia.gov/ cia/publications/factbook/index.html; and NationMaster.com, "Education Statistics: Literacy, Total Population by Country," Web page, www. nationmaster.com/graph/edu_lit_tot_pop-education-literacy-total-population.

7. Gail Russell Chaddock, "US Notches World's Highest Incarceration Rate," *Christian Science Monitor,* August 18, 2003.

8. Joseph Nye, *Soft Power: The Means to Success in World Affairs* (New York: PublicAffairs, 2004).

9. Data on worldwide opinion of the United States, and explanation of data, from Kevin Sullivan, "Views on U.S. Drop Sharply in Worldwide Opinion Poll," *Washington Post,* January 23, 2007, available at www. washingtonpost.com/wp-dyn/content/article/2007/01/22/AR200701 2201300.html?referrer=emailarticle.

10. "[W]e must consider that we shall be as a City upon a Hill. The eyes of all people are upon us. So that if we shall deal falsely with our God in this work we have undertaken and so cause him to withdraw his present help from us, we shall be made a story and a by-word through the world. We shall open the mouths of enemies to speak evil of the ways of God and all professors for God's sake. We shall shame the faces of many of God's worthy servants, and cause their prayers to be turned into curses upon us till we be consumed out of the good land whither we are going." From John Winthrop, "A Model of Christian Charity" (1630), in *Readings in the History of Christian Theology,* ed. William Carl Placher (Louisville, Ky.: Westminster John Knox Press, 1988), 108–109.

11. Alexis de Tocqueville, *Democracy in America* (New York: Signet Books, 2001); text originally published in 1835 (volume 1) and 1840 (volume 2).

12. The Architect of the Capitol, Capitol Complex, Telegraph Centennial, available at www.aoc.gov/cc/plaques/telegraph_cent.cfm. Morse's own account of his role in inventing the telegraph was that: "I have made a valuable application of electricity not because I was superior to other men but solely because God, who meant it for mankind, must reveal it to someone and He was pleased to reveal it to me." From M. Norvel Young

and Mary Hollingsworth, *Living Lights, Shining Stars: Ten Secrets to Becoming the Light of the World* (West Monroe, La.: Howard Publishing, 1991), 202.

13. Condoleezza Rice, speech at Southern Baptist Convention annual meeting, Greensboro, N.C., June 14, 2006, available at www.state.gov/secretary/rm/2006/67896.htm.

14. James Madison, "Federalist No. 51," in *The Federalist Papers*, ed. Isaac Kramnick (Harmondsworth, England: Smith, 1987).

15. The renowned Protestant theologian Reinhold Niebuhr put it this way: "Loyalty to the truth requires confidence in the possibility of its attainment; toleration of others requires broken confidence in the finality of our own words." From Reinhold Niebuhr, *The Nature and Destiny of Man*, vol. 2, *Human Destiny* (Louisville, Ky.: John Knox Press, 1996), 243, quoted in Anatol Lieven and John Hulsman, *Ethical Realism: A Vision for America's Role in the World* (New York: Pantheon Books, 2006), 72. My thinking on the relationship between democracy and humility also draws on Martha Minow, "Should Religious Groups Be Exempt from Civil Rights Laws?" lecture at Princeton University, Princeton, N.J., May 2006, in which she described a key role of humility in a democracy: "Humility is of course a virtue within many religious traditions. I think it is also central to the liberal commitment at the core of constitutional democracy, though less commonly so seen. For the virtue of tolerance at the heart of freedom of speech depends on acknowledging that our truths may be wrong, and deserve the test of the marketplace of ideas."

16. Franklin D. Roosevelt, quoted in Tom Barry, Laura Carlsen, and John Gershman, "The Good Neighbor Policy: A History to Make Us Proud," International Relations Center Special Report, August 2005, available at www.irc-online.org/content/commentary/2005/0503ggn.php. I am indebted to the authors of this article for some of the points in this discussion. The International Relations Center's Global Good Neighbor Initiative has a wealth of information and good ideas on the concept. See its Web site, http://ggn.irc-online.org/.

17. Herbert Hoover, quoted in ibid.

18. FDR, Inaugural Address, March 4, 1933, available at www.yale.edu/lawweb/avalon/presiden/inaug/froos1.htm.

19. Luis Quintanilla, *A Latin American Speaks* (New York: Macmillan, 1943), 156.

20. Barry et al., "Good Neighbor Policy."

21. Ibid.

22. Saavedra Lamas, untitled article in *La Prensa* (Buenos Aires), January 23, 1936, quoted in Ellery C. Stowell, "President Roosevelt's Proposal of an Extraordinary Pan-American Conference," *American Journal of International Law* 30, no. 2 (April 1936): 270–273.

23. FDR, Inaugural Address.

24. Franklin D. Roosevelt, Second Inaugural Address, January 20, 1937, available at www.bartleby.com/124/pres50.html.

25. U.S. General Accounting Office, "Estimated Costs of the Kyoto Protocol," report GAO-04-144R (Washington, D.C.: General Accounting Office, January 30, 2004), available at www.gao.gov/new.items/d04144r.pdf.

26. A taste of the controversies can be found in U.S. General Accounting Office, "Estimated Costs of the Kyoto Protocol," ibid.

27. See Keith Bradsher and David Barbosa, "Pollution from Chinese Coal Casts a Global Shadow," *New York Times,* June 11, 2006. For a detailed discussion on the economic costs of global warming, see Nicolas Stern, "Stern Review on the Economics of Climate Change," HM Treasury report commissioned by the Chancellor, November 2006, available at www.hm-treasury.gov.uk/independent_reviews/stern_review_economics _climate_change/sternreview_index.cfm.

28. Harry S. Truman, "Thanksgiving Day, 1945, by the President of the United States of America: A Proclamation," Washington, D.C., November 12, 1945, available at www.pilgrimhall.org/ThanxProc1940. htm.

CHAPTER 7: FAITH

1. Pew Global Attitudes Project, "Among Wealthy Nations, U.S. Stands Alone in Its Embrace of Religion," report (Washington, D.C.: Pew Research Center, December 19, 2002), available at http://pewglobal. org/reports/pdf/167.pdf.

2. Garry Wills, *Under God: Religion and American Politics* (New York: Simon and Schuster, 1990), 16.

3. Patrick J. Deneen, *Democratic Faith* (Princeton, N.J.: Princeton University Press, 2005), 15.

4. Wills, *Under God,* 384.

5. See generally Deneen, *Democratic Faith.*

6. Abraham Lincoln, "The Perpetuation of Our Political Institutions," address before the Young Men's Lyceum of Springfield, Ill., January 27, 1838, available at http://showcase.netins.net/web/creative/lincoln/speeches/lyceum.htm.

7. "The Examination of Mrs. Anne Hutchinson at the Court at Newton, 1637," available at Commonwealth of Massachusetts Web site www.mass.gov/statehouse/statues/hutch_transcript.htm.

8. Patrick Henry, "Give Me Liberty or Give Me Death," speech, March 23, 1775; Thomas Paine, First Crisis Paper, December 23, 1776.

9. Martin Luther King, Jr., "I Have a Dream," address, Washington, D.C., August 28, 1963, in "A Call to Conscience: The Landmark Speeches of Dr. Martin Luther King, Jr.," project of Stanford University and the Martin Luther King, Jr., Research and Education Institute, available at www.stanford.edu/group/King/about_the_project/address_at_march_on_washington.htm.

10. Carl Schurz, "True Americanism," speech at Faneuil Hall, Boston, April 18, 1859, in Speeches, Correspondence and Political Papers of Carl Schurz, ed. Frederic Bancroft (New York: Putnam, 1913), 61.

11. See George W. Bush, "President's Remarks at the 2004 Republican National Convention," Madison Square Garden, New York, September 2, 2004, available at www.whitehouse.gov/news/releases/2004/09/20040902-2.html.

12. Abraham Lincoln, Second Inaugural Address, Washington, D.C., March 4, 1865, available at http://memory.loc.gov/cgi-bin/query/r?ammem/mal:@field(DOCID+@lit(d4361300)).

13. Learned Hand, "The Spirit of Liberty," speech at I Am an American Day, New York City, May 21, 1944, available at International Freedom Center, "Words of Freedom" compilation, www.ifcwtc.org/words22.html.

14. Barack Obama, keynote address, Democratic National Convention, Boston, July 27, 2004, transcript, Washington Post, July 28, 2004, available at www.washingtonpost.com/ac2/wp-dyn/A19751-2004Jul27?language=printer.

15. Arthur M. Schlesinger, Jr., "Not Right, Not Left, but a Vital Center," New York Times Magazine, April 4, 1948, sec. 6. I am indebted to Peter Beinart, "An Argument for a New Liberalism: A Fighting Faith," The New Republic, December 2, 2004, for pointing me to Schlesinger's article.

16. See Peter Beinart, *The Good Fight: Why Liberals—and Only Liberals—Can Win the War on Terror and Make America Great Again* (New York: HarperCollins, 2006).

17. Pew Global Attitudes Project, "U.S. Image Up Slightly, but Still Negative: American Character Gets Mixed Reviews," report (Washington, D.C.: Pew Research Center, June 23, 2005), available at http://pew global.org/repts/display.php?ReportID=247.

18. My account of Qutb's life and the quotations from his writings are drawn from Lawrence Wright, *The Looming Tower: Al-Qaeda and the Road to 9/11* (New York: Knopf, 2006), 10–31.

19. Madeleine Albright, *The Mighty and the Almighty: Reflections on America, God, and World Affairs* (New York: HarperCollins, 2006), 281.

20. John F. Kennedy, Commencement Address, Assumption College, Worcester, Mass., June 3, 1955, available at www.jfklibrary.org/Historical +Resources/Archives/Reference+Desk/Speeches/JFK/JFK+Pre-Pres/ 002PREPRES12SPEECHES_55JUN03.htm.

CONCLUSION

1. Sudarsan Raghavan, "Violence Changes Fortunes of Storied Baghdad Street," *Washington Post,* September 18, 2006.

2. Peter Wallsten, "Falwell Says Faithful Fear Clinton More Than Devil," *Los Angeles Times,* September 24, 2006.

3. John Cassidy, "The Ringleader: How Grover Norquist Keeps the Conservative Movement Together," *The New Yorker,* August 1, 2005.

4. Lewis H. Lapham, *Pretensions to Empire: Notes on the Criminal Folly of the Bush Administration* (New York: New Press, 2006).

5. Clint Willis, *The I Hate George W. Bush Reader: Why Dubya Is Absolutely Wrong About Everything* (New York: Thunder's Mouth Press, 2004); Clint Willis, *The I Hate Dick Cheney, John Ashcroft, Donald Rumsfeld, Condi Rice . . . Reader: Behind the Bush Cabal's War on America* (New York: Thunder's Mouth Press, 2004); and Clint Willis, *The I Hate Republicans Reader: Why the GOP Is Totally Wrong About Everything* (New York: Thunder's Mouth Press, 2003).

6. George Washington, Farewell Address, 1796, available at www.yale .edu/lawweb/avalon/washing.htm.

7. Bill Moyers, "Yearning for Democracy," *Context: A Quarterly of Humane Sustainable Culture* 30 (fall/winter 1991): 14–17, reprint of a speech

given to the Democratic Issues Conference of the National Legislative Education Foundation.

8. Ibid., 16.

9. Ibid., 15.

10. Quoted in Michael R. Gordon, "Military Hones a New Strategy on Insurgency," *New York Times,* October 5, 2006.

11. These examples come from Stephen Flynn, *The Edge of Disaster: Rebuilding a Resilient Nation* (New York: Random House, 2007). Flynn makes a much larger and very compelling argument about the democratization of information as our best guarantee of homeland security.

12. Israeli supreme court decision of September 6, 1999, concerning the interrogation practices of the General Security Service (also known as Shin Bet). *Public Committee Against Torture v. Israel* HCJ 5100/94, 37, available at http://elyon1.court.gov.il/files_eng/94/000/051/a09/94051 000.a09.pdf.

13. Thomas Smith, "Why Should I the World Be Minding," date unknown, in *America in Poetry,* ed. Charles Sullivan (New York: Abradale Press, 1992), 14.

14. See, for example, Michael Signer, "A City on a Hill," *Democracy* 1 (summer 2006): 33–44.

15. Carl Schurz, "True Americanism," speech given at Faneuil Hall, Boston, April 18, 1859, in *Speeches, Correspondence and Political Papers of Carl Schurz,* ed. Frederic Bancroft (New York: Putnam, 1913), 51.

Acknowledgments

MY GREATEST DEBT in writing this book is to Tom Hale, who shared both the pleasures and the pains of researching and writing this book as he moved from Princeton to Beijing to London, and from former student to valued colleague and friend. Christened Thomas Nathan Hale and descended from a brother of Nathan Hale himself, Tom's commitment to the values that animate this book matches my own. Tom and I are both grateful to my wonderful agent, Will Lippincott, and to the world's best editor, Lara Heimert, and to the entire production team at Basic. As she did with my first book, Terry Murphy helped every step of the way, taking on countless tasks. The final stage of any major project comes down to a small support group emailing at all hours of day and night; this was mine.

Amid the late nights, early mornings, and many long plane trips spent writing, my life would have simply ground to a halt without Nancy Everett, my indispensable executive assistant who remains absolutely unflappable and completely supportive no matter how crazy life gets. Marianne Goldfarb keeps the front office running smoothly, providing everything from sympathy to regular infusions of sugar. Kate Reilly, like Tom Hale before her and Liz Colagiuri today, worked for me for a wonderful year; they all made it possible for me to "outsource my memory" and escape much of the anxiety caused by endless lists. And to all of the administrators at the Woodrow Wilson School who may not have realized that they were making it possible for me to write a book as well as lead the School, you are the best team any dean ever had.

Intellectually, this project has multiple sources. Serge Schmemann asked me to write the op-ed for the *International Herald Tribune* that first allowed me to voice my anguish as an American traveling abroad. Bill Burke-White and I taught a freshman seminar at Princeton where we read the memoirs of secretaries of state from Jefferson forward. That intellectual journey opened my eyes to the many forgotten or distorted preachers and practitioners of fundamental American values. A number of the students from that seminar provided valuable research assistance in the early stages of the book: Ross Liemer, Avinash Murthy, Omer Ziyal, Sarah Zaslow, Amanda Rinderle, David Maass, Lilian Timmerman, and especially Samantha Lomeli. At the same time, John Ikenberry and I launched the Princeton Project on International Security, which assembled almost 400 top foreign policy thinkers over the course of two and half years and produced a final report in September 2006. John, Elizabeth Colagiuri, and Tom Wright were my constant and invaluable companions and co-conspirators in making the Princeton Project happen and in drafting the final report. Many of the ideas we developed there appear in a different guise here.

Equally important as sources of inspiration were many of the people who make my life possible, as crazy as it often is. At home, Ludmila and Radovan Olexa, who have become part of our family and have taught our children to speak English with Slovakian accents. Their uncle Milan came to America in 1968, fleeing Communist rule when Slovakia was still part of Czechoslovakia. Luda and Rado came four years ago when Milan won the green card lottery. Their life now spans both continents; they are in regular contact with their family back home as well as here and spend much of their summer back in Slovakia. They see much that is good here, but if they need real medical care they must wait until their annual visit to what is still their home—the Slovakian health care system is effectively subsidizing us. And then Aziz El Badaoui, my Moroccan hairdresser who has moved me in ways he could not know as I wrote this book. Aziz who, when he was studying to become a citizen, told me: "I love your history. It's so short and cute!" Who worked night and day to open a beauty salon of his own, and who said to me shortly before he took his oath of citizenship: "it's my *dream,*" with his hand pressed over his heart.

Alongside the speeches and quotations and inscriptions from famous American men and women, many of the sources for this book come from my family. Like all families, my family maps a small part of America as it is today and as it is becoming. In the generation past, Edward R. "Butch" Slaughter and Mary Hoke Slaughter, on my father's side; Jean Limbosch and Henriette Limbosch on my mother's—grandparents who opened their worlds to me on both sides of the Atlantic. In the generation present, my priceless and beloved parents, Ned and Anne Slaughter; my mother-in-law, Francesca de Gogorza Moravcsik; my brothers, Hoke and Bryan Slaughter, who are my lifelong support system; my sisters-in-law, Laurel

Beckett Slaughter, Jennifer Ciocca Slaughter, and Julia Moravcsik, who have connected us to their Irish, German, and Italian families and who have become the sisters I never had. My uncles, Alexander Slaughter and Jean-Michel Limbosch; my aunts, Mary Peeples Slaughter, Mary Hoke Slaughter, Poucette Dumon Limbosch, and Christianne Neuray Limbosch; and my cousins, David Slaughter, Patrick Limbosch, Jean-Frederick Limbosch, Caroline Limbosch Van de Velde, and all their families.

I wrote this book above all for the next generation. For my sons, Michael Edward Hoke Moravcsik and Alexander de Gogorza Moravcsik, whose very names reflect their multiple national heritages (and some marital log-rolling). They are directly responsible for my deep knowledge of Harry Potter and *Star Wars*. Even more important, our ongoing discussion of who we are and what we do and don't do as a family, of values and character and responsibility, has provided an invaluable counterpoint to my reflections on what we as Americans should and should not do as a nation. For my nephew, Sean Bowling, and my nieces, Elizabeth Skye Slaughter, Gwenyth Anne Slaughter, Jane Kavar Slaughter, and Elizabeth Odry Slaughter, each named in part for grandmothers and great-grandmothers, each already weaving her distinctive thread into the family tapestry. And for my adopted nephew to be. Like Terry's kids, Sammy and Emmy, adopted from a Romanian orphanage, and like the many Chinese baby girls that friends of mine have made part of their families, my nephew stands for a new American relationship to the world. He will bring his culture and homeland directly into our family, through our imaginings of his birth family and our desire to explore his dual heritage. My generation has traveled from a time when adoption was hidden and stigmatized to an age when so many of us who could have or do have our own biological children, or who could adopt much closer to home, decide instead that they want to reach out to the world and offer a better life to babies born in far less fortunate circumstances. Instead of letting immigrants from the world over come to America and make it as best they can, why shouldn't America reach out to other nations and vastly improve our own lives in the process?

Finally, to my wonderful husband, Andrew Moravcsik. He thinks this venture is "noble but quixotic," yet as with so many other things that I plunge us into, he supports me anyway. His skepticism keeps our household lively; his wit keeps it full of laughter; and his love helps keep it whole. Without all of that, I could not do anything that I do.